FREEDOM IS

FOR THOSE WILLING TO DEFEND IT

STORIES OF MEN IN WAR ◆ HELENE ENSIGN MAW

Printed in Canada

Typesetting and graphics: Roy Diment VRG, rdiment@shaw.ca

National Library of Canada Cataloguing in Publication Data

Maw, Helene Ensign
   Freedom is for those willing to defend it : stories of men in war
ISBN 1-55369-292-6
   1. Veterans--United States--Biography. 2. United States--Armed Forces--Biography. I. Title.
U52.M39 2002   355'.0092'273   C2002-901130-2

TRAFFORD

This book was published *on-demand* in cooperation with Trafford Publishing. On-demand publishing is a unique process and service of making a book available for retail sale to the public taking advantage of on-demand manufacturing and Internet marketing.**On-demand publishing** includes promotions, retail sales, manufacturing, order fulfilment, accounting and collecting royalties on behalf of the author.

Suite 6E, 2333 Government St., Victoria, B.C. V8T 4P4, CANADA
Phone   250-383-6864   Toll-free   1-888-232-4444 (Canada & US)
Fax   250-383-6804   E-mail   sales@trafford.com
Website   www.trafford.com
TRAFFORD PUBLISHING IS A DIVISION OF TRAFFORD HOLDINGS LTD.
Trafford Catalogue #02-0105   www.trafford.com/robots/02-0105.html

10   9   8   7   6   5   4   3

DEDICATED

TO THOSE

WHO UNDERPRIZE

LIBERTY

CONTENTS

VIETNAM WAR

Instruction to the Reader

Stories were written in first person to preserve emotion and uniqueness of each veteran's story as observed during personal interviews. Italics appear where I have inserted commentary pertinent to a battle, a territory, or history.

Author.

ACKNOWLEDGEMENTS

I express my gratitude to the veterans who have related their war experiences to me in personal interviews for this book. My work was to organize and edit their stories for publication. Each contributor approved his story for accuracy and authenticity.

They, and all veterans, deserve our country's deepest tribute for their service.

I value the meticulous proofing provided by Linda Watson and Carolyn Morgan and to Charles Tate for a final edit of the manuscript; for veterans Roger Maw and John Maw for their astute attention to content details.

My appreciation to Garth and Maydene Baxter, Helen Dibblee, and Lamar Baxter for referring me to veterans that have had unusual war experiences.

And my devotion and appreciation to my husband and adviser, Robert, who ate peanut butter and honey sandwiches for many suppers.

*

ix

PREFACE

Their leader, never more dangerous to the enemy than now, had commandeered all boats up and down the river to prevent the enemy's attack. He would use those same boats to strike while the enemy reveled in the last dregs of Christmas night. These noble men in rags boarded boats moored on the river and bent to their oars protecting their weapons with meager rags from wind whipped sleet and plowed their boat bows against the river ice. Each of the twenty-four hundred men carried a few personal possessions, a blanket, a spoon, a plate; they shared canteens. To have joined in the attack were Brigadier General Gates and his brigade, but as the hour approached Gates claimed illness and he and his brigade stayed in camp. Ens. George Ewing appointed to lead the third brigade concluded the floating ice too hazardous and they too remained at camp.

Crossing the river at midnight, the shoeless soldiers marched nine miles in a snowstorm arriving outside enemy fortifications at daylight. Boldly they attacked and captured the stronghold, defeated their surprised enemy and killed or captured approximately fifteen hundred. Two of Washington's soldiers died from exposure during the bitterly cold night, and two others were wounded in the battle. With prisoners in tow they retraced the nine-miles, returned to boats and recrossed the river and returned to campfires of those who remained at Valley Forge. Then assembling his entire army, Washington retraced the route and entrenched at Trenton.

Cornwallis, comfortably encamped at New York with amenities for the winter in the customary British style, was rousted by news of the Trenton attack and assembled his men to counterattack. Cornwallis chose to encamp on the outskirts of Trenton as night approached and attack Washington across the Assumpink River at first light claiming, "We may easily bag the fox in the morning." But wily Washington, leaving campfires burning, slipped away in the midnight hours of January 2-3, and marched on Princeton routing three British regiments moving to reinforce Cornwallis.

Washington's army fluctuated between 20,000 and 5,000 as short-time enlistments came due. To feed this army required between 34,577 and 8,600 pounds of meat and 168 barrels of flour a day, and it fell to Washington to provide it as no central military supply existed. The un-united Colonies had only sporadically filled supply and replacement quotas. Foraging parties were sent to scavenge the countryside for food as shortages were particularly direful from December to February 1776-1777. It was during this period Washington pledged his own private fortune to pay the soldiers' wage, since the soldiers had not received their promised pay from congress, an example followed by other officers, while this uncommon man asked for no pay. He had early on formulated rules by which he measured men. The first was fortitude under fatigue and privation, courage second; hardship, poverty, and actual want he considered the soldier's best school. Washington's tatty food rations were the same his men received.

There were women there, officers' wives, who cooked, laundered, patched, mended and nursed. Martha Washington frequently accompanying her husband, labored among the sick and wounded with the other wives. During one of our longest wars General Washington prayed for divine guidance.

These men of mettle have often rallied my soul to weep and marvel at their nobleness. The stories that follow are of men who have also endeared my deepest respect and gratitude for preserving the standard of liberty and lending their dignity to this country's noble beginning.

ILLUSTRATIONS

MAPS

I BRING TO YOU THIS BRIGHT BOUQUET
BEFORE WINTER FALLS ON LEAF AND BOUGH.
THESE LAST EARTH-BLOOMS I BRING TO YOU,
FOR IT IS THE DUSK OF AUTUMN NOW.

TIME HAS ASSUAGED THE ACHING HEART—
HAS SHIELDED ME FROM BITTER PAIN,
JUST AS THIS CRIMSON ROSE LEANS FAR
AS IF TO HIDE YOUR COLD-CARVED NAME.

DO I FEEL YOUR TOUCH? DO I HEAR YOUR VOICE?
IS THERE A NOSTALGIC SADNESS IN YOUR TONE?
DO YOU SEE THESE LAST BROWN LEAVES THAT FALL
CARESSINGLY ACROSS YOUR GRANITE STONE?

Alda Larson Brown

WORLD WAR 2

CHAPTER 1

LT. COLONEL
CHASE J. NIELSEN

Lt. Colonel Chase J. Nielsen
U.S. Air Force

FREEDOM IS FOR THOSE WILLING TO DEFEND IT

I was on the first bombing raid over Tokyo four months after the attack on Pearl Harbor.

When the Japanese bombed Pearl Harbor on December 7, 1941, it began a succession of victories for the Japanese. After President Roosevelt radioed that news from the Pacific was "all bad," Americans became fiercely outraged and quietly demoralized. In the first three months, Japan militarily captured and occupied Guam (U.S.), Wake Island (U.S.), Gilbert Islands (G.B.), Hong Kong (G.B.), Singapore (G.B.), Java (Dutch), Bali (Dutch), Timor (Dutch), the Burma Road which was the main supply route into China; coastal cities of China; the Celebes (Dutch), and Bataan in the Philippines (U.S.). General MacArthur withdrew from his home at Manila in late December declaring it an open city.

Disgruntled citizens offered large sums of money to anyone who could devise a plan to attack Japan in retaliation. Schemes were proposed, but no one resolved the primary problem of how to get aircraft carriers to invade Japanese waters far enough to strike Tokyo with short-range Navy fighter-bombers, nor did the Army's medium-range bombers have the fuel capacity to fly from the closest US airbase on Midway Island. One plan proposed the use of commercial airplanes. Though they were unsure how bombs would be dropped on the target, I guessed they anticipated just kicking them out.

Spurred on by malcontent, an unconventional idea erupted, hatched by Admiral Ernest J. King, staff member Captain Francis S. Low, and air operations officer Captain Donald B. Duncan, whereby Army Air Force bombers would replace Navy fighter planes on an aircraft carrier. This unorthodox Army and Navy coalition was presented to Army Chief of Staff General George C. Marshall and Chief of Army Air Forces General Henry "Hap" Arnold who reviewed it with perspicacity and assigned the project to chief of experimental flying Lieutenant Colonel Jimmy Doolittle.

A veteran of World War I with a Doctor of Science in Aeronautical Engineering, Lieutenant Colonel James Doolittle had flown just about every aircraft. He had demonstrated aerodynamic theories by racking up records as the first pilot to fly across the United States in less than a day, the first blind flight completely on instruments, and the first pilot to fly an outside loop. By evaluating aircraft designs, Doolittle settled on the B-25 for the mission and plunged into reconfiguring the design to increase fuel capacity. It necessitated lightening the structure by removing the tail gun and lower aft gun turrets. In consequence of these changes, the fuel capacity nearly doubled, increasing from 640 gallons to 1141 gallons. By reducing power settings, which in turn reduced cruising speed, fuel consumption could be kept at 85 gallons per hour. With these modifications, the aircraft could fly approximately 2300 miles.

In February of 1942, Doolittle visited the 17th Bomb Group stationed at Columbia, South Carolina, the only bomber wing with B-25s, to hand pick volunteers. I had nearly completed pilot training when I mashed up a plane and had my flying status revoked. It resulted in my entering navigational training instruction at Columbia,

South Carolina where the Bomb Group practiced bombing and combat maneuvers flying the new B-25 Mitchell bomber. News spread quickly when Doolittle arrived asking for volunteers for a dangerous ninety-day mission outside the United States. In training for two and a half years by then and reaching my twenty-fourth birthday, I eagerly anticipated action. I volunteered.

Our top-secret flight training began with vigorous admonishments by Doolittle stressing that the mission was fraught with unanticipated risks and dangerous hazards. Concluding, he emphasized that to even speak of our training would endanger the lives of many. It gave us the feeling of pride to be chosen to associate with the distinguished Colonel Doolittle, and from the start began calling ourselves Doolittle Raiders.

At a secluded airfield at Eglin Air Force Base, Florida, we practiced low level bombing carrying 500-pound bombs. We soon learned that when dropping a 500-pound bomb from an altitude of 1500 feet, the force of the explosion made our knees buckle when standing in the aircraft. When Navy Lieutenant Henry L. Miller from Pensacola showed up claiming he would instruct us how to get a B-25 off the field in 500 feet or less, we speculated that we had volunteered to take off from a pitching aircraft carrier. But we learned after four weeks' training with Lieutenant Miller that in an eight-knot wind with throttles in full power, as soon as we released brakes, the aircraft would just about jump out from under us.

Proficient in short take offs, we left South Carolina and practiced our low-level flying on a southerly route over the United States to McClellan Air Force Base near Sacramento, California, to outfit our aircraft with new three-bladed propellers. When leaving Sacramento en route to Alameda to begin the mission, the crews admittedly conspired with one another, deviated from the flight plan and our recent arduous training, and with gleeful hearts flew our gleaming aircraft under San Francisco's Golden Gate Bridge while rapturously wobbling our wings.

Each of us had grown increasingly fussy about the integrity and condition of our smooth purring planes and paced as we nervously watched the Navy crane grasp and pluck each B-25 off the pier and plant a 25,000 pound plane on the aircraft carrier *U.S.S. Hornet.*

Pilot Ted Lawson, flying the *Ruptured Duck* on the mission, described his aircraft as more than an inanimate mass of material, intricately geared and wired and riveted into a tight package, it was a good, trustworthy friend. I had similar feelings about our aircraft named the *Green Hornet*. There had been twenty-four planes and twenty-four crews during training, now we were pared down to sixteen crews and aircraft, each crew of five having two pilots, a navigator, bombardier, and gunner.

Our mission was clear—bomb Japan.

THE PLAN

When the *U.S.S. Hornet* approached within 400 to 500 miles of Japan from the east, Doolittle and his crew would soar off the carrier at eight at night leading the raid. They would reach the objectives around midnight and drop incendiary bombs on Yokohama, Tokyo, Nagoya, Osaka and Kobe to mark the targets. Following with primary and secondary charted targets, the remaining fifteen aircraft would follow Doolittle's lead, each carrying three 500-pound bombs and one 500-pound incendiary cluster bomb.

Because of limited fuel capacity in the B-25s, none of the planes or crews would return to the carrier after the raid, but would set a course southwesterly toward Free China, cross the East China Sea, and land approximately sixty miles inland from the China coast at Chuchow, Lishui. Meanwhile, American pilots flying C-47s would cache 5-gallon cans of gas along designated secluded airstrips where the B-25 pilots would land, refuel, take off, and fly eight hundred statute miles farther west across China and rendezvous at Chungking. Colonel Doolittle expected to land his plane first at Chuchow and the rest of the crews could home in on his radio signal to the fuel caches.

Extra B-25 crewmembers stood by on the *Hornet* in the event one of us buckled or became ill, but our aircraft had an eager crew. I wanted to go. I wouldn't have traded my navigator's chair on the *Green Hornet* even if I could have foreseen the eventual outcome. We named our aircraft the *Green Hornet* as it sat on the gigantic new

Navy carrier *U.S.S. Hornet*. Rather fitting we mused, not just because the *Green Hornet* evoked the popular radio program of the day, but because it seemed decorously appropriate for our first flight from the deck of the *U.S.S. Hornet*. The carrier had also racked up firsts as the United States' newest christened carrier. This was its first voyage into combat, and first Navy carrier deploying Army bombers.

Shelved for the mission, the top-secret Norden bombsights had been replaced with what we jokingly referred to as the twenty-cent'r. The bombsight amounted to a simple notched sighting lever attached to a metal face with etched degree numbers. Engineered by the mission crew pilot Captain C. R. Greening, it adequately served for our low-level bombing.

THE RAID—18 APRIL 1942

During the first two weeks at sea, studying intensified for the navigators. We practiced celestial navigation, created our own maps on grid paper, and plotted geographical coordinates of coastal areas, radio stations, and towns. There were enough maps of Japan available, but no detailed maps of China. Some of us felt the National Geographic had better maps than we had been provided, so we ripped out pages from current issues. The *Hornet* received daily coded transmissions from a submarine submerged in Tokyo Bay. *U.S.S. Thresher* lay undisclosed in Tokyo Bay during daylight and surfaced each night to make observations of shipping traffic, weather, and locations of barrage balloons that were anchored over military targets to block passage of aircraft. We plotted the new information daily.

On 14 April the carrier *U.S.S. Enterprise* and eight accompanying warships joined our convoy in mid-ocean to give the *Hornet* protection until we neared our point of departure 400 nautical miles off the coast of Japan. The *Enterprise* would circle out and wait at a rendezvous point for the *Hornet* on its return trip to the US. The convoy of two carriers and accompanying sixteen cruisers and destroyers comprised the greatest striking force in the Pacific that the United States had in that first four months of the war in the Pacific.

Admiral William F. Halsey, Jr. on the *Enterprise* commanded the task force.

Enemy patrol boats were sighted within forty miles of the task force and endangered the success of the mission, and our course changed several times to avoid detection. But on the morning of 18 April a Japanese patrol boat spotted us. The cruiser *U.S.S. Nashville* within the convoy fired at and sank the patrol boat within minutes. But Admiral Halsey, unwilling to risk the chance that the patrol boat had radioed Japan and disclosed our position before it went to the bottom of the sea, gave the order to launch the B-25s off the *Hornet's* deck and proceed with the bombing mission immediately.

It was Saturday morning, 18 hours earlier and about 400 miles sooner than the original planned take off. With this shift in plans, we would attack in broad daylight vulnerable to antiaircraft and attack by enemy fighter planes.

Thirty-foot waves broke over the bow of the *Hornet* and the deck, slippery with salt spray, pitched beneath my feet. With headwinds at 12 knots and the *Hornet* going full speed ahead at 37 knots, it was impossible to stay on my feet. I slid down the deck on my hands and knees pushing my gear ahead of me in the general direction of the *Green Hornet*. Several sailors seeing my predicament rushed to help. During the last minutes before take off, ten additional 5-gallon gas cans were loaded into each plane, and the fuel tanks topped off. With thumbs up, Doolittle wished us all good luck, promised to throw a big party when we rendezvoused in Chungking, revved his engines, and cleared the *Hornet's* deck at 8:20 in the morning.

Sixth plane in the line of sixteen, the *Green Hornet* lifted off the deck in perfect form and in rapid succession all the aircraft were airborne within an hour after Doolittle soared off the deck. I estimated we had 2300 miles to fly, 800 miles from the carrier to Tokyo and 1500 miles from Tokyo to Chuchow to refuel. In the cockpit were Lieutenant Dean E. Hallmark, pilot, and Lieutenant Robert J. Meder copilot. Bombardier Sergeant William J. Dieter sat in the Plexiglas nose. Engineer-gunner Sergeant Donald E. Fitzmaurice was aft, and I had the navigator's chair.

Nearing Tokyo, six Japanese aircraft flying in formation at 16,000 feet streaked northward in the opposite direction. A few scattered rain clouds along with our flying twenty to thirty feet off the water obscured our passage. Our firepower had been greatly compromised to increase fuel capacity, and we felt grateful to elude the enemy. Broomsticks had been stuck into gun ports where the rear waist gun turrets had been removed to make it appear the aircraft had full firepower. We were vulnerable with only a short flexible 30-caliber gun on a swivel that we could stick into three different ports in the nose, and a 50-caliber gun turret in the waist of the plane.

About 600 miles from Japan we tuned our radios into a local Tokyo radio station, JOAK that was still broadcasting. With our radio direction finder we tuned into the station and homed in on it all the way to the target. Flying over Tokyo's streets fifteen to twenty feet above the rooftops, bystanders waved at us, secure in their minds that we were Imperial Japanese aircraft.

One of the bombs destined for Tokyo had medals and ribbons attached to it, metals previously presented by Japanese officials to US sailors visiting Japan on a goodwill tour. In an explosive gesture, we were returning them, plus a little interest earned at Pearl Harbor.

Prior to reaching our target sites, antiaircraft batteries began sporadically firing up flak at us. Gaining our bombing altitude of 1500 feet, Dieter found our primary target, which was the Tokyo steel mills, and released our bombs.

Collectively the Doolittle Raiders bombed factories, warehouses, gas plants, dock areas, oil storage tanks, power plants and power stations, steel mills, tank factory, oil refinery, merchant ship, arsenal, and aircraft factories in the Tokyo, Yokohama, Nagoya, Kobe, and Osaka areas. Every bombardier found his targets and released

> Historians can reckon for all time that the precise moment of the beginning of the end of Japanese dreams of world conquest is a half hour after noon on April 18, 1942. For it was at that moment that Staff Sergeant Fred A. Braemer, Doolittle's bombardier, opened the B-25's bomb bay doors, adjusted the twenty-cent bombsight, and drew a bead on a large factory. Seconds later all four bombs were gone and Doolittle headed for the rooftops of downtown Tokyo, amidst intense but inaccurate anti-aircraft fire. (Glines 24-25)

their bombs. A few aircraft were perforated with bullet holes; one of our planes bagged a Japanese fighter plane, but the bombing went off as scheduled.

The Japanese had decoded messages from the *Hornet* and *Enterprise*, and a Japanese reconnaissance plane had sighted our convoy within 700 miles of Japan. Knowing US planes could only fly 320 miles before returning to a carrier, the Japanese delayed action. Consequently, the mission was the surprise that Admiral Halsey and Lt. Colonel Doolittle had anticipated.

Freed from the last 500-pounder, we made a beeline south away from Tokyo and focused on the equally hazardous leg of the mission: finding Free China and an unlighted dirt landing strip in the dark to refuel.

We had exceeded our fuel consumption estimates by leaving the *Hornet* early and by bucking 25-knot headwinds. Innocuous clouds churned into storm clouds and it began to rain, and the farther west we flew the worse it got. We passed the tip of the Honshu landmass heading over open water of the East China Sea. I figured we had been flying for twelve hours by then; it was 9:30 at night. We were all pretty anxious about our diminishing fuel. An hour later a fuel light lit up on the pilot's instrument panel, one wing tank gauge read empty, and still no sight of coastline. Pilot Hallmark reached up and flipped off the warning light—he didn't want to be reminded. We slipped into our life jackets aptly named Mae Wests out of veneration for a voluptuous celebrity of the same name (a Dolly Parton of another era), hopeful for landfall before our fuel ran out. About ten minutes later our engines sputtered and quit. We braced ourselves for the crash into an angry sea frothy with whitecaps.

We hit the water so hard the left wing ripped completely off. Hallmark was thrown through the windshield, seat and all. I hit my head that knocked me out momentarily, and when I regained my senses, I was waist deep in water and going down fast. I grabbed the crash axe and broke out the window overhead and pulled myself up on top of the plane. Copilot Meder, already out and bleeding from injuries, braced himself on top of the fuselage. Bombardier Bill Dieter had stayed in the nose of the plane in order to give direction and warning while flying over several small islands along the coast. Consequently, when we hit, he took the full brunt of the crash. By the time I got out on top of the aircraft, Dieter floated up between the wing and the fuselage badly injured, and I grabbed his Mae West and pulled him up. Fitzmaurice surfaced and climbed up on top, bleeding from a deep hole in his forehead. With precious few moments left before the plane completely submerged, we seized the life raft from its hatch compartment. I grabbed the CO_2 bottle to inflate the raft and the lanyard broke off flush with the bottle. I grasped the emergency kit and pulled out the hand pump, but the plane pitched and rolled throwing me off balance. I cut the rope from around the life raft to lash us together, but by then we were awash in waves. The aircraft plunged, and I lunged and swam to get out of the sucking swirl.

I was alone. The rain had subsided. My nose felt broken, and a gash on my arm stung from the salt water. I began an awkward swimming stroke, my arms constricted by the Mae West, my mind racing refiguring our estimated arrival time, air speed, and calculating how far I might be from shore. Then I refigured it all over again. If accurate, we ditched about four miles off the coast of China, yet no lights appeared anywhere; not even moonlight—I couldn't see anything. I didn't know if I was swimming seaward or shoreward. Finally, I gave up and just rode the peaks and troughs of the waves. Again and again I dropped my feet down hoping to stub against rock. I started yelling, but heard nothing. Hours went by in hostile silence. Haunted by self-doubt, I got my .45 off my belt and jacked a shell into the chamber hoping a couple shots might give me a bearing, but all I got was a soggy click. Because the web belt weighed me down, I unbuckled it and let the .45 and ammo sink. A few minutes later I remembered that my hunting knife was attached.

ONLY A NAILCLIPPER

In the darkness without warning, I came onto fishing nets suspended from floating bamboo poles six to eight inches in diameter. The nets presented a wall that I couldn't force down far enough to climb over, and since I had just let my knife drop, I didn't have anything to cut through them. I shoved a nervous hand into water-filled pockets and found a nailclipper. It took patience to cut a hole through several strands of net large enough to wriggle my six-foot frame through. Then I half-swam half-floated until I heard waves breaking on the beach. I dropped my feet down with great relief that solid earth lay beneath my feet, though now undertow swept me away from the beach. Hearing splashing against rocks, I worked my way toward the sound, found sea rocks and laboriously pulled myself up. I lay exhausted and wondered what in hell I was doing there— alone, six thousand miles from home, didn't know where I was, didn't know where my buddies were, didn't know the language with only a nailclipper to defend myself. I sought a place to hide and in the dark lost my footing and fell into a rock abyss, hitting my head and passing out. When I regained consciousness, it was daylight, but luckily I hadn't been discovered.

I eased myself up where I could see out and looked down at the beach below, now alive with Chinese fishermen readying their boats for the day. I had come on shore on the south side of a cove three miles across. The shoreline, rocky for half mile to the west, receded into pine trees covering a gentle slope. Farther west, a small village of fifty houses edged the water and boats rocked gently against their moorings along the waterfront. My blood froze when I spied two Japanese motor launches with their tiny red "meat ball" flags fluttering from the fantails. Obviously this village wasn't in Free China. Working my way uphill on hands and knees through bamboo brush, I stopped out of sight to reconnoiter. Two motionless orange objects lay on the beach some distance from me that could be the Mae Wests on my buddies. I had to find out. Working my way back down on hands and knees, keeping my head down, and stealthily crossing a rice paddy dike, I got within thirty feet of the beach. Thinking I could identify the orange objects from there, I cautiously raised my head. First thing my eyes fell on was a pair of canvas split-toed shoes and leggin'-covered legs directly in front of me. Reticently I raised my gaze, the legs belonged to the most pockmarked face I'd ever seen.

"Stand up, or I shoot," his Oriental eyes squinted tight.

I stood up, and didn't know what to do. I was twice his size, but he had a rifle barrel pointed straight at my stomach. I glanced past him down to the beach and recognized the two Mae Wests were on Fitzmaurice and Dieter.

"You American? You Japanese?" he said in Pidgin English.

I looked right at him and said, "I'm American. You Japanese? You Chinese?"

He moved his chin toward his shoulder and spat, and said, "Me, Chinese. We go see boss."

As I looked past him toward the beach again he said, "They dead. Bury them after hour. You go with me."

We were heading back across the rice paddy and up the area I'd just crossed when we heard the whine of boat engines coming into the bay. "You American and me Chinese," he said, "Japanese kill us both." He held me down in the brush, lit a cigarette and watched. I figured if he didn't want the Japanese killing either one of us, he must be a friend.

Rain fell on my head and face as Leggins eventually marched me up the path to the Chinese garrison. The clapboard barracks were laid out in a square with all the buildings aversely leaning inward toward an open-air center. Inside were a bunch of languid soldiers informally talking. They seemed in good humor, so I indicated I wanted soap. I still had saltwater on my skin that itched miserably. I took the soap, went outside, stripped down and took a shower in the rain. Evidently, that was the first time they'd seen anyone take a shower. They laughed like it was the funniest thing they'd ever seen. But funnier still, before I was through showering, there were about fifteen Chinese that stripped down and were out there in the rain showering with me.

The boss turned out to be a young Chinese captain by the name of Ling. I could tell he was the boss when he came into the room because he had shiny leather boots and a clean uniform. Leggins was his interpreter as I tried to make him understand I was with other Americans, our plane had gone down at sea, and I wanted a power-boat to get to Wenchow, about forty miles to the south, to get inland to Free China.

I had been piecing bits of observations together regarding the Chinese coexistence with the Japanese in the village, and it appeared that the Chinese led precarious lives fearful for their women, families and themselves from their long-time enemy the Japanese, and would face death if they were caught helping me. Japan and China had been warring neighbors for centuries.

Through Leggins I learned the Chinese had found pilot Dean Hallmark and copilot Bob Meder, as he led me to another building farther up the hillside in the village. As I stepped into the dark doorway of the building, Dean Hallmark, not knowing who approached, hid behind the door with a poised club to bludgeon the intruder to death. I caught a glimpse of a moving shadow and stepped aside, and to the utter surprise of both of us after our discovery, clasped each other in a bear hug. Hallmark suffered from wounds on his knees from the plane crash. After a short time, Leggins escorted Bob Meder in and we all excitedly talked at once. Encouraged by each other's presence, we compared what had happened since being washed off the aircraft. That night Captain Ling and Leggins led us to the spot where the bodies of Fitzmaurice and Dieter lay. The Chinese prepared wood boxes, and we gently laid them to rest, burying them in high ground. We prayed silently with deep reverence and respect for our buddies who had given all that they were able to give for their country.

THIRTY JAPS AND A MACHINE GUN

That night Captain Ling took us aboard a sampan anchored off a small village to hide us from Japanese patrols. During the night a Japanese patrol boat hailed the sampan to board and search it. The three of us dove through the open trap door into the bilge in the lower section of the sampan and covered ourselves with grass mats. The hatch was shut and we lay in darkness. Anguished moments passed, then the trap door opened and a big rifle descended held by a small Jap soldier. He came down in the bilge and began poking around in the dark. I sucked in my breath and held my throat stifling a retching stomach overcome by the smell of human waste floating in the bilge. He forcefully jabbed the grass mat that covered me, but I squelched an involuntary cry. The patrol left after a thorough search of the boat not any too soon. Unable to hold back a vomiting spasm

The Japanese... waged ruthless experiments in biological warfare against the Chinese. Some of it was retaliatory and directed against Chinese villages suspected of helping American fliers during the April 1942 Doolittle raid of Tokyo. In areas that may have served as landing zones for the bombers, the Japanese massacred a quarter-million civilians and plowed up every Chinese airfield within an area of twenty thousand square miles. Here as well as elsewhere during the war, entire cities and regions were targeted for disease. We now know that Japanese aviators sprayed fleas carrying plague germs over metropolitan areas like Shanghai, Ningpo, and Changteh, and that flasks of disease-causing microbes—cholera, dysentery, typhoid, plague, anthrax, paratyphoid—were tossed into rivers, wells, reservoirs, and houses... millions more perished from starvation and disease caused in large part by Japanese looting, bombing, and medical experimentation. If those deaths are added to the final count, then one can say that the Japanese killed more than 19 million Chinese people in its war against China. (Chang 216-217)

any longer, I doubled over and contributed a tad more to the odoriferous sludge.

The next morning Ling anchored in Wenchow harbor and went into the walled-in city of Wenchow to determine the Japanese' intent and military force. On returning, he grimly expressed grave concern for our welfare and his own. He told us that the Japanese, outraged and humiliated that Americans had bombed the Imperial City of Tokyo, were deploying land and sea patrols vengefully hunting us down. We remained on his sampan that day and when night came we were disguised in monk's robes and rowed to shore. We walked hunched over trying to foreshorten our large frames so as not to stand above our robed Chinese friends, and placed ourselves within the moving center of the group. We entered the walled city, past tin-roofed wooden shacks to a building in the center of the city. The Chinese turned their faces away as we passed them, fearful of consequences of Occidentals among them. We were led into a dark building empty except for one man. We were introduced to English-speaking Mr. Wong who told us of the hardships and sadistic treatment the Japanese imposed on the Chinese. They assaulted young Chinese girls until dead, used children and infants for bayonet practice, and beheaded boys and men with Samurai swords.

We hadn't talked long with Mr. Wong when a frightened Chinese soldier in half-flight swung open the door and spoke excitedly in Chinese. We understood that the Japanese had entered the village and were marching toward the building where we were. Wong rushed us out, and we fled through an alley.

I peered around a corner. Japs were setting up a machine gun on a tripod. Wong pushed us into a nearby building, but the room, big and empty, had nowhere to hide. Hallmark headed for a corner still limping from knee abrasions, and we hurriedly piled old sacks and rags over him and pushed up a bench in front. There was no choice except to hide in the rafters. Meder swung up into the rafters in one corner and I pulled myself up in another and tried to stifle my excited breathing. Even in the dim light, we had only half a chance of not being seen if the Japs came in. Wong sat quietly on the floor in the middle of the room mindlessly laying wood for a fire.

A few minutes passed then the door flung wide and a dozen Japanese soldiers crowded into the room. One Jap held a submachine gun at his hip while an officer went right to the corner where Hallmark hid and uncovered him. It appeared that he was directed to the spot.

"Where are your two buddies?" the Jap interpreter spoke good English.

Now standing, Hallmark uttered, "What two buddies?"

The Jap officer then turned on Wong and began beating him. As the Jap cocked his arm back to strike Wong, his eyes shifted upward and observed me hunched over the rafters above him.

"Get down now, or I shoot! Now, you are prisoners of the Imperial Japanese Army!" he exclaimed to me.

I could only conclude, it had been a sell-out.

From Wenchow, we were taken to Shanghai by Japanese patrol boat. Through an interpreter, a Japanese officer fired off questions. To all of them my reply remained the same, "If you are an officer, you would know that the only information I will give you is my name and rank."

Dragged into a small room and placed on a table, torture then began. Around the table were winch-like devices on all sides. Leather straps were placed around my ankles and wrists and a collar placed about my chin and the rear part of my head. My legs and arms were all hooked up and the winch turned until my body was pulled and stretched above the table. I felt my head was going to detach from my body when they cinched the winch at my head. The collar around my chin and head made it difficult to breathe and cut off circulation. Just prior to blacking out, they released the harness and pushed me into a chair, and as my blood returned to my head and eyes, I could see and hear again. The interpreter barked that I was foolish to take any more punishment because my buddies had already talked and they knew the whole story.

"Tell it to me and I'll see if it's right," I said. The four big guys worked me over again, while the officers laughed.

"It is useless to continue, we will execute you right now," the interpreter said.

Handcuffs were clasped on my wrists and they marched me outside. Then removing the handcuffs, they stretched my arms out spread eagle against the wall and pinned a target on my chest. Leg irons were attached to both my legs and a blindfold placed over my eyes. Then they began asking me questions about the mission. At the same time, I could hear an army squad marching out. I heard the rifle butts hit the flagstone path, and I knew what that meant. It was ready, aim, fire and that's it! Within those seconds my life flashed before me. Flashed most prominently were things I had yet to do. I wasn't afraid of dying, but what hit me forcefully was who would ever know what had happened here? And the sad thing, was how were my mother and father going to ever know what happened to me!

Several minutes seemed to pass as my brain sent flashing black and white pictures speeding through my consciousness as my life flashed before me. An interpreter came out and spoke to the Japanese officer, who then spoke to me.

"We are the Knights of Bushido of the Order of the Rising Sun. We don't execute at sundown, we execute at sunrise. If you don't talk by morning, we'll execute you in the morning!"

They took me back to the cell. I hadn't noticed the peg high up on the wall of the cell. The guards lifted me up so the chain between my handcuffed hands hooked over the peg just high enough that my feet couldn't touch the floor. I can't remember how long I hung there. I believe I blacked out for most of the night. When they took me down the next morning, I thought both arms would fall off at the shoulder sockets. They questioned me again, but I never did tell them anything regarding the mission or the war effort. So they took me back to the cell and pegged me back up on the wall again and left me there.

At six the next morning the Japs were back, pulled me down off the wall, and put a blindfold over my eyes. My arms by then had become totally useless. I didn't know what was going to happen to me next.

"You have a last reprieve," a Jap officer said. "We have orders to fly you to military headquarters in Tokyo for interrogation."

My buddies and I were flown to Tokyo and experienced hell from the KempeiTai military police. We were all given the same torture. Bamboo splints were jammed under my fingernails, then set on fire while they asked me questions. They stuck large splints between my fingers, compressed my hands while pulling them out one at a time, and when I didn't answer their questions, they smacked their hobnailed boots against my shins until they bled. They burned the bottom of my feet with charcoal. The guards had me squat down, put bamboo poles about two to three inches in diameter behind my knees, then the guards jumped up and down on my thighs until my kneecaps sprung. They beat my back with a rubber hose until lacerated as raw as hamburger. They forced me down to the floor with a guy on each side of me holding my arms down, wrapped a Turkish towel around my face and poured water in the towel. Just before I drowned, they brought me up, asked questions, and then forced me back down and started over again. Grinning and watching with a watch in his hand, the Jap knew exactly when I would lose consciousness. I never did tell them anything.

One day they sat me down at a table opposite a Jap officer and on the table was a stack of documents six or eight inches high. He flipped through the papers pausing now and then so I could read them as he turned over the pages. One piece of stationery had *U.S.S. Hornet* as its heading.

The interpreter began, "What is a hornet?"

With a bit of glee, I said, "A bee."

I could see that the documents were maps, charts and crew lists that had been taken from some of our downed aircraft on the mission. One document listed the crews on the raid by name, rank, serial number, airplane tail number, and crew position. After showing me these, the Jap officer ran his finger across the name Doolittle.

"Do you know him?" inquired the interpreter.

"Yes," I said.

"We captured him, and we executed him." And then he ran his finger down the list and drew his finger across another name, my name.

"I know *you* know this guy!"

I responded spartanly.

During the next interrogation they brought out their information file on the *U.S.S. Hornet* and showed me documents and pictures of the *U.S.S. Hornet* from the day the keel was laid to the christening of the ship and the celebration. Yet the questions continued. How big is the carrier? How many guns does it have? What fuel capacity does it have? How many aircraft can it carry? To each of these questions I said, "I'm not a Navy guy, I don't know." The first words I learned in Japanese were, I don't know, and I don't understand. Each time I said it they responded with angry kicks to my shins. We endured day and night interrogation in this manner for four weeks.

Though we had very little opportunity to verbally communicate with one another, nevertheless we reached a group decision that since the Japs had all the information about the raid, there wasn't any need for us to take any more punishment. After that we responded to questions when it was obvious the Japs already knew the information.

Our unwashed bodies had become riddled with sores. Fleas, lice and rats plagued us all the time in our cell. The fleas would crawl up our pant legs and lay eggs along the seams, and when they hatched out, they could really make us dance. A pack of rats lived just beneath the floor. We took turns keeping the rats away while the others slept.

To add to their individual and collective miseries, all eight of the men had dysentery . . . They had not had a bath, shave or change of clothes since their capture and their beards and hair were now long and matted. The odor of their own bodies, the stench from the *benjo,* a hole in the floor serving as a toilet, and the humid atmosphere of the airless, lightless cells became overpowering. The only relief from this form of torture was the hours of questioning. (Glines 65)

Food and water became our chief concern. The food consisted solely of weak tea and watery rice. The rice, mixed with worms, maggots, and other unidentifiable bugs, provided the only protein. I decided to eat everything given me because I wanted to survive. My buddies were convinced likewise, and soon worms became a delicacy. I was driven by a desire to make our captors accountable, and I endured their beastly treatment determined to live and testify of it. While in the Tokyo prison I found a nail and scratched my name and the names of the men in prison with me on a floorboard of my cell and in every cell I occupied after that.

A hundred and twenty days after our capture we were allowed our first bath. One by one we were marched to an upstairs room and allowed to languish in a tub of hot water with plenty of soap. I had my beard clipped and a hair cut. Guards gave us clean clothes, and we had our first good meal. I felt certain we were going to be executed.

They moved us to Shanghai to a room in the Kiangwan prison where a military tribunal was assembled. We stood before the tribunal, with the exception of Hallmark who was gravely ill and brought in on a stretcher, and heard the court proceedings spoken in Japanese. An interpreter informed us we had been sentenced and the tribunal had issued an order for our execution. They had taken the execution order before the Emperor and he negated the execution commuting the sentences instead to life imprisonment. Unaware at the time, the sentence commutation to life imprisonment was not afforded to all of us as we learned later. Pilot Lieutenant Hallmark, pilot Lieutenant Farrow, and his engineer-gunner Sergeant Spatz, crewmembers of the sixteenth plane in the squadron who bailed out and were captured near Nanchang, were taken to Kiangwan Cemetery in Shanghai and executed on 15 October 1942. No explanation ever devolved why they were singled out.

THE BLACK DEVIL

We began our life-sentences in Kiangwan military prison in Shanghai in solitary confinement. On rare occasions we were allowed outside for a half-hour with our buddies, but never allowed to talk to them. Months dragged on, winter cold became unbearable in our unheated concrete cells, and extra blankets were denied us. Exactly one year to the day that we had soared from off the deck of the *Hornet*, they moved us to a new prison in Nanking, where we expected our fate would be death to commemorate that anniversary. Yet we were again placed in solitary confinement. The isolation, probably our worst punishment, blurred days into blurred months until we suffered with hallucinations. Thoughts of food consumed me. I dreamed about food, and planned delicious food to eat when released.

When fall came, and I felt the harsh cold of winter again, I had the feeling I could not survive another winter. In October (1943) Bob Meder began to show the advanced stages of beriberi. Though difficult for him to walk, he still came out in the exercise yard whenever we had a thirty-minute exercise period. We weren't allowed to talk there, but did so when the guards weren't looking. On one particular day in October, I stood near Meder and he leaned over and whispered, "Say a prayer for me." I talked to him and tried to give words of encouragement. We always did our best for each other. The chief guard hollered for me to stop, but I continued talking quietly to Meder. Tension mounted when George Barr, Jacob DeShazer and Bob Hite, members of Bill Farrow's crew, were removed from the exercise yard, but I continued to attend to Meder, helping him get up, and assisting him down the hall to his cell. By that time the chief guard was in a rage. As I passed him, he lashed out with his fist and caught me squarely in the face. I staggered under the blow, but kept my temper. I let go of Meder, calmly set down the bucket in my hand and with all the strength I could muster, snapped my right fist forward and caught him square on the jaw, knocking him against the wall. Stunned and humiliated, he recovered and tried to strike back at me with his steel sword scabbard. Each time he lashed out, I dodged and dropped into a fighting crouch. After a few minutes, the guard withdrew and I suppose I was the obvious victor. From that time on when a guard pushed or shoved me, all I had to do was drop into a fighting crouch and he would back up a respectful distance. That guard never showed up again. The Japanese had obviously not been trained to fist fight. After that incident they called me the Black Devil, although they knew I was usually pretty mild mannered.

Later that day a doctor came and gave Meder injections and treatment and he improved for a time, but on 11 December he passed away. I didn't know it until later when I heard a commotion down at the end of the hall. Finally a guard came and unlocked my cell and the cells of DeShazer, Hite and Barr and led us into the cell of Bob Meder. He lay in a wood casket in a respectful repose with flowers on his chest. It was a gut wrenching shock—a vivid reminder of our own frail vulnerableness. Later cremated, his ashes were returned to the prison. Discouraged and disheartened, yet beyond grief, I moved into action and demanded to speak to Honcho Donno, the number one man. He came into my cell with an interpreter and through him asked me what I wanted to discuss.

"I'm going to talk to you in English because I know you understand English," I began, "and if you don't want your interpreter to hear what I have to say to you, you can excuse him," I continued.

He looked around at the interpreter and said, "You may be dismissed."

I directed my gaze firmly on him, and my pent up thoughts formed my words. "We are upset about your letting Meder die. The treatment that we're getting isn't as good as we treat animals. If we are going to continually be treated like dogs, we're going to continually act like dogs. And if your guards get messed up once in a while, you'll know why. I can't see any reason when we are soldiers and we're fighting a war that we have to be treated inhumanely. We want to have better food for sustenance, we want heavier clothing to stay warm, and we would certainly like something to read, or do some

kind of work, be it a menial task." The food never got any better, nor
did we get warmer clothes, but we were given four books written in
English, and that's really what we needed. We passed the books
among us and it helped us all, and our attitudes changed. One of the
books was the Bible. I read from the 23rd Psalm, "Yea, though I walk
through the valley of the shadow of death, I will fear no evil: for
thou art with me; thy rod and thy staff they comfort me. Thou
preparest a table before me in the presence of mine enemies; though
anointest my head with oil; my cup runneth over. Surely goodness
and mercy shall follow me all the days of my life: and I will dwell in
the house of the Lord for ever." We memorized passages and it nour-
ished us. Some of the verses that I hadn't understood before became
clear.

Once again relocated, this time we were transported to Peking
(Beijing) by train to the harsh and regimented FengTai prison near
Tianenmen Square. Again we were placed in solitary. There were
months and months that I thought through all the events in my life,
and about growing up and about my mother and father. After that I
designed a home just the way I wanted it from the ground up and
nailed in every board. Meder had been good at getting us into mind
games, but he was no longer with us. For months and months, I
would rethink thoughts, then say to myself with disgust and des-
peration, I've already thought through that!

ARE YOU AN AMERICAN?

One day I heard commotion out in the hall beyond my cell and
looked through the narrow slit in the door. I saw a bunch of guys in
khaki uniforms talking American. I had been in solitary confinement
for more than two years and I could only think it was another
subversive trick by the Japanese to torment me. The khaki uniforms
approached my door and the guy in command unlocked and opened
it.

"This guy looks like an American. Are you an American?"

I didn't say a word.

Finally, I rasped, "Where were *you* captured?" He studied me intently. I had a beard that was so long that I could wring both hands around it to shake the fleas out. My face was chalk white behind my black beard my six-foot frame a skeleton.

Raising his voice, the khaki uniform said, "*Who* are *you*?"

"I was with a lieutenant colonel by the name of Doolittle several years ago, and I got captured by the Japanese in Wenchow," in a voice made hoarse from disuse.

He eyed me suspiciously, then warned the other uniforms, "You guys better watch *him*, he's off his trolley. Those guys were all killed years ago."

I'd found my voice by then, "Come down the hall, and I'll show you three more guys that were with me." We went down the hall and opened the cells of Lieutenant Robert L. Hite, Lieutenant George Barr, and Corporal Jacob DeShazer.

"The war is over," the khaki uniform exclaimed.

I didn't understand.

"You're free!"

*

Editor's Note:

Chase Nielsen and three other crew members were imprisoned for over three years and four months. Within ninety days following his release, Colonel Nielsen returned to the Japanese War Crimes Trial in Shanghai where he was the first witness against his captors. A board cut from the floor of the prison cell in Shanghai where he had scratched the names of C. J. Nielsen, R. J. Meder, Geo. Barr, R. L. Hite, J. D. DeShazer into the wood with a nail was condemning evidence, since the Japanese captives claimed the airmen were never prisoners.

"During the time of the War Crimes trial, I went down to the village where I had first beached and with the Graves Registration people we searched for the remains of my dead crew members. After we got the remains of Donald E. Fitzmaurice and William J. Dieter, I obtained the remains of the three men that had been executed: Dean E. Hallmark, William G. Farrow, and Harold A. Spatz; the remains of

Robert J. Meder; and also the remains of Leland Faktor, a member of pilot Lt. Robert M. Gray's crew. They had all been cremated. All of the remains were brought back to the United States and buried in Arlington National Cemetery with the exception of Sergeant Spatz whose remains were buried in the National Cemetery at the Punchbowl in Honolulu."

All sixteen aircraft and crews in the Doolittle mission were forced to crash land or bail out in Japanese occupied territory or in the China Sea with the exception of pilot Ski York and his crew who landed in Russia. All eighty crewmembers were recovered from China within twelve days after leaving the Hornet with the exception of the crews of pilots Dean Hallmark, Bill Farrow and Ski York. York and his crew were imprisoned in Russia for thirteen months until they escaped and were able to find their way back to the United States. Lt. Colonel Doolittle, recipient of the Congressional Medal of Honor for leading the successful mission, was later commissioned brigadier general, continued to serve in the war effort, and lived to see his ninety-sixth year.

On returning to the United States, the crewmembers were transferred to other military assignments and many were killed in action in other theaters of war before the war ended in 1945. The U.S.S. Hornet was lost in the Battle of Santa Cruz on 26 October 1942.

During the dark years of his imprisonment when the world was unaware whether Colonel Nielsen was living or dead, the Air Force presented the Distinguished Flying Cross in a posthumous ceremony received by his mother on behalf of her missing son. Colonel Nielsen was also the recipient of the Purple Heart with Oak Leaf Cluster, Commendation medal with Oak Leaf Cluster, and many other medals including The National China Pao-Ting medal that was pinned on his chest personally by Madam Chiang Kai-shek. Besides serving in World War II his military career spanned the Korean and Vietnam wars. He again obtained pilot status and flew in the Strategic Air Command for thirteen years piloting B-29s, B-50s, B-36s, and B-52s and held various staff and command positions until he retired from the U.S. Air Force on 30 November 1961. Continuing his career with the government as an industrial engineer, he was involved in measuring workloads and establishing manpower requirements, retiring in 1981 from Hill Air Force Base Ogden, Utah.

Born and raised in Hyrum, Utah, Colonel Nielsen graduated from Utah State University with an engineering degree in May 1939. He and his recent bride Phyllis Henderson reside in Brigham City, Utah. He has two sons and a daughter, eight grandchildren, three step-children and four step-grandchildren.

I asked Colonel Nielsen one final question: How do you feel about serving our country and how do you feel when you see the American flag?

"I was never prepared to be a prisoner of war, but it has given me a much deeper appreciation for my fellowmen and the country I live in. I enjoy my freedom. I think it's the greatest country on earth and I would go fight for it any day that they needed me. Freedom is for those who are willing to defend it. I feel my buddies died to help perpetuate the freedom that we enjoy today.

"Let us have as our objective our country's welfare, and with the blessings of God, may our country become a vast monument to wisdom, peace, strength and liberty upon which the world may gaze in admiration forever.

"And, I don't think my buddies died in vain."

*****

SOUTHEAST ASIA 1968

Chapter 2

Sergeant Bauduy R. Grier

Sgt. Bauduy R. Grier
498th Squadron, 345th Bomb Group,
5th Bomber Command, Army Air Corps

ADRIFT

The luckiest guy in our crew the morning of 10 March 1945, was navigator Robert Wandry who learned at the last minute he could go back and hit the sack—only the lead squadron navigator was required for the mission. Amidayo Fincenti our engineer and Jimmy Lane our tail gunner hoisted themselves up through the hatch after me. Already aboard, on his second mission, copilot Charles Raney sat next to the pilot in the cockpit. We waited for the signal. Then our squadron of B-25s took off at sixteen-second intervals from a short dirt runway, previously a Jap fighter plane airstrip at San Marcelino on Luzon. Too short for a regular take off, pilot Benjamin Franklin Chambers revved the B-25H to full throttle exactly the way Jimmy Doolittle had roared off from the *Hornet* to get airborne three years earlier. Our mission was a routine hunt for Japanese ships ply-ing the shipping lanes to and from Japan. From Luzon we flew west across the South China Sea flying the right wing position to the lead aircraft on my seventeenth mission.

Flying toward the French Indochina coastline (now Vietnam), we came upon a luckless Japanese oil tanker stuck on a sandbar fifty yards off shore from the island of Hainan. We flew within a few feet above the ship and dropped a bomb that bounced on the water, drove into the hull and the ship exploded in flames. A second later we heard and felt a big WHOOMPH! Usually equipped with a forty-five second delay fuse, that day our bombs detonated on contact and exploded directly beneath us as we flew in just above the ship's mast. In the waist of the plane, the concussion felt like someone hit the bottom of my feet with a baseball bat.

I flipped on the mike and asked the pilot, "Ben, everything okay?"

"Yeah, we probably have a big dent from the concussion in the belly," he drawled.

We flew along the coastline scanning for another prey, finally rendezvousing with our squadron and turning east back across the South China Sea toward our air base on Luzon. With tension and action of the morning behind us, I settled back in my radio seat and pried open my K-rations when I heard a rumh rumh rumh and black smoke streaked past the side window. I radioed Ben again.

"Ben, everything okay?"

"Yeah—Bauduy (BOdee), we have a problem with the left engine. The hydraulic lines are broken and I can't feather the prop—probably vibrations from the bomb concussion broke hydraulic lines. Nothing I can do about it—the prop is windmilling and slowing us down—we're losing altitude, and it looks like we're going to ditch."

"We'll throw stuff out the back to lighten the plane," I offered. We had flown training missions many times on one engine; our two Pratt & Whitney's were always reliable.

"Well, you can do it, but I don't think it will help," Ben responded.

Jimmy and I threw the .50 caliber guns out, the radio set went next, and anything not lashed securely we tossed out. Ben's message came only a couple minutes later.

"Get yourself ready to ditch," Ben radioed calmly.

Jimmy and I fastened our Mae Wests. I took an axe and broke out the Plexiglas in the side window ready to dive out when the plane hit the water. Then sat against the bomb bay bulkhead with Jimmy bracing against me. Jimmy was a big guy from Tennessee, bigger than me all the way around. We had been friends for the past two years chiefly because we were both positioned in the waist of the plane—Jimmy as tail gunner and I as radioman. Each mission we flew together he'd say, "Bauduy, you know I can't swim a lick. You gotta take care of me buddy—you're a good swimmer and ya'll been a lifeguard."

I kept my headset on. "Okay, we're 500 feet," copilot Raney's words were calm, "300," the words came in staccato intervals, "200—100—brace yourself we're going to hit."

I threw off my headset. "Jimmy, buddy, this is it!" We hit the water with a force that felt like a car hitting a concrete wall at hundred miles an hour, then everything went black.

I regained consciousness when water surged around my waist. Jimmy, also knocked out, squirmed in front of me about the same minute. Jimmy dove through the side window inflating his Mae West on the way out. I threw a small one-man raft out the window after him set to deploy on impact. I glanced toward the cockpit already underwater, and bellowed and hollered hoping for some response at the same time yanking on the lever to release the main life raft. During training, the hatch would swing up and around and the raft would inflate automatically. Now in the frenetic moments before the plane sank, the raft compartment jammed, opening only a few inches.

The plane had plowed into a big swell and flipped nose down in the water angled in a 45-degree dive—I had to get out fast. I dove through the open window and swam hard afraid of the sucking back-water of the lurching aircraft. I could have beaten Mark Spitz' Gold Metal Olympic time that day as I busted waves right past Jimmy. Then I heard from behind me.

"Bauduy come back! I can't swim!"

Jimmy was floating in the shadow of the looming tail. I thought the world of my buddy Jimmy, I just never figured out how he passed flight training without learning to swim—we were required to swim fifty yards. I swam back to him. Jimmy hadn't snatched the one-man raft I had thrown out for him and it had disappeared.

From a report of Captain Elmo L. Cranford, lead pilot of the squadron that day:

[Cranford] and his other wingman had stayed with the damaged B-25 during the ditching and watched as the plane sank in about 90 seconds. Cranford could see Grier and Lane struggling below in the sea, which was running in very heavy swells before a 30-knot northeast wind. The two B-25s had little gas to spare and remained overhead for only three minutes after the plane sank. A ground station was notified of the details and location of the ditching before the planes continued on their way. (Hickey 273)

At Luzon a rescue effort was immediately launched, but when extensive searches over the next several days produced no results, the crew was given up for lost.

"We don't have time to fool around," I yelled, "we've got to do this as quick as we can—please do everything that I tell you, and maybe we'll make it—maybe we won't. First, put your head back and don't worry about getting water in your face or your mouth, you can spit it out, your life jacket is holding you up. When your head goes back, your feet come up, and when those feet come up you start kicking as hard as you can—don't stop until I say stop!" He did what I asked, and I started pulling a hard sidestroke. He kept kicking, and I pulled him along by his collar. We were fifteen feet from the plane when the tail rose up vertically then plunged down and disappeared.

LOST AT SEA

Alone bobbing on twelve-foot swells, I thought, what am I going to do now? I'm scared, my buddy can't swim, and we're three hundred miles from the nearest land.

Then up through a mass of air bubbles popped the inflated life raft landing right side up fifty feet away. It was a miracle! The force of the water had opened the jammed door, the raft inflated, and popped up to the surface.

"Whow! There it is!" I yelled, but it was going one way on the waves and we were going opposite with the current. "Jimmy! The only possible chance we have is that raft. We got to get that raft!" From debris surfacing from the sinking plane, Jimmy had grabbed onto a floating oxygen bottle and wouldn't let go.

"Jimmy, that oxygen bottle will hold you up for as long as you can stay awake," I yelled. "You've got to come with me!" But he wouldn't respond. I tried making him angry by threatening, hoping it would force him out of his frenzied death grasp on the oxygen bottle, but he wouldn't react.

I whirled around and swam for the raft. Halfway, I snagged onto the small one-man raft thrown out for Jimmy and hung on to it, at least we had one. Then threw it ahead of me ten feet in the direction of the larger raft and swam toward it, my inflated Mae West encumbering my arms with each stroke. Within three feet of the big raft, I lunged just as a wave swept over my head and the raft skidded ahead twenty-five feet. Stroking hard, I finally grasped the rope encircling the raft and heaved myself over the bloated side, but the unyielding life preserver pushed me away. Anxious to rescue Jimmy, my fingers fumbled with rigid life jacket clasps. Grasping a penknife from my pocket, I cut the straps and slipped out of it throwing it into the raft, grabbed the one-man raft and tossed it in, and climbed aboard. I broke open a bag lashed to the bottom of the boat containing provisions, joined two-section oars together, rammed them into oarlocks, dug a paddle deep in the water and swung the raft around.

"Jimmy," I hollered, where the hell is Jimmy? "Jimmy!" I couldn't see him. My oars dug deep, "Jimmy!" and turned this way and that. "Jimmy!" ocean swells were impossible to row through—I searched—but Jimmy had slipped beneath the waves.

Distraught and fatigued, I lay in the bottom of the raft sobbing, vomiting swallowed salt water, and sobbing again—I had saved Jimmy then lost him!

Limp and doubled over from exhaustion, I felt the same as I had after winning swimming meets. "Bauduy," I bellowed through sobs, "you better pull yourself together 'cause you're goin' to be out here for a long time."

Looking at my GI watch it had stopped on impact at 1:27 that afternoon. I turned the watch hands to see if it would run again and they stopped at 6:10. I tucked it away.

Checking the survival pack, there were six pints of canned water, candy and chewing gum, vitamin tablets, fishhooks, pork rind bait, fish net, a book *How to Fish*, Catholic and Protestant versions of *St. Matthew,* and a small book of Jewish prayers, a whistle, zinc oxide, sulfanilamide, a sail, and one flare; in my pocket a penknife, and in my wallet a hundred dollars.

Accustomed to sailing, I calculated my position in the China Sea while attaching the plastic sail to a mast fashioned from oar sections and secured it in a ready-made housing in the raft's center section. My brain cleared and emotions calmed as my hands worked with ropes and sail. I would set a course eastward until I made landfall on one of the seven thousand islands in the Philippines. By sailing three miles an hour for ten hours daily, in ten days I could sail three hundred miles to the Philippines. The China coast was closer, though predictably unfriendly, and I dismissed that landfall. I set my course east, felt the northeasterly wind on my cheek, and began tacking against the wind with an oar for rudder. My success depended on my discipline to conserve six pints of water.

My flight jacket and shirt had vanished. I ripped my torn pant legs off at the knees. I lashed my shoes securely in the front of the boat aware I would need them to walk through jungle when I reached an island. Quite unexplainably, my socks were gone, though my shoes had remained on my feet. The one-man raft produced a slicker with hood that I slipped on, then slathered my face with zinc oxide to prevent sunburn. The weather was hot, though wind and salt spray kept me comfortable enough, except when storm clouds threatened squalls. I read *How to Fish*, both versions of *St. Matthew*, and the Jewish prayer book every day. Though I hadn't been a religious person, often I thought about God and contemplated praying, but I wasn't sure how, or if I was good enough to save—so I just kept to my calculated sailing schedule.

I awoke each morning at sunrise, or earlier if I hadn't slept well, riveted to the east watching a blazing fireball fight out of a watery horizon to course across the azure sphere and demarcate a new day. Yet the days and long nights fused, each one like the last. I sang to keep myself company, most often singing two of the more popular songs *Don't Fence Me In* and *There Will Be Some Changes Made*. I languorously lay in the bottom of the raft beneath tarp, yellow side up. Though when enemy planes appeared overhead I flipped blue side up to fade into the sea. I rationed drinking water, swallowing one small sip every three or four hours.

Lured by what appeared to be floating cellophane candy wrappers, I curiously grasped for them and received a jolting shock and stinging finger from a Portuguese Man-o-war. My finger swelled from the poisonous sting and on the following day I punctured it with a fishhook, squeezing and wrapping it with a scrap of pant leg. I had received cuts to my forehead and knee when the plane ditched, and slashed my hand while cutting through life preserver straps with my penknife. All of them healed within a week.

I tried fishing, threading the leathery pork rind bait onto the over-sized fishhooks and jigging them. Invariably I caught fish so large they jerked the line clear from my hands. Smaller fish wouldn't bite, but using the fish net, I netted a nice eight-inch catch. It had been several days since I'd eaten anything. I severed head and tail, carefully slit and cleaned the belly and began scaling it when it slipped from my hands over the side into the water. Quickly I grabbed for it, but jaws of a big fish snatched it first.

One morning while lying in the bottom of the raft squinting at cloud forms, I recognized the formation of my squadron flying from east to west. I jumped up—I had seen them once before, but now they were closer, and thinking this was my best chance to use my only flare, I shot it off. The squadron turned and headed toward me. They had seen it! I flapped the tarp in the air—yet they flew on. After all, I justified, a small dot on a sun glazed ocean is impossible to see. During training exercises our crew had to locate a raft moored in the Gulf of Mexico, and even though we knew the coordinates, we couldn't find it. Japanese bombers frequently flew over, and I watched confidant now that they wouldn't see me either.

Four or five times swells crashed over the bow washing me overboard, but after the first flailing dunk and race to retrieve the raft, I tethered myself to the boat.

On the eighteenth day I went berserk with thirst and drank the remaining two pints unrestrained. The water gently slaked my thirst refreshing me. Though later I moaned, "You dumb idiot." From then on my eyes scanned clouds for rain, and there were two or three rainsqualls, each one yielding a mere half-cup of slightly salty water that collected in my outstretched slicker.

INDELIBLE DREAM

Several months prior to flying that fateful mission, I had a dream—an unusual dream—more like a nightmare—that indelibly stuck in my memory in detail. In the dream I flew a mission in which the plane crashed at sea, and I was alone on a raft for twenty-one days. Well, there I was, just the way it happened in the dream. I pulled out my watch again—the hands had rusted in place at 6:10. I had the impression I might be rescued on the twenty-first day around six o'clock.

Without water for the next couple of days, my parched throat finally overpowered my better judgment, and I drank seawater, dissolving candy Charms in it to disguise the salty taste.

Water calmed to tabletop smoothness—a sign that land must be near—or was that my indomitable spirit keeping hope alive? A shark circled and lazed in the shade of my sail. When it approached too aggressively, I thumped it on the nose with my fist. A bamboo tree floated by—the China Sea was dirty with all kinds of floating trash. Again, I drank seawater. It was the twenty-first day. Nightfall descended without rescue.

During the next day a waterlogged two-by-four floated toward me with two sea crabs resting on it. I paddled closer, picked the three-inch crabs off the board, shelled and ate them, washing them down with seawater.

I had always believed in God. I began to seriously think about Him then, and felt impressed to pray. I felt despair, and knew I would die if not rescued quickly. I had never prayed before, but I began aloud, "Dear God, I haven't been what you would call a real good person. I don't know if I'm worth saving, but I would certainly like to be. If you could see your way clear, I would like to make it, however, 'Thine be done.'"

Next evening with the seas still placid as a millpond, I lay in the bottom of the raft napping, always with one eye open, the tarp pulled over me for shade. The sun was low on the scarlet horizon when I felt humming vibrations through the bottom of the raft. I jumped up scanning the sky.

Unknown to Grier, the U.S.S. Sealion, a submarine out of its regular patrol area, was en route to Subic Bay in the Philippines, when it received orders to rendezvous with the U.S.S. Guavina.

The submarine *U.S.S. Sealion* under Commander C. F. Putman was cruising 130 miles off the China coast and about 225 miles [east-southeast of Saigon]. Earlier in the patrol the *Sealion* had torpedoed an [unmarked] Japanese merchant ship carrying allied prisoners of war. The sub had rescued about a hundred out of the water and taken them to Australia. As it cruised toward the rendezvous point, the watch spotted a yellow life raft at five miles through the high periscope. No life was evident aboard, but Putnam investigated anyway. (Hickey 297)

A ship was coming directly at me! I lunged to the front of the raft reaching for the whistle in the raft pocket and blew hard—an S O S and kept blowing, hollering and waving. It was—a—submarine. I hailed, "Hey, where you going? Help! Don't leave me!"

From the conning tower the skipper hollered, "Don't worry, we're not going to leave you. We're coming around easy. We don't want to knock you over and lose you."

"Okay," I hollered back, "Hey, what day is it?"

"April second—Easter was yesterday; the Marines invaded Okinawa. How long have you been out here?"

"Since March tenth," I yelled, and pulled out my watch, the hands still rusted tight at 6:10. "What time is it?"

"1807," hollered the skipper—6:07 P.M—rescued just three minutes short of the time rusted on my watch.

The *Sealion* made a wide U-turn and inched up within twenty feet from me when a sailor hollered, "Can you catch a line?"

"Sure, throw it here," and he threw a line with a weighted ball on the end, and I jumped and caught it nearly careening overboard. I tied the rope to the raft and they pulled me onto the bulging side of the submarine hull where several hands reached down and grabbed the raft and pulled it onto the deck.

"I can walk, leave me alone," I said testily, and took a step and collapsed. Six guys caught me and gently lowered me down through the conning tower. Below deck I stood up asking, "You got a drinking fountain onboard?" and veered toward it on wobbling legs.

"Get him off of there, he'll get sick," the chief pharmacist mate warned.

It took a guy on each arm and leg to pry me loose.

Adrift without benefit of a centerboard, I hadn't sailed east at all. After twenty-three days, I had drifted south on the current 550 miles from the point the plane submerged, and was rescued 225 miles off the coast of Saigon, (South) Vietnam.

My shorts drooped over my protruding hipbones. I weighed eighty-five pounds, having lost forty pounds. A sailor in the only bed in sickbay crawled out and I crawled in. Other than sunburn over my entire body, saltwater ulcers big as boils on my legs, arms, buttocks and back, a half-inch beard, and a thirst that couldn't be quenched, I was okay. Though, I had the worst case of hemorrhoids the doc had ever seen—having gone nineteen days without relieving myself because of dehydration. The sailors made this airman welcome and comfortable, and outfitted me with Navy dungarees, even providing a pillow to sit on. The doc gave me a shot of morphine so I would sleep, but it didn't phase me; I was high on life. Later he slipped me two sleeping pills, but I couldn't sleep.

"Anyone here from Delaware?" I ventured. Wilmington was such a small town nobody was ever from there, so I always said Delaware.

"Yeah," the cook spoke up, "I'm from Hocession."

I had caddied at Hocession's Hercules Country Club golf course to earn spending money during my boyhood years just four and a half miles from where I lived. "Your family owns the general store in town, right?"

"Right," he said.

Already I had a buddy from my hometown. "Any chance of getting me some water?" I pleaded. A few minutes later he came back with a frosty metal pitcher full of ice and water. It was great, until (true to the doc's warning) I began vomiting into the trash can.

The submarine submerged and cruised toward the point of rendezvous with the sub *U.S.S. Guavina*. When we surfaced adjacent to the other submarine, five airmen transferred onto the *U.S.S. Sealion*. Coincidentally, they were all airmen from my bomb group who had floated in the water for twenty-four hours. Though remarkable that we were plucked from the sea, it was extraordinary that my country had between sixty and eighty US submarines continually patrolling the South China Sea to recover downed airmen.

Arriving in Subic Bay, Philippines, I mailed off a gift of the hundred dollars to my mother and father instructing my dad to buy a new suit (which could be bought for $50 in those days), and mother a new dress; and when I got home I would take them out to dinner, an uncommon event during wartime.

When reporting the plane crash details to my commanding officer, he said, "You shouldn't have been sent overseas since you had three brothers in combat."

I could only respond irately, "Thanks for telling me, now."

Granted convalescent leave after a week in the hospital, I sent a telegram to my mom and dad when to expect me. Arriving home, we had a joyous reunion, though my mother pleaded, "Please don't send us another telegram."

*

Editor's Note:

The Griers' family of four sons and a daughter served overseas during World War II. Prior to Bauduy's return, Mr. and Mrs. Grier had received a war telegram notifying them their son Warren was killed in action in Germany and buried in Holland. Previously, telegrams were received by them that George, a Pfc. in the Army and Silver Star recipient, was wounded in Germany. Son, Wayne, staff sergeant in Patton's Third Army and recipient of a Bronze Star, sustained injuries after his entire squad was killed in crossfire. Daugh-

ter, June, staff sergeant in the Women's Army Corps (WACs), served overseas in Africa and Italy for twenty-seven months. In retrospect we might say Sergeant Grier was a "Private Ryan" having had three brothers and a sister serving overseas simultaneously with him. He was discharged in December 1945 after serving two and a half years.

Bauduy Grier was accustomed to swimming and sailing during his youth. During his high school and college years as a champion swimmer and diver, he bagged the Middle Atlantic Conference diving championship for three straight years. While attending the University of Delaware, he broke swimming pool records four times and school records eight times. In dual team swimming meets, he won thirty out of thirty-five races, coming in second in the other five.

Graduated from the University of Delaware, he majored in mechanical engineering, and is retired from Hercules. Sergeant Grier has three children, Stephanie Williams, Jane Layman, Bauduy Grier, Jr., and four grandchildren. His present wife, Monir Eghbal Kitabchi native of Iran, was a volunteer administrator for Iran's orphanages in Tehran during the reign of Shaw of Iran, reporting to Queen Soraya, and subsequently to Queen Farrah. Monir's father, Eghbal, owner of the leading publishing house in Iran, wrote and published Discovery of America, *the first book written in Iranian about the United States. Because he favored western culture and US politics, he sent Monir and her son, Massoud (Massey) Parvar, to the United States to complete Massey's education.*

*****

Sgt. Bauduy Grier Army Air Corps,
prior to crash
Courtesy of Bauduy R. Grier

Sgt. Grier in Navy dungarees
Courtesy of Bauduy R. Grier

Bauduy Grier Championship diver,
broke U of Delaware dive records;
took Middle Atlantic Conference 3
years. *Courtesy of Bauduy R. Grier*

CHAPTER 3

SERGEANT
GRANT P. PARKINSON

Sgt. Grant P. Parkinson
2nd Bn, 3rd Regiment,
3rd Marine Division, Marine Infantry

THE SOUNDS AND SMELLS OF WAR I KNOW SO VERY WELL

Guam 21 July 1944 0800: Enemy shells spanged around my head as 3rd Battalion Leathernecks grappled with combat packs, tossed them over the sides of Higgins boats, and jumped into amphibious tanks mid the awkward rise and fall from ocean swells. By the time we had crossed the last three hundred yards of coral reef, men on both sides of me were bleeding and dying. The amphtracks pulled up on the beach, and I jumped over the side. Enemy bullets whistled past me while I helped lift those that were wounded back into the amphibian to return them for medical aid. Then I dove for cover behind a coconut log on the beach. Attacking a hundred yards from Adelup Point the first day of the Guam invasion, we took cover all along the beach as gunfire pinned us down for several hours. I lay on wet sand, ocean waves slapping at my boots. The Japanese were well dug in above us on Fonte Ridge, sitting up on the cliffs shootin' down at us like they were shootin' squirrels.

Our Navy ships in the bay had shelled and bombed our landing zone at Red Beach #2 for seventeen days before the invasion. It must have been a fierce battle because the Japanese hadn't buried their dead yet, and they lay rotting in the sun, the feculent stink of decaying flesh loathsome in my nostrils.

"Parky," someone barked at me, "get those tanks unloaded." It was dusk by the time the tanks were ready to drive up the beach to shell and strafe ahead of us. We ran behind them and fought our way to the base of Chonito Cliffs and the base of Fonte Ridge. Darkness overcame us there and we dug in for the night.

Before daylight, we began the precipitous climb hand over hand up the lava rock cliffs above us. With flame-throwers and grenades, we cleared the enemy from caves and crevices. The Japanese would rather die than surrender. So we did what we had to do. At the same time that we were crawling up the rock, Navy fighter pilots strafed the cliffs and shot rockets into the ravines ahead of us, flying in so close their ammo clips fell on our helmets. Our ships fired artillery that exploded the cliffs above us. It was perilous climbing just dodging friendly fire, but at the same time the Japs were rolling grenades over the edge of the cliff on us. Snipers had us in their crosshairs and many around me tumbled from the cliffs. With help from Navy aircraft and artillery from ships in the bay, we seized the Japanese fortifications at the top by the end of the second day. There were over two hundred Japanese found dead in the ravine. Our casualties were yet to be counted.

We secured the ridge and waited until other battalions joined us and tanks arrived with them. On top, the terrain leveled out into grass covered rolling hills with clumps of coconut trees and jungle brush. The camouflaged Japanese were everywhere yet out of sight. We formed a skirmish line and each squad fell in behind a tank and moved forward shelling and strafing while we flushed out stragglers. Suddenly, the tank in front of me stopped and I was a target. A Jap machine gun opened fire. I hit the ground dropping down next to Roth, my friend from Pennsylvania, and we nodded in recognition of the caliber of the gun. The machine gun rattled again, and I felt bullets pulse across Roth's back as he humped up and then sagged. I thought this is it! If that Jap raises his gun an inch I'm dead. Not waiting an instant, I moved for better cover, then looking back over my shoulder watched a corpsman reach Roth, but I knew he was dead.

Within the skirmish line, we moved aggressively across the semi-open terrain ignoring enemy sniper fire. Not all my buddies made it across the fields and their blood stained the volcanic earth. As the fighting died down at dusk, we speculated that we would dig in on the edge of Fonte River Canyon.

At twilight the peaceable evening sounds were audible and my thoughts quieted in the stillness. I reflected on my good-natured friend Roth dying next to me. It struck fear to the very heart of me.

We dug in. Dug in meant a foxhole big enough for three men, five to six feet wide, six feet or more long, and a foot deep with the fresh soil piled up front facing the enemy, or the direction you thought they would attack. About the time we were satisfied with the size, we heard that hot coffee was available from a temporary mess unit located back across the same open terrain we had covered that afternoon. We hadn't had anything hot for several days and four of us ventured out a hundred and fifty yards back. We filled two five-gallon gas cans with coffee and started lugging the full cans. Out in the open, half way back, snipers started firing at us. Unwilling to give up the coffee, we juggled the sloshing cans between us on a dead run while rifle bullets twanged just above our heads. The coffee was good and hot, but it tasted of gas.

That night on the edge of Fonte Canyon over cups of coffee, we spoke of our wounded buddies and others, like Roth, who had died, and listened to jungle sounds reverberate louder as the night quieted. Distantly, there were staccato sounds of a machine gun and an occasional mortar exploding where fighting hadn't quit for the night.

By midnight the second day of the invasion, casualties in our regiment had reached 815 killed, wounded or missing. We were paying with blood for that meager earth.

The peanut-shaped island of Guam, thirty-two miles long and four to eight and a half miles wide, is a piece of United States real estate in the Marianna Islands acquired in 1898 because of its strategic military location in the Pacific. The Japanese navy had attacked and seized Guam on December 8, 1941, one day after attack-

ing Pearl Harbor, and all the U.S. Marine and Navy personnel stationed on Guam when occupied by the Japanese had been taken prisoner, tortured, or beheaded.

The next morning descending from Fonte Canyon by an easier route than the cliffs we had scaled, I witnessed an astounding spectacle. Looking down from a ridge trail into the desolate ruins of Agaña, once a metropolis of 12,000, the Japanese soldiers were holding a full-dress ceremony on a bomb-pocked avenue of the capital city, or what was left of it. Flashing Samurai swords gleamed in the sun as they paraded wearing full combat regalia. We ordered an artillery concentration, but it was too late to catch the prideful retreating Imperial enemy.

We were taken off the front lines for the day and put in reserve to give us a chance to rest up before returning. Working through trees and low brush half way down the ridge, we came onto a small Jap field hospital with four or five abandoned beds. The Japs had left in a hurry evidenced by a dead soldier still lying on the operating table. We moved down off the slope to the bottom of the canyon and out into the open at the edge of the city. Agaña was now a dead city, and buildings and homes were masses of abandoned ruins. Skeletons of victims, killed during the race to evacuate the city, remained in motionless flight near carports and patios. We cautiously moved through Agaña checking for snipers.

We moved on through Agaña without incident and re-entered the jungle. After two or three miles, we stopped for a break by a house in a small clearing. We were resting, relaxing and eating rations, taking it easy while probing around the dilapidated house. An old grass roof from a collapsed shed lay on one side of the clearing. Suddenly, a Jap jumped out of the rubble and aimed his rifle right at me. He had been hiding when we came upon him. I couldn't figure why he singled out me to aim at among our guys present, but maybe because I'd grabbed my rifle and was aiming at him. Without hesitating, I fired first. It all happened in a couple seconds. Even while relaxing, our reflexes were taut.

Later in the afternoon we moved up and took a position on the front line again. That night we dug in at an area partly covered with brush that was facing a slight incline. As we dug our three-man foxhole, we noticed a lot of wood ticks as big as my little fingernail. I could pick them up, fold them four ways, set them down, and they would crawl off. The only way I found to kill them was to rip them in two.

It was a moonless night with brilliant stars, and around midnight, my companions and I heard commotion in the next foxhole down the line to our right. A moment later hell broke loose in the camp as screaming Japs attacked, overran our line of defense, and surrounded us. One Marine saved his life by reaching up and grabbing the Samurai sword of an attacker just before he swung it to behead him. With badly cut hands, the Marine fought in his foxhole until his buddy overpowered the Jap. Later in the night during a second attack, Japs ran screaming through our camp again. Three of them stopped and looked down into the foxhole behind us, which was our command post. They were made to realize their mistake immediately.

At 0300 not too far behind our lines, we heard someone call cadence in Japanese. The Imperial enemy had assembled fifteen or twenty Jap soldiers into formation and were marching them through our lines. Marine guns opened fire. The night was chaotic. All the while we were swatting at the blood-sucking wood ticks.

Next morning our defense line was entanglement of war paraphernalia and the dead. We moved into the jungle on patrol to find our attackers that were moving toward the north end of the island. During the day, we captured a Jap supply dump along with a 10 x 10 storage building stocked with sake in small fancy bottles. I had suspicioned that the Japanese were often insanely drunk. While we rested, temptation overcame at least one Marine. Then moving through dense and tangled foliage at the north end of the island, we approached a small banana grove half-acre in size and our CO ordered us to dig in for the night. During our foxhole excavations, we discovered that our field telephone lines had been cut. The telephone lines were laid along the ground to keep our company in touch with battalion headquarters and the Japs had obviously found and severed them. My lieutenant called me over.

"Parky, take two men and follow the lines back and find out what's happened." My entire squad was now down to Brewer, Higgins and myself. I said to them, "Let's go," and the three of us started back through the jungle following the phone line moving slowly and quietly. We had gone only two hundred yards when we heard Japs talking. We couldn't understand them, but knew we were walking toward them, and by the sound there were quite a few.

Brewer climbed a big tree. From a rather high perch, he excitedly whispered, "There's a bunch of them but I can't get a count."

"Well," I whispered, "be quiet and get down before they shoot you down." Brewer slid down the tree, and we headed back to camp to report. We concluded we had bypassed them earlier in the afternoon, and they had moved into the area we had just passed through, discovered our phone line, and cut it. Too dark to take a patrol out to get the Japs, the CO waited until morning.

As usual it rained that night. I lay in water in the foxhole that caught the rain and from freshly dug dirt splashed rivulets of mud on me. It was a usual occurrence. During the night the rain stopped, but it was a dark, moonless night. In the quiet I could hear the ocean waves breaking on a beach in the distance. We were taking our turns on watch, two trying to sleep, while one kept alert for an hour at a time, when around midnight we faintly heard engines starting up—not ours—I could tell by the sound. They kept getting louder and louder. We had dug in on the edge of a banana grove, and circling the trees was an old dirt road, or what was left of it, for it appeared not to have been used for some time. Right in front of our three-man foxhole, a bomb shell had exploded leaving a hole in the middle of the road about three or four feet deep and six to eight feet wide in a "V" shape.

Listening to enemy tank engines grow louder and closer, I sweat nervously. A few minutes later their silhouettes loomed in front of us. Two tanks at the corner of the banana grove went around the far side to miss the trees, and two headed in our direction. The tanks had a 37mm cannon and a mounted machine gun. All we had were rifles, B.A.R.s, carbines, and one inoperative bazooka that had shorted out in rainwater. In those moments I aged and felt old.

The tank tracks clanked toward us. One tank dropped into the "V" shaped shell hole and the engine killed. A Jap soldier was standing half exposed out of the tank so close I could have reached out with a stick and hit him. It sounded like he was giving his driver hell in Japanese and soon the tank re-started and backed out of the shell hole, this time heading around the left side straight for our foxhole. The Jap harangued his driver again, this time the tank stopped, backed up and proceeded around the shell hole on the far side from us. They had not seen us, and we held our breaths and crawled out of the foxhole and crept into the banana grove. Two tanks went by our side of the grove and two went along the backside and moved off into the jungle. We relived that close call several times that night.

At first light we heard a battle off in the distance. Later in the day we passed by the same Jap tanks, and they had encountered devastating flame-throwers from our Marine battalion. The Japs were expected to die in battle rather than dishonor themselves by surrendering.

During the next two or three days while headquarters decided where to send us next, the division photographers came to take a picture of our company, and we got together in a small jungle clearing. Prior to landing on Guam there were three hundred-fifty men. We were now eighty-nine men. I was in the 4th platoon, which originally had forty-nine men when we hit the beach, now just seven of us were left the rest wounded or killed.

We moved north and bivouacked on the highest point on Guam atop 861 foot Mt. Santa Rosa and from there began day and night patrols. I was an NCO in charge of a fifteen-man patrol. We got as many Japs during patrols as we did during the invasion campaign. As a rule, we would get in single file along the jungle trail with a scout in front who had guts and steady nerves. Back of him was the man in command, and behind him the main body of the patrol about ten feet apart spread out fifty to a hundred feet. Several times on patrols the enemy would hide out and let our lead scout go on by, then ambush the main body of the patrol.

It was on one of these patrols that I had wrenching chills and dry-heaves, while engaging the enemy in a hot gun fight. The Japs retreated and disappeared into the jungle, and we searched the rest of the day for them. Returning to camp in late afternoon, and while I was making my report to the lieutenant, dry-heaves hit me again. He asked what was happening and I told him about the chills and fever plaguing me during the day. The debriefing immediately stopped and a corpsman called. After asking me a couple questions, the corpsman took my temperature then informed my lieutenant I had malaria. I was carted off with my gear to a field hospital in Agaña. While at the hospital I swallowed lots of quinine, fruit juices and plenty of good chow spending eight to ten days recovering. By that time my chills and fever subsided and my strength returned.

I rejoined my outfit and continued leading patrols for another two months. On night patrols we went into the jungle where we knew Japs frequented along a known trail and waited sometimes all night, hoping Japs would walk into the ambush, which they often did. We killed many during these patrols, and they got some of us.

"In twenty-one days, the Third Marine division had overrun and captured sixty square miles of territory… During the last phase of the campaign, the Division had buried 3,264 Japs and estimated that an additional 2,000 remained to be buried following the announcement that the island was secured. Cost of the operation to the Third [Division] was 3,626 casualties, including 619 killed in action." (Aurthur 162)

With the island secured, the patrols came to a halt, and we began training for the next campaign. By then attacks of malaria came every six to eight weeks. Each time I spent a few days in the hospital then rejoined my outfit to continue training. We were advised in our next invasion we would land on an island that didn't have much vegetation, consequently, training continued in open terrain. One day we were in a skirmish line crossing a large open grass field when a Jap soldier jumped up out of hiding and started running across it. We didn't have any live ammo, which didn't stop one Marine, rather than watch him go, chased after him and downed him with his rifle stock. The poor guy was half starved. We had given him a chance to stop, but he wouldn't.

Our training continued into the first part of February 1945, until ordered to pack our combat pack: one blanket, poncho, change of clothes, rations, rifle and ammo. The rest of our gear was stuffed in our sea bag and put in storage. We boarded the *USS Callaway,* a troop ship, on 9 February 1945 and moved out into the bay at Apra Harbor and waited for the rest of the invasion force to form up. It was during this wait that another malaria attack hit me. When I was in the throes of convulsive heaves, my lieutenant approached.

"Parky," he said, "What's the problem?"

"I'll be okay in a few minutes," I gagged. But he took me down to sickbay. The medic took my temperature and a blood smear.

"Take this man ashore, he should be in a hospital, not going into combat," he concluded.

I complained—I didn't want to leave my outfit, but no one listened. There was a strong bond among us in the squad—we had taken care of each other. I well remember giving my extra socks and clothes to men in my squad and returning my rifle to the gunnery sergeant. Walking up the ladder from the hold, the fellows all waved good-byes. That was terribly hard for me—to leave my buddies like that. A few minutes later a special boat came out and took me ashore to the naval hospital near Agaña.

The next morning, 16 February, my unit steamed out of the harbor for the next invasion, and the infamous battles yet to be fought on Iwo Jima.

At the hospital, I had a chance to think about my wife and baby and those powerful emotions of home would rush through me until I had to dismiss them. I enjoyed watching women nurses, listening to a radio, and eating good chow. We had been on C-rations for the entire three weeks of the invasion, some days a lot of us didn't have water to drink. I reflected it had been two and a half years since I had been sworn into the Marine Corps on 21 September 1942. Again my thoughts switched to home. My wife Millicent holding our baby, and my mother, my brother, and his wife had been there to say good-bye to me. After fourteen months of training, without a furlough, I had gone directly overseas to New Zealand. After several more months of training, I landed on Guadalcanal 6 July 1943 to practice assault landings for the Bougainville invasion.

I had been in the antiaircraft battalion of the 3rd Marines then. The tropical island of Bougainville was an impenetrable jungle of bottomless mangrove swamps, crocodile infested rivers, and insects.

The wild aborigines were headhunters, not to mention 40,000 Japs who could slash your head off with one swipe of a Samauri. On 1 November 1943 we had been strafed and bombed while waiting for our wave to build-up before landing on Bougainville. When we finally hit the beach, we wallowed in the surf while getting trucks and 40mm antiaircraft guns to shore while enemy aircraft strafed us and Jap troops fired at us from the beach. As soon as we got the guns set up, we returned fire. I saw the worst dogfight in the sky that first day. I witnessed our fighter planes and the Jap planes shooting each other down and planes exploding in mid-air. The air was full of disintegrating aircraft parts—wings, fuselages, props and engines, and men free-falling through space. Some men had parachutes and some didn't and Jap planes strafed them as they descended. It was a brutal sight, unfortunately, forever captured in my memory.

Someone shook my shoulder and the musings over Bougainville subsided. I was on my way to Hawaii to the naval hospital near Pearl Harbor at Aiea Heights. While waiting for transportation to the naval hospital we were taken to the mess hall at Hickam Field where the mess officer made ham sandwiches for us. We started eating when he said:

"Any of you guys like a drink of milk?"

I hadn't had fresh warm milk since I left New Zealand, twenty months ago. He took us back into the kitchen and there were seven or eight ten-gallon cans of fresh milk that had been delivered from a nearby dairy.

"Help yourself!" he said.

It was cold, and I believe the best milk I had ever tasted. Those ten-gallon milk cans brought back memories. They were just like the ones I had poured buckets of fresh milk into during my early years milking cows on the ranch.

I left Pearl Harbor arriving in San Francisco on 11 March 1945, and since the hospital treating malaria patients was in Oregon, I boarded a C-47 along with fifteen other guys and flew to Klamath Falls. The barracks were all new, located in a beautiful pine forest, and the chow was the best I'd had in the Marine Corps. I had barely settled in when my first thought was to phone Millicent. I hadn't talked to her for over two and a half years. It was not long after that,

I was given my first leave: a seventy-two hour pass, plus a thirty-day leave. So I caught the bus for home. There're a lot of telephone poles and small towns between Oregon and Utah, and time to get nervous about meeting my wife. It took a long time to contemplate that I had a son who was already three years old.

And then I saw my wife Millicent. Inexpressible feelings of delight went through me. The next day I saw our boy, Grant C., a fine looking boy, and I felt real proud.

It was good to be home.

*

Editor's Note:

The 2nd Battalion, 3rd Regiment reinforced, was awarded the Presidential Unit Citation for action against the Japanese forces when capturing Fonte Ridge, Guam.

The US was compelled to reimburse the British government for every coconut tree cut down on Bougainville during the war. It was the U.S. Marines that had invaded, dug in and fought for Cape Torokina, Hellzapoppin Ridge, Hill 1000, Hill 600, Hill 500, Cibik's Ridge and in fact all the British island of Bougainville.

Sergeant Parkinson was in the Marines for three years. Prior to enlisting, he was employed as an aircraft sheet metal mechanic, repairing aircraft at Hill Air Force Base (known then as U.S. Army Air Corps). Being a war defense job, there was little likelihood he would be drafted. However, the summer of 1942 proved a restless time for the country and for him. Those were years when men felt deep responsibility to do their part for their country, and though he had a wife and child, he chose to enlist in a specialized branch of the service. His fourteen months of training gave him experience with hand to hand combat, use of bayonet, pistol, rifle, machine gun, B.A.R., 40mm antiaircraft guns, 30 caliber and 50 caliber machine guns, and making repairs and maintenance on all of them. His training included ambush and attack tactics, scout and sniper training, rappelling off cliffs, and fording streams.

Sergeant Parkinson is presently a retired rancher and farmer with his beloved wife, Millicent Carlsen Parkinson, and live on the origi-

nal two hundred acre homestead which Grant's great grandfather Timothy Parkinson homesteaded.

His son Grant C. followed in his father's footsteps and served in the Marines in the Guantanamo Bay, Cuba stand-off. His son Stephen served in the Navy in Vietnam and his son Timothy served in the Army in Vietnam. Besides three sons, they have a daughter Christine; and a daughter Laurrie, deceased, and twenty grandchildren and ten great-grandchildren.

I asked Sergeant Parkinson, "How do you feel when you see the flag?"

"I don't think young people realize the blood that has been spilled for it. I don't know how to describe my feelings."

"Tell me more," I said. "When you saw the flag being raised on Bougainville and Guam, how did you feel?"

"It would give me a thrill, that's all there is to it. It was an emblem. My crew and I would reflect, There it is! We've done it again! I'm not fancy with words, but there is something there that I just can't describe, a feeling inside me that this is the way it should be, and I was proud to be an American. Very proud."

*

If I get to heaven's gate St. Peter I will tell,
One more Marine reporting Sir, I've done my time in Hell.

*****

Invasion of Agana, Guam 1944
Third Marine Division, Infantry Press First Edition, 1948

Invasion of Bougainville at Cape Torokina, Solomon Islands, 11/1/43
"The Jap Air Force was there to meet us, as well as Jap troops on the beach."
Third Marine Division, Infantry Press First Edition, 1948

Photo taken in jungle clearing following the liberation of Guam, August 1944. Ninety Marines out of the original 350 survived. Grant Parkinson was 1 of 7 survivors from his platoon of 49 men.

Photo courtesy of Grant P. Parkinson

CHAPTER 4

LIEUTENANT
LOUIS M. BAXTER

Lt. Louis M. Baxter
353rd Bomb Squadron,
301st Bomb Group,
15th Army Air Corps

NOWHERE TO HIDE

I can go home after today if my luck holds out for one more mission. I'm the guy that sits in the glass nose of a B-17.

Because my .45 was bulky and noisy, I quit carrying it on my third or fourth mission and carried my knife instead. It's silent if I have to use it. My well-oiled combat boots sit next to me in the plane, tied together with rawhide laces. I hope to sling them around my neck if I have to jump. Flight boots are often jerked off when parachutes open, and I want to walk out, if I can. Bombardiers are scarce. They don't last long in the glass nose of B-17s when German fighters make head-on attacks.

I had to force myself to get in the plane today. The Linz Oil Refinery in Austria is our target, and it's never an easy one. Mostly I'm anxious because this is the last mission I have to fly before I go home.

But the mission began with trouble when we barreled down the runway with a full load of gas and bombs and couldn't get airborne because our tailwheel came off. The strut holding the wheel had dug into the metal ramp runway, jolting and jerking the aircraft. We had reached a critical amount of runway before the plane finally lifted.

Gaining cruising altitude of 27,000 feet, we headed due north over the Adriatic Sea from our base at Foggia, Italy. I was feeling tired and burned-out. A big party awaits me tonight at the base when we return, and I can go home after today if my luck holds out for just one more mission. The fifty-one missions I've flown as bombardier have spanned only six months, but in that time I've aged well beyond my twenty-two years—a full ten years claim Army psychiatrists. But I say, ten years each time my name appeared on the Battle Order. Only six other officers besides myself have completed fifty missions during my time in the squadron while the rest have been shot down, killed, field injured, or for other reasons can't fly anymore.

When I joined my crew six months ago, I was a young kid. All of us officers enjoyed excellent accommodations on the *Sea Perch,* and pilot Jimmy Cole and I had shared a stateroom. Jimmy was so short he had to use two seat cushions to fly a B-17. But while we lounged in comfort and had six to seven course meals three times a day, the enlisted men, crowded into a stinking hold existed on poor scanty rations. Jimmy and I and two other officers loaded all the beef and ham sandwiches we could carry under our flight jackets and took them down to them.

Zigzagging across the Atlantic on a troop ship avoiding German subs, I felt the danger that would follow me for the next six months. Then on the hot morning of 9 June 1944, after a ten-day stop over at Oran, Algeria, our ship slowed while entering the Naples harbor and I went up on deck for a view. Aghast at the devastation and partially submerged shipwrecks that pockmarked the harbor, I watched our ship *Durban Castle* jockey along side a capsized hull, then anchor, and we disembarked onto the dry side of a rolled ship onto shore.

During a five-mile march to a train station, Lieutenant Lucky, who was carrying a case of popular records, record player, and duffel bag, collapsed from heat exhaustion just two miles into the march and Jimmy and I retrieved much of his load for the remaining three miles. Boarding cattle cars at the station, the tired train clacked east a hundred and eighty miles as we swayed in a hot airless car until reaching our base at Foggia, Italy.

OUR SQUADRON CAMPED IN AN OLIVE GROVE

We reported to the 301st Bomb Group just outside Foggia, a town in the lower quarter of Italy near the west coast of the Adriatic. Our 353rd Bomb Squadron was encamped in an olive grove, and on arriving we were told to relax and await orders for our first combat mission.

Because of shortages, six of us shared one tent, including pilot Jimmy Cole and Lieutenant Lucky. The tent had a dirt floor, one light bulb dangling from the center pole, and a stove made from empty oil drums fueled by 100-octane gasoline piped from a tank that hung up one of the olive trees. Whenever the fire went out in the stove, it was the newest man's job to re-light it. This all worked quite well until a new officer came in and tried to light it while drunk and the explosion blew him out the tent door. After that our tent had a black coating of soot inside.

We were split up and placed with experienced crews for the first three missions. Our first target was the Budapest Oil Refinery in Hungary on 14 June 1944, and we had to fly the tail-end Charlie position, the unenvied last place in a formation of forty planes. Just two or three miles after takeoff, a plane in our squadron caught fire and the men tried to bail out at 3,000 feet, but four of them couldn't get out of the burning plane. I learned after the mission that my friend Rissio was one of them.

We flew over the Adriatic, spread out and test fired our machine guns. In the nose of the plane were two swing guns, one on each side of the aircraft. Because the guns were mounted on heavy springs, movement of the plane slammed the gunner against the side of the aircraft. I spoke up and claimed the guns were about as useless as teats on a boar hog and after that mission, we flew with a crew of nine instead of ten. After checking the guns, we climbed on course to bomb the Budapest Oil Refinery.

Flak was heavy, and we had no fighter escorts to assist us. Exploding shells from 88mm and 105mm antiaircraft cannons blackened the sky. It's hard to describe my fear when flying through flak. The closest is a feeling of fear, hatred, and anger that churns together in my stomach and seizes my gut into knots. We all experienced extreme fear and it was difficult for a man to control it, and affected each of us differently.

Two B-17s were shot down by flak in front of me. One plane exploded killing everyone on board, and from the other plane I counted only seven parachutes. When landing at the base after the mission, I learned that our crew gunner Rissio was one of the men that couldn't get out of the plane that caught fire shortly after take off. Rissio had family in Rome and had talked about getting a pass into Rome to visit his grandfather.

The crew went to Rissio's services. Fingerprinting the dead before they lay them to rest was customary, and I volunteered. As I pressed his fingers, my fingers sank into Rissio's burnt flesh. I explained to my crew afterwards that I wouldn't attend their services if they got killed, not out of disrespect, but because it tore me apart. The chaplain read a short service off a form, yet to my way of thinking a sincere prayer would have been more appropriate. Rissio was buried in the military cemetery at Bari, Italy. It hardened me, and I realized my slim chance of getting out of this war alive.

Weather conditions kept us grounded for the next seven days until 22 June when I flew my second mission. At briefing we were told the target was the Foronova Di Earo Marshaling Yards, Italy. We lost one plane from our squadron, but our bombs hit the target.

The following day pilot Jimmy Cole was lost on a mission. I folded up his belongings from our tent. I heard that no one got out of his plane, but years later, I learned Jimmy had bailed out and had been captured by the Germans.

Out of the thirty men that reported with me ten days earlier, there were only twelve men still flying, and I had forty-seven missions yet to fly.

On 24 June, I flew again, and we knocked out the Piatra Railroad Bridge in Romania. This was an easy mission because there was no flak and nearly all of our 86-ton of bombs hit the target. Our Bomb

Group was flying every day since the weather improved.

NOWHERE TO HIDE—26 JUNE 1944

I was appointed lead squadron bombardier and our target was the Lobau Marshaling Yards in Vienna, Austria. After the general briefing where we were shown the target and told what flak and fighters to expect, everyone was excused except lead pilots, lead navigator, and lead bombardier. Strike photos, altitudes, corridors, bombsight settings, wind conditions, and two alternate targets were given us in case we couldn't hit the primary target.

As we entered the target area, flak exploded all around us, and as I dropped our bombs, our number one engine was shot out. Seconds later an 88mm cannon shell went through our left wing leaving a hole the size of my head. It would have been the end of all of us if the shell had exploded. Then returning to the airfield, we couldn't get our landing gear down. We headed for a beach on the Adriatic about forty miles south of our front lines and braced ourselves for the crash. Everyone except the pilot and copilot sat in a row against the wall behind the bomb bay bulkhead with legs spread and bodies tight against each other as we approached the beach. The plane hit the water with a jolting bang, took a leaping bounce, and hit again, making a terrible crunching noise as it crumpled to a stop on a sandy beach. We moved fast and cleared the hatch. We had radioed ahead and a truck was waiting and returned us to our base. My nerves were shaky and I felt damn lucky to get back alive. I needed a rest, yet my name appeared on the posted Battle Order to fly again the next day.

It was on this mission that we had as our guest an Infantry captain who flew in our plane as waist gunner. Because there had been contention between the Army and the Army Air Corps that had reached the point where men were fighting each other, the higher-ups decided to send an officer and enlisted man from the Army to fly with us for a couple of missions. At the same time an Air Corps officer and enlisted man spent a week in the trenches on the front lines. It was hoped that the two services would gain a higher respect for each other. We left on this mission with twenty-eight bombers and returned with just eighteen. After landing safely, the visiting officer commented.

"I have encountered several heavy artillery shelling on the ground, but nothing nearly as intense as we flew through today. On the ground we can jump into a foxhole, or hide, but you guys have nowhere to hide. I will never again get into an airplane as long as I live."

TAKE ME OUT AND SHOOT ME

An hour after we got into formation on the way to our target the Rakos Marshaling Rail Yards in Hungary on 27 June, we flew into cloud cover and saw B-24s returning. We figured they had received a recall, and we questioned why we hadn't. Somewhere in the clouds the lead squadron with planes following had made a wide U-turn. Tension mounted as we strained our eyes watching for head-on aircraft. Suddenly, we broke out into clear blue sky and flew directly into a squadron of thirty to fifty German fighter planes.

I called out, "Bandits 12 o'clock high." The fighters seemed to be as surprised as we were and it gave us time to get to our guns. They dove in on us, attacking head-on. I could tell the old fighter pilots the way they barreled in on us, while the inexperienced ones hesitated a few dives before firing. They shot out two of our engines and riddled us with bullets.

"What should we do?" The pilot shouted at me.

I shouted back, "Dive for that cloud below."

The pilot countered, "What about our other planes?"

"There's only one other plane left, and he can follow us down," I yelled. The pilot rolled the plane into a dive just as the third engine took a hit. We were about 27,000 feet when the fighters first hit us and came out of the lower clouds at 14,000 feet. I glanced southward and saw twenty of our planes struggling in on the target with about the same number of German fighters flying on their tails like a swarm of angry bees.

With but a single engine running, the pilot hollered to me, "We're going down, what're you goin' to do with the bombs?"

"Follow the PDI," [pilot direction indicator] I hollered. I hadn't started this blasted war, but I was going to take as many of the enemy with me as I could. With bomb bay doors open, I set the Intervalometer that spaced the ten, five hundred-pound RDX bombs at 200 yards apart. I sighted in on the main street of Budapest and let 'em go. As we got past the city, the pilot shouted orders.

"Prepare to bail out!"

I grabbed my mike and yelled, "Bail out? Hell! I just bombed that city! If those Germans get their hands on me, they'll hang me. Everyone get *ready* to bail out, but try to get as far out in the country as possible, then we'll bail out two at a time. We might have a chance of walking back to our base." We were about 7,500 feet and losing altitude, and we began throwing everything out to lighten the aircraft—guns, ammunition, our twenty-seven pound flak jackets and anything that wasn't tied down.

"Get ready to bail out, as I start number two engine. If it catches fire, we gotta' get out in a hurry," the pilot hollered into his mike. He lowered the bomb bay doors, so we could jump. We were all praying as he tried to start engine #2. It turned over, belched a large cloud of black smoke and started. The pilot got two-thirds power out of the engine, and raised the bomb bay doors. We approached the Yugoslavian coastal range of mountains with only enough altitude to skim the tree tops. Landing at our base field over an hour late, they had already listed us as missing in action. Our Bomb Group had sent out twenty-eight planes that day and only fourteen returned.

I was jumpy, irritable, and couldn't relax; and went over to the mess hall and got something to eat, and then to the Officers Club to play Bridge. I couldn't keep my mind on the cards and happened to throw them down on the table just as Major Block passed by. He asked me to have a walk with him.

"What's the matter with you Baxter, can't you take it?" he began.

"Major," looking him straight in the eye, "I'll fly one more mission, and if it's anything like my last two, you can take me out to that big tree and shoot me."

"From your squadron only one other man flew both missions and came back alive," he revealed.

Lieutenant Lucky was killed. I packed up his belongings from our tent, and gave his record player and records to the enlisted men's new clubhouse in memory of Lucky. I couldn't get my mind off my last two missions and the images of three B-17s exploding within a few hundred yards of me with no survivors. I also learned that my friend McKay, a tail gunner, was killed on his first mission out of England.

I walked over to my tent glad there was no one there. I got down on my knees and called out to my heavenly Father to help me before I cracked up. I don't recall hearing a voice, but the message came clear to read my patriarchal blessing[1] I had been given and carried with me. I dug deep in my duffel bag and found it in my Book of Mormon. Within it I read if I was called into the front lines, I would be protected. I put my things away, lay down and slept as peacefully as a lamb.

SALUTED THE COLONEL—IN MY SHORTS

On our return from our mission, we saw new silver B-17s parked in our area on the airfield, and I exclaimed, "Man Oh man! Our new planes, the B-17G models with a chin turret under the nose are here at last." As it turned out they belonged to the Eighth Air Corps based in England that had landed at our airfield. Martin and Stressing, two officers I had trained at Rapid City, were among them.

The next day I was awarded another air medal and then went to the ocean swimming with the boys. We relaxed and talked about the fun we had together in Rapid City. They couldn't believe the losses we had sustained during the past two days. I let them believe that was normal, as we claimed we did the work, and the Eighth Air Corps got the glory. When we returned from the ocean, I told Major Block that I was ready to fly again. I wanted to get the missions over with as soon as possible. Later in the afternoon my name appeared on the Battle Order for the next day.

On 30 June, at the same time Eighth Air Corps bombed Berlin, our target was Blechhamer North Oil Refinery, Germany, and I was squadron lead bombardier. Fortunately for us the German fighters went after the Eighth Air Corps, and we lost only one plane from our squadron of forty.

1 July, we had to abort the mission, and I dropped our bombs in the ocean.

2 July, our mission to bomb the Brod Marshaling Yards inYugoslavia was a milk run. I didn't fly again for a few days and had nothing to do but lay around and take the boys' money playing Bridge.

7 July as deputy lead bombardier for the Group, we bombed Blechhammer North Oil Refinery, Germany again, a tough target rated as a double mission. The Germans rebuilt after we had bombed the last time, and so we bombed it again, dropping chemical bombs this time.

8 July, we bombed an airfield near Zwolfaxing, Austria, about seven miles from Vienna, using fragmentation bombs tied in 200 pound clusters. When these hit they exploded like huge hand grenades tearing apart anything in their path. A few of our fighter planes went in ahead of us and kept the German planes on the ground until we came within range and started bombing. Then approaching the target, we flew through dense explosions. Intelligence reported the next day we had wiped out nearly two hundred German airplanes. After the mission, I took two new bombardiers up to check out their bombing accuracy to give them ratings. I was squadron bombardier after just three weeks.

9 July was a great day for the 301st Bomb Group. We celebrated the Group's three hundred and first combat mission with a big party, and the next day Secretary of War Simpson came for formal inspection of the troops. I was exhausted from flying tough missions the past two days in addition to spending another five hours checking out two new bombardiers. I cleaned up around my area in the tent and told the boys I would not attend the 8 A.M. inspection. After I heard the last man leave our tent, I went to sleep again. Shortly after 8 o'clock someone snap-rolled my bed, and I landed on the dirt floor. Looking up, the first sergeant was grinning at me. Well, that riled me just a bit. I expect he could see I was just a little bit upset.

"The adjutant captain has ordered me to get you out of bed," he barked.

Now I didn't much like the butt-kissing non-flying adjutant, so I raised my voice just a bit so everyone could hear me and shouted,

"Don't you ever again come into my tent without my permission." Then added a little louder as the sergeant was disappearing, "And tell that yellow-belly captain to stay out of my way." As I gathered up my dusty bedding, I knew I must learn to control my temper better.

I just got to sleep again when someone yelled, "Attention!" I opened one eye, and never have I seen so much brass—all the way from colonels to General Twining, who was in charge of the Fifteenth Air Corps. I knew I must be in trouble with so many ranking officers in my tent. I was sure they were not there to present a medal. I got up and saluted them in my shorts.

"Lieutenant Baxter, why didn't you stand inspection?" demanded Group commander Colonel Batjer.

"Begging your permission to speak sir, the last two days I flew two very tough combat missions, and yesterday I checked out those two new bombardiers. I'm scheduled to lead the Group on tomorrow's mission, and damnit! I need some sleep! We all have to make judgments, and it was my judgment that winning this war was a darn site more important than standing an inspection. I'm sorry if I have shown poor judgment."

"I agree with your good judgment, Lieutenant Baxter, get back to sleep," Colonel Batjer retorted.

I hadn't acted by the book, but it sure felt good. Once those non-flying officers realized that men would rather take a court martial any day than fly another combat mission, they may become good officers.

I didn't fly again until July 14th. Cruising toward an oil refinery in Budapest, our ball turret gunner got sick and we returned to base. It turned out he had an appendicitis attack.

15 July, we bombed the Americano-Romano oil field at Ploiesti, Romania. By the time we arrived, there was a smoke screen covering the target, but we dropped our bombs in the center of the area, and huge black clouds of smoke bellowed up through the smoke screen. The antiaircraft flak around oil refineries was always intense, and that day was no exception. Coming off the target I was unable to get the bomb bay doors closed, and the drag made by the open doors slowed our plane, causing us to fall behind the rest of the squadron.

Without protection from the squadron we were vulnerable to enemy attack.

I decided to hand crank the bomb bay doors shut. I took off my flak jacket, parachute, and Mae West life jacket, and headed for the open bomb bay. The quarters were just too tight to work with those strapped to my body. I instructed the flight sergeant to hand me a new oxygen bottle every thirty seconds, since I didn't want to run out of oxygen, pass out, and fall out the bomb bay without a parachute. I got out on the six-inch catwalk, leaned over the open bomb bay and looked down at the ground 28,000 feet below. I said a brief prayer and started cranking up the doors with the hand crank. It took me five minutes of hard cranking to get the bomb bay doors closed. The pilot then poured on more power, and we were able to catch up with the Group and resume our lead position. The Group lost several planes, as was usual on a Ploiesti raid, but no one was injured in our plane.

I was outwardly calm now while flying our missions, though never cocky, and guys were noticing the change.

"You don't get scared up there do you? —you joke and kid around with us," commented one.

"You bet I get scared up there," I said. "I think my religion helps, or anyone that relies on God."

We had an atheist in our Group who was barely eighteen years old and had already finished college—a brilliant young man. One day we got talkin' about religion and God.

"You gotta' prove everything to me," he said.

"Well, you're a scientist, aren't you?" I said.

"Yeah, you know that."

"Well," I said, "you have your laws of physics, and then you have your theories. Now tell me what's the difference?"

"A law happens every time the same way," he said. "You can prove it with a formula and it's going to happen every time. That's a law."

"But you have theories, too," I prodded. "Explain to me what a theory is."

"A theory is an explanation of how something *may* happen," he said.

"Well, you say you don't believe in God because I can't prove to you there is a God. Can you prove to me the theory of evolution?"

"Yes—" and then he stammered, knew he couldn't, and was silently thoughtful.

"The way I look at it" I said, "if I believed as atheists believe, it doesn't help me. But believing in God, gives direction and comfort in my life." Well, I hadn't convinced him. We went through a couple of real tough missions, and one day I walked into the tent and saw him down on his knees praying. When he was through, I asked, "I thought you were an atheist?"

"I thought I was, too," he replied.

AWARDED THE DISTINGUISHED FLYING CROSS

17 July, last night Axis Sally in her broadcast from Vienna said: "Three Hundred and First Bomb Group, when you come into Vienna tomorrow, we've got a nice warm reception for you. If you'll check the clock in the Officers Club you'll find it's exactly fifteen minutes slow."

She was right. It was fifteen minutes slow, and we never knew who changed it. True to her warning, Vienna had a reception waiting. Our target was the railroad round house and repair sheds in Vienna, which was always a tough mission. I led the Group of three hundred and sixty airmen, and it weighed heavily on me. As we approached the primary target, clouds obscured it, so we bombed our secondary target, which was Vienna. The reason we bombed Vienna was in retaliation for reports that Austrian farmers impaled our parachuting airmen on their pitchforks as they came down. We had previously dropped leaflets on Vienna threatening to openly bomb the city unless they stopped it.

It was a rough mission, and I lost two men from my tent. I packed up their belongings and sent the packages to their homes. It was tough on us. We ate and slept with crew buddies, flew with them, played cards—and actually I think we were closer than most family members were because our lives depended on each other every day. I felt sorry for the men who were married, worrying whether or not they would return home to their wives and children, I tell you, it tied knots in my gut and changed me.

18 July, I was deputy Group lead bombardier and our mission was the Mimmingen Airdrome Field, Germany, and though we lost planes, it was considered a successful mission.

19 July, our mission was to bomb the Milbertshoven Ordnance Depot in Munich, Germany. When I returned I received a Dear John letter from my girl back home. Well, it wasn't exactly a Dear John— it just said she thought we should just be good friends now. She was, after all, an extra beautiful girl and eighteen years old, and she apparently wanted to date those draft dodgers back home. I was doing my best trying to stay alive in combat, and my girl wanted to replace me back home. It wasn't something I got over easily.

30 July, Major Block was pilot as we led the Group to the Brod Marshaling Yard in Brod, Yugoslavia, and successfully dropped our bombs on the target, though we lost a plane from our squadron. We were approaching our field to land when Major Block told everyone to land except for our plane and his two wingmen. Our squadron encampment had been buzzed twice by P-38s, which flew in just above the treetops, scared hell out of us, and blew dust all over. Now, it was our turn. We flew over their encampment with our props in high pitch and gave them a real good dusting. They didn't bother us again.

DARK ALLEYWAYS OF NAPLES

After completing half of my missions (difficult missions were counted double), I was due for rest and recuperation in Naples for ten days. Lieutenant Cameron and I sailed to Capri and stayed at the best hotel on the island, compliments of Uncle Sam, and sailed in the bay, kayaked and paddled to the grottos, hiked up the mountains, and visited old art museums. I loved this island, and even today often see it in my dreams. The facilities on Capri were strictly for Air Corps personnel, and the Navy guys on leave from destroyers docked in the harbor were a disappointed bunch because they couldn't get into the dances. I invited a group to my room for a party. My suite was large enough to accommodate thirty or forty men, and since it had a huge balcony overlooking the dining and dancing area of the hotel, we could hear the music, and we had a good time.

The dreaded day when I had to catch the boat back to Naples was approaching too quickly. That last night in Naples I couldn't sleep for thinking of the combat missions that were ahead of me. Even though we had been warned not to go out on the streets of Naples after dark, I was restless and took a walk along the beach in the sand. Feeling tired after about three miles, I headed back to the hotel, choosing an alley to cut down the distance. As I continued down it, the alley got narrower and narrower and darker and darker. Ahead, about a block away, three silhouettes jumped into the shadows of the alley. I walked over to the wall and struck a match, pretending I was lighting a cigarette when I saw four figures behind me move. I recalled stories I had heard about American soldiers getting beaten up, robbed, and left naked in the streets. Well, this wasn't going to happen to me without putting up a fight. I blew the match out and stuck my right hand with my thumb extended into the lightweight pea jacket I was wearing and continued down the alley at a fast pace. When I got within thirty feet of where I saw the three guys hide in the shadows, I shouted in a rough voice loaded up with foul language:

"Take off, or I'm gonna start shooting!" I heard a noise and men broke and ran down opposite ends of the alley, and I breathed a great sigh of relief, since I had no weapon.

INVASION OF SOUTHERN FRANCE

12 August, I returned to my squadron by truck and started to unpack when a jeep drove up and I heard an order addressed to me.

"Lieutenant Baxter pack up clothing and personal supplies to last you five days, and come with me."

"Where're we going?" I asked.

"Group headquarters."

After assigning quarters, he told me to report for briefing in an hour. My next mission was the invasion of Southern France.

"Your planes will be the first aircraft over the beachhead, and Baxter, you're the Group lead bombardier."

I studied maps, beaches and surrounding areas for two days. Timing was crucial for success of the mission. Air corridors were established for each Group. Our Group would go in at 16,000 feet, drop 100-pound bombs at 50 yards apart starting 500 yards out in the ocean then on up the beach for a 1,000 yards. Our sole purpose was to enable our troops in the landing barges to get a foothold on the beach.

15 August 1944—D-day on Beach #261, San Rafaël, France. About three hours before take-off a major from the Fifteenth Air Corps headquarters replaced me as Group lead bombardier. Majors loved recognition, and this was his big chance; I was deputy lead, and Cameron was pilot. As we flew over the southern coast of France, there were hundreds of ships and troop-landing barges lying in the Mediterranean. We were the first aircraft to the beachhead that day. I didn't know it at the time, but my cousin Darwin Baxter was in one of the landing barges assaulting the beach. We did a near-perfect job of bombing and the troops got established on their beachhead. It was an unusual eagle's eye view of the sea battle.

August 16 was a great day for me. I led the Group on a mission to destroy a railroad bridge about five miles north of Violin, France. This was the last bridge standing as General Patton's army had the Germans running backwards in an all-out retreat. We arrived in the target area, but because of a broken cloud cover, we couldn't see the bridge. Then clouds separated just long enough for me to get a glimpse of the bridge over #2 engine. I told the colonel to bank the plane sharply while holding the formation together, and make a 360-degree turn. I hoped it might be possible to hit the target before the clouds closed in again over the bridge. The pilot completed the 360-degree turn, and I took control of the plane from the bombsight. Even though we had a very short approach to the bomb run, we knocked out the bridge.

On landing, I learned I had been promoted to First Lieutenant and awarded the Distinguished Flying Cross for this mission, and General Twining complimented our Group for a job well done. The general said hundreds of motorized vehicles, including tanks, and hundreds of German troops had been captured because the bridge was destroyed. It was nice to be rewarded for a good job.

I had another head cold, and it was impossible to fly high altitude in an unpressurized airplane with a cold without taking a chance of breaking an eardrum, so it was 23 August when I flew again. Our target was South Vienna Industrial Center in Vienna. Lieutenant Stanley Bear was Group lead bombardier, and I was deputy lead again. The German antiaircraft flak wasn't too accurate and yet we lost two planes.

While debriefing the gunners after this mission, I learned that a sergeant, one of the ball turret gunners, fired his guns prior to take-off while he was checking them out. This was extremely dangerous because hundreds of men were on the airfield. After briefing, I asked him to come over to my desk, and I talked to him about it and ended with, "Mistakes are bound to happen, but make darn sure this never happens again."

24 August, the same gunner did the same thing. After briefing all the other gunners, I had the problem gunner standing before me again. I looked up, gave him my disgusted look, and asked him to have a chair.

"Anybody could make one mistake, but only a damn fool makes the same mistake twice. Something's bothering you and I wanta' find out what it is." I explained everyone got scared up there, and told him I wasn't going to make a decision on his case, he was. All he had to do was decide between flying his combat missions, and getting broken in rank from staff sergeant to buck private, and doing KP seven days a week until the war ended. "You're a good man, not a coward. Let me know by noon tomorrow your final decision," I said. I suggested he might want to pray about his problem, that pray-ing helped me.

The next day the sergeant came to my tent and we went outside.

"I prayed about it, and I want another chance," he said.

He went on to become one of our best gunners.

27 August, Captain Story, a bombardier, was not too well respected in the Group since he couldn't hit a target, and we were getting tired of his excuses. A typical Captain Story mission was that some bombs hit the target, but most bombs fell short. On this day he was flying as

Group lead bombardier and I was deputy lead. It was our third mission to bomb the Blechhammer Oil Refinery in Germany. Customarily, I gave our crews a countdown by the second before our bombs were to be released. This day was no exception, I counted twelve, eleven, ten, and just as I said nine, Captain Story let his bombs go.

"You sorta missed it that time Baxter," Colonel Henry, the lead pilot, radioed me.

"No, sir," I snapped back, "he dropped those bombs early and they hit at least a half mile short," which they did, and only scared hell out of the oil workers. We lost five planes on the raid and missed the target. I was upset!

That night the big shots down at Group really got into a rhubarb about what Colonel Henry said his bombardier told him. They sent a jeep for me and got me out of an excellent Bridge game to go down and back-up what Colonel Henry had said about the bombing. Now I found myself in a no-win situation between a colonel and a captain, and it was Captain Story's word against mine. Captain Story claimed his plane got hit causing his bombs to fall early. I might have let that pass by, except he made an arrogant remark.

"Some bombardiers just think they're a lot better than others," he said.

Now, I didn't particularly like this guy's crust and that remark riled me just a bit.

"Captain Story," I told him, "some bombardiers *are* better than others. I've instructed for five months and know this to be true." This heated up Captain Story, and he sneered.

"Well, what d' *you* think happened?"

"You must not have been on the target, since if you were, the bombsight would have automatically released your bombs," I said. Irritated, I added, "I'm going to take a walk and cool off." I resolved never to get into a wrestling match with a skunk because there's no way to win.

30 August, the target was Noyi-Sad Marshaling Yards, Hungary, and I was Group lead bombardier. Weather was stormy, and we turned back without finding our target. Colonel Henry thought we should save the taxpayers' money by not jettisoning our bombs, and I was the unlucky guy that had to replace the pins back in the bombs. We

came in for a landing and the colonel set the plane down easy. With a full load of bombs and a half load of fuel, we kept rolling and rolling—well beyond the end of the runway. Finally, we stopped when we hit mud. That was the last time I ever heard anyone suggest we land with three ton of bombs on board.

1 September, the target was the Nis Airdrome, Yugoslavia, and the Germans were expected to have a small number of fighter planes at this air base. They often hit us as we were starting out on a long mission and then hit us again just about the time we thought we were home safe. I flew lead bombardier, and we clobbered the target. Intelligence reported that nearly thirty enemy planes were destroyed.

6 September, our target was the Orada Railroad in Romania, and I flew deputy Group lead. We did an excellent job of bombing. The plane piloted by commanding officer Major Block was shot down and he didn't survive. He was a good person and an excellent officer.

10 September, the target was the Lodua Oil Refinery in Vienna, and our squadron led the Group. Flak was unbearable during the bomb run, and our wingman's plane took a direct hit in front of my eyes. Before it exploded, its crew bailed out. As we approached the target, our aircraft was bouncing around in the turbulent air and the pilot couldn't get the four engines running smoothly. We had just three minutes before we were over the target. Frustrated, I lost my temper, grabbed the mike, and hollered into it.

"Colonel, if you can't fly the damn airplane, let the copilot try."

Well, Colonel Henry forgot to take his finger off his radio button, so we all heard his reply over the communication system. He cussed me, he cussed the plane, he cussed the Germans, but he got the plane under control, and we hit the target dead center. As the pilot banked the aircraft and headed home, we started counting the new bullet holes in our plane when we discovered our ball turret gunner had been wounded.

On the return flight I had time to think over my terse words to Colonel Henry. He was back for his second tour of combat duty, and I had reason to believe I was in trouble. As a safety measure when we landed, I jumped out and rode in the truck with the enlisted men back to our quarters. Later that night, Colonel Henry came to the table where I was playing Bridge and asked if he could buy me a drink. I left the table and walked with him. I started to apologize for my actions on the bomb run when he stopped me.

"Lieutenant Baxter, we were on the bomb run, and the bombardier has full control of the airplane. I want to apologize to you. You showed a lot of leadership in a difficult situation and from now on when I fly, you fly with me."

I let out my breath—but after all, anything the Army could do to me could not possibly be as bad as flying another mission. Four of our planes in the Group were lost that day.

15 September, Intelligence reported a German submarine in dry-dock for repairs at Salamis off the tip of Greece. I led the mission as we flew over the desolate terrain. The submarine made a clear target and we put it out of action.

17 September, our target was the Rakos Marshaling Yards in Budapest. We bombed this target three months previously. The Germans had rebuilt it, and we bombed it again. At the target site, flak was concentrated on us and four planes were shot down even though we had P-51 and P-38 fighters flying escort. German fighter planes only had time to make one pass at us before our fighter escorts were on their tails.

September 20, we bombed Budapest again hitting the railroad bridge on the edge of the city with no planes lost. This was counted as my fortieth mission, and I was awarded an air medal, and my last ten missions loomed ahead of me. They were referred to as whiskey row—because at this point men began to think they had a chance to make it home, and began drinking heavily.

23 September, our target was the Brux Synthetic Oil Refinery in Czechoslovakia, and one of my toughest missions. The exploding flak was black and heavy around us, and we lost three planes. Pilot Toronto and assistant squadron bombardier Stanley Bear were both shot down. They had been with me from the first day of combat duty and were my close friends and crew buddies during thirty missions together.

October 12, after three weeks of rainy weather, I was in the sky again leading the Group in a bombing raid of German troop concentrations near Bologna, Italy.

THE SILVER STAR

13 October, at briefing I nearly fell off my chair when I heard we would be the only bombers over Germany that day, our mission Blechhammer South Oil Refinery in Germany. Because the Eighth Air Corps was weathered in and B-24s didn't have long-range fuel capacity, the mission fell to us. Even with two hundred fighter escorts and two hundred and forty B-17s, the odds were not in our favor. We could expect at least three hundred and sixty German fighter planes to attack us.

We took off shortly after sunrise and headed due north, spread out, and tested our guns with our aircraft leading the Group. We were a couple of thousand feet above the Alps when the Swiss notified us over the radio we were flying over their neutral territory. We radioed back, "We know it."

"We are going to have to fire on you," the Swiss responded.

"We know it," we replied. They fired antiaircraft shells that fell far short.

"You're firing too low," we radioed.

"We know it," was the doleful reply.

I listened to the sound of our four synchronized engines—that beautiful purr a B-17 makes when everything was going right, and had time to silently praise the men that kept our planes in repair. The first and second Groups went in over the target and encountered heavy flak. As they banked, I led our Group in. It was a surprise to us that we received only a dozen bursts of flak and not a plane in our Group was hit, but the next three Groups were shot up. The Fifteenth Air Corps lost fifteen planes, including one crew that had claimed if they ever got over Switzerland, they would land and sit out the war. I guessed we hadn't taken them seriously enough. Now there were only six men remaining out of the thirty men that had reported to my squadron in June with me.

On our return, Colonel Henry asked me how we could reduce losses and I told him my theory and belief.

"There are flak alleys within the target areas where gun emplacements are placed along roadsides," I explained. Later, he told me he had recommended me for the Silver Star, which I received.

On 23 October bad weather had grounded us for several days until someone had the harebrain idea to send up four planes over Germany, regardless of the weather, just to harass the workers at the Roseheim Marshaling Yards in Germany and disrupt their arms production. We referred to them as lone-wolf missions. Again we learned the Eighth Air Corps was grounded because of weather and the job fell to us. Planned as a night mission, four planes would be the only aircraft over Germany, the first plane leaving at 8 P.M., and the other three planes following at two-hour intervals. Men from our squadron were to make up the crew of the lead plane, and I was told to choose the bombardier. After asking two men to volunteer and receiving two turndowns with crazy looks, the word got out, and I couldn't find a bombardier.

Since our Group was using this wild idea for the first time, I reasoned it had a chance for the first plane to get through and home safely. I called Colonel Moorman, Group CO, and told him I couldn't find a bombardier, and I was volunteering.

"No way, I can't spare you, get someone else," he retorted,

I reminded him that he owed me a favor, and added I only had five more missions left, and wanted to get them over.

"Hell," he said, "this is no favor, but if you are crazy enough to fly it, go ahead."

Ours was the first plane out. We took off in a rainstorm, praying we could find our airfield when and if we got back, and flew three and a half tense hours in silence. Just after we dropped our bombs, the sky clouded over before I could photograph the bomb strike, though I felt confident we hit the target. We got home safely. The second plane went out and returned. The third and fourth planes went out and were never heard from again after crossing the front lines. The next week another four planes went out, and none of them were heard from again. From our tent, Lieutenant Bill Moffett volunteered for one of the missions. He didn't make it back. I packed up a bag of his personal belongings and sent them home.

17 November—that brings me to my current and last mission we flew today, which was trouble all the way. Besides the tailwheel

falling off before we were airborne, early in the mission fifteen German fighters hit us, shot down two of our planes, and damaged two others so they had to return to the base. Our fighter escort didn't join us until we were well into enemy territory. As we came within range of our target in Linz, we encountered heavy flak and lost three more planes. Approaching the target site, a piece of flak went through the nose of the plane just missing me as I bent over on the bombsight. When I leaned backward to get the target photo, another large piece of flak tore through the nose of the plane just where I had been two seconds earlier, ripping another large hole in the Plexiglas nose. In spite of those obstacles, I made an excellent bomb strike and started to relax, when another piece of flak tore through the nose of the plane and hit me directly in the chest and knocked me over the back of my chair.

Lying on the deck I thought it had finally happened to me on my last mission. Wiggling my toes and fingers, they responded, and moving my arms, hands, feet and legs, they felt okay. As I checked out body parts, the navigator behind me watched in shock while I slowly rose and crawled back to my gun turret. A few minutes later we were free from fighter attack, and I looked around to see what had hit me. A piece of flak weighing about half a pound lay nearby. I picked it up and immediately dropped it as it burned my hand. I concluded a piece of flak that had been shot up was falling down when we flew into it. Because it had hit my flak jacket, my life was saved. Then when we landed, we didn't have the tailwheel, of course, and the aircraft tail strut tore up the runway, but the pilot brought us in.

I sadly recount the friendships of lost buddies. The loss etches deeply into my soul, and it's impossible to be the same person that I was six months ago. I packed my belongings, took my knife out of its sheath and thought it was good I didn't have to slit any throats with it. I turned in my electric flight suit and bulky sheepskin flight clothes to supply. While folding up my electrically heated flight suit, I noticed a two-inch slit where a piece of flak had come up from under the plane and hit me in the buttock. Blood had run down my leg then, and the Air Corps wanted to give me the Purple Heart for that.

"No, thank you!" I had responded. "I don't want to explain where I was wounded in the war for the rest of my life."

*

Editor's Note:
Lieutenant Louis Maughn Baxter served five and a half years in the Army Air Corps and returned to Utah where his roots were deep in the soil of his beloved fields and mountains of Cache Valley. He graduated from Utah State University majoring in Dairy Production and minoring in Animal Sciences. He and his wife Norma Cooper Baxter have three children, Connie, Douglas, and Robert. Douglas served in the Air Force and Robert served in the Navy. They enjoy eleven grandchildren and four great-grandchildren, and presently reside in Hillsboro, Oregon.
I asked Lieutenant Baxter to describe his feelings when he saw the flag.

"Well, coming back from combat each night when the flag was lowered, we'd turn toward the flag and salute it wherever we were. We were living in such undesirable conditions, I'd remember what home was and tears would come to my eyes. I loved and respected and honored the flag and nobody better destroy it, or do otherwise in my presence today."

*****

---

[1] *Genesis* 49:25-26; *Doctrine & Covenants* 124:92

Bombardier photo of bombing raid Budapest, Hungary.
Railroad Bridge over Danube River, 9/20/44
Courtesy of Louis M. Baxter

Bombardier photo of bombing raid Salsburg Railroad Yards,
Germany 11/17/44. *Courtesy of Louis M. Baxter*

78

CHAPTER 5

SERGEANT
J. DARWIN BAXTER

Sgt. J. Darwin Baxter
36th Infantry Division, U.S. Army

TRUSTING MY INSTINCTS

Driving past the Coliseum and under the arches of Titus and Constantine, we were making history during the early summer of 1944. The Germans had declared Rome an open city and surrendered it rather than have art treasures and monuments destroyed by street fighting and bombing. Instead of fighting on the front line, the 36th Infantry Division paraded in a victory celebration. Rome's citizens cheered us, waved homemade flags, and bands played as we paraded down the main avenue.

INVASION OF SOUTHERN FRANCE

A short time later I was transported to Naples and our ship steamed out of the bay of Naples and headed south toward the Mediterranean along with hundreds of other US war ships. By then I learned we were the invasion troops getting in position for the invasion of Southern France. The night before the beach landing, frogmen swam to shore to dismantle mines on the beaches, but the mines were too numerous and only one area was cleared before daylight. During that same night, our paratroopers and glider infantry had landed and set up roadblocks to prevent the Germans from moving reinforcements to the battle area.

The invasion of Southern France took place near the seaport of San Rafaël, just west of those fancy towns on the French Riviera. On the morning of the invasion, 15 August 1944, I watched from a landing craft as formation after formation of US aircraft flew over and dropped bombs that exploded on the beaches ahead of me. As the planes disappeared, Navy destroyers and heavy cruisers moved up firing barrages of artillery onto the beach. More Navy ships moved closer to shore firing missiles that had been newly invented.

I was one of the first to hit the beach from our landing craft, and headed toward cover, but was immediately commandeered to lay metal mesh grid-work so that trucks, big guns, and tanks could move to shore. I was exposed to enemy fire, and felt relieved when I finally moved on up into brush. Huge artillery guns mounted on train cars shelled our ships then entered a tunnel to reload, reappeared and fired again. There were dozens of Germans wounded on the beach and our medics picked them up and carried them to flat boats where they were taken to larger ships and US doctors. Meanwhile, our lead riflemen spotted German soldiers under a double track railroad bridge hiding from the bombing and coastal shelling. Some of the Germans lay dead, others were wounded or so demoralized they couldn't fight, and waved their undershirts at us to surrender.

Before sundown, I moved to the top of a small hill overlooking the beach and watched our LST's unloading supplies when a lone German aircraft slipped through the clouds and made a direct bomb hit on one of our ships. A black explosion erupted from the ammunition being unloaded and on reflex, my hands reached for my gaping mouth. It was a shock and seemed like a movie playing out in front of me, except I was caught up in the acrid smoke. I felt a long way from my home in Cache Valley—herding cows and working in the hayfields.

The following day trucks drove us a short distance to San Raphaël, which our companion regiment had just liberated. Once again, as in Rome, we were welcomed as liberating heroes. We marched through the streets and the town's people cheered and greeted us with kisses on both cheeks, threw flowers on us, and gave us cantaloupes, watermelons and wine. As they cheered, we recognized the words, "Vive la France, Libérer! la libération! Americain!" The French hated the Germans because of the brutality they had experienced from German occupation troops. Even before that there had been centuries of border disputes and festering hatred.

Skillfully executing the beachhead landing with few casualties, men of the 36th were soon regrouped and briefed on the next day's attack. Assigned to the newly organized Butler Task Force, we advanced swiftly north through hilly and mountainous terrain to block the German retreat up through the Rhône River valley. Our task force of armored scout cars and trucks headed north through the mountains paralleling the Rhône River. From the mountainside, I observed German soldiers and armament retreating northward. We destroyed German trucks and tank convoys with the help of the Air Force, and mile after mile of the main highway became a mass of tangled burning enemy tanks, wheeled vehicles, and human tragedy. Germans were fleeing up the mountainsides, which was risky for them since the German Gestapo was not far behind ready to execute them if they were caught without their officers. The Germans feared the Gestapo more than they feared our Infantry.

We kept the enemy on the move. My squad and I were in a truck moving along slowly through a field, when an artillery shell exploded a quarter mile in front of us. Our truck stalled and wouldn't restart and another round of artillery exploded between the previous round and us. I knew the third shell would hit our truck and we took off running. I ran toward a farmyard about thirty yards away, scaled a rock wall and landed in an empty farm watering trough just in time to hear the next loud explosion. It hit our truck and blew it to smithereens, including my camera and fountain pen, gifts from my brother, but we were unhurt.

It took the 36th Infantry Division six weeks to advance 400 kilometers north to Grenoble, France, all the while liberating small towns along the way. Since the French felt great animosity toward the Germans, we were able to trust the French. Within our company was a French interpreter who would frequently phone the next town to inquire if there were any Germans in that vicinity. If they answered no, we knew it was safe to move ahead at full speed. The French had two resistance forces, the FFI, or Free French of the Interior, and the Maquis; one was Communist, and the other anti-Communist, but both worked for our side.

MARCHING THROUGH FRANCE

In October (1944) Shorty Odom and I, attached to an anti-tank platoon, were resting in an open farming area south of the Vosges Mountains in France when orders came to transport fifteen fresh replacements to the front. To lessen the chance of ambush, we waited until night then the guys loaded into the back of the truck. Shorty drove, and because we couldn't use headlights, and I was determined to spot our turn-off in the middle of Laval where we were to turn left to battalion headquarters, I stood out on the running board directing him. We drove into the demolished town on rubble-strewn streets and zigzagged through the dark town while I tried to recognize a landmark. Unknowingly, we missed our turn-off and instead advanced toward the German front. BANG! The left rear tire hit a German mine, the truck exploded into flames and men were thrown from the truck with their clothes on fire. I was blown into the air landing on the road. Through the ringing in my ears from the explosion, I heard Shorty shout, "Get off the road!" I rolled down into a barrow pit. The Germans shot flares up and sprayed us with machine gun fire, and wounded and dead lay everywhere on the road. Seeing the flares and flames, our medics at battalion headquarters located us and cared for the wounded and dying. Shorty and I were unhurt.

Each infantry company had sixty to eighty men and two machine gunners with light air-cooled machine guns. I was a machine gunner and squad leader. In the training manual I had read that a machine gun was a defensive weapon, not an attack weapon. A machine gunner is put in to stop an enemy's forward attack, but I learned quickly that things were different in the field.

It happened outside the town of Bruyers, France, where combat engineers were attempting to build a bridge all the while drawing heavy enemy fire. Tanks were idling waiting to cross the bridge as soon as the last plank was fastened, but the engineers were pinned down by enemy artillery fire. An officer in command came up to me.

"Baxter, we're short on infantrymen, and the riflemen have all been killed or wounded, and it's not safe to attack. We want you to go out there," and he drew an X on a map, "and attack." He continued, "Take the other machine gunner with you, and I want you to go along this road to the edge of the wheat field toward the next town. There are a few trees here and there for cover, and we'll have another attack group ready soon to move up and take the town. We can't get the bridge built until we reduce the enemy fire coming from that town."

It looked dangerous to me as we were mostly out in the open, but we moved ahead along side the wheat field anyway. All at once we heard the chatter of machine gun fire. Bullets hit the ground ahead of us, but not close enough to hurt, so we continued. Then an artillery shell exploded directly in front of me. I hit the ground, then scrambled into the hole the artillery shell made and my buddy followed. I wondered what had happened to the rest of the men that were supposed to attack since we were the only ones out there.

We lay there in the hole, pounded by artillery explosions until finally a runner came up and hollered at us.

"The captain says you're supposed to attack!"

I fired right back, "Well, you go back and tell him we're pinned down and can't move ahead."

Above the next blast, "Well, he won't like that!"

"Well, you go back and tell that officer to show us how!" And he left. We feared artillery and mortar fire more than rifle and machine gun fire. Explosions from 88mm artillery shells seized us with fear. In about fifteen or twenty minutes we heard our tanks rumbling up. We were disgruntled to learn we had been a diversion to draw enemy fire away from the combat engineers completing the bridge.

A tank rolled up and a guy shouted, "Hey, you guys run behind us, we're going into that town." I sprang up and ran behind the tank smelling the diesel fumes, but the warmth from the engine felt good on my face and hands. It was November. The tanks rolled into Bruyers and shot up the second story buildings to flush out snipers. The houses touched each other and the cobblestone streets narrowed and from out of them the French Resistance appeared in civilian clothes.

A Hunch

By December of 1944, we were getting more resistance and taking more casualties as we advanced closer to the German border. Within fifty kilometers southwest of Strasbourg, France, at a road junction close to the town of Sélestat, my battalion, including myself, was ambushed as we approached toppled pine trees lying across the road. The Germans fired down on us from a position uphill. The order came for my platoon to take it out. Platoon leader Lieutenant Dixie Davis was a rancher from Oglesby, Texas with a wife and young child, and a nice guy with a good heart. He repeatedly said that if we were sent out on a dangerous mission he would go in first. I led our platoon of sixteen guys and hiked up the mountain in the shadows of the forest, intending to circle back around and come down the mountain behind the Germans. We stealthily walked in silence, rifles ready, single file spaced a few yards apart going downhill. A burst of machine gun fire broke the silence of the forest, and we hit the ground. Bullets sprayed around us and pinned us down. We couldn't see them, but they knew exactly where we were. I was forward, the first man in the lead, and I felt I didn't have a chance.

All at once a German corporal jumped out of a bush right in front of me with his hands up and surrendered. Hoping to stay alive, he quickly knelt down and drew a map in the dirt of the exact position of the machine gun. By this time Lieutenant Davis had come forward and said, "Baxter, take the prisoner back to battalion headquarters, and I'll take the lead."

Reaching battalion headquarters with the POW, I placed him in the major's charge, and rushed back up the mountain to rejoin my platoon. In my absence Lieutenant Davis had gone ahead alone to sneak behind the machine gun position. We estimated there was a machine gunner in a command post and about forty German riflemen in foxholes, dug in and camouflaged. We listened to the steady rhythm of the ra-ta-ta-tat of the machine gun bursts. Then it quit. On a hunch that the gun had jammed, Bill Fuller and I rushed forward firing our Tommy guns from the hip, spraying every bush and tree while dodging bullets from the German riflemen. We shot up the command post, killed the German machine gunner, and killed or captured about thirty Germans. Others escaped through the forest. The command post comprised a four-foot high log hut in the brush, and behind the log hut was Lieutenant Davis. After circling around to get behind the machine gun to take it out, he met enemy fire and lay dead. True to his word, he went in himself rather than send in one of his men.

THE GERMAN SIEGFRIED LINE

It was March of 1945 when the men of the 36th attacked northward, crossed the Moder River and then around the west end of the Haguerau Woods. Our regiment led the way with my company just behind the lead company. We advanced across a grassy knoll in single file, spacing ourselves about ten yards apart to avoid casualties from artillery or mortar fire when our advance was stalled. It was reported that retreating Germans had blown up a bridge that crossed the Zintel River and we would be delayed. I sat down to rest. I felt nervous about the woods to my right. Though officers reported the woods had already been cleared and declared safe, I still felt nervous. Trusting my instincts, I talked another guy into checking it out with me. Leaving machine gun behind, I pulled my .45 off my belt, and moved toward the trees. Just before we reached the tree line we heard gunfire up ahead. I ran for cover. Then there was silence and I couldn't see anything but shadows and tree trunks. All at once in front of us thirty Germans stood up with their hands held high and hollered, "Kamerad, kamerad" which meant to us, "We surrender, we surrender." Approaching closer, two German officers lay dead obviously shot a few moments before we approached. A German chaplain came forward who spoke English.

"We had an argument over whether or not to surrender," he began, and we saw you headed straight toward us and quickly settled the argument."

They had two of their machine guns aimed straight toward our line of men on the trail. There was a lot left out of the training manual, and I learned to trust my instincts in order to stay alive.

With the rivers Moder, Sauer, and Zintel crossed, we reached the German border at the town of Wissembourg. Two miles ahead the much-dreaded Siegfried Line German defense was lined with dragon teeth of cement pyramid structures and concrete pillboxes. In front of these fortifications, a deep channel was dug to trap tanks if the dragon teeth didn't stop an attack. We attempted to tunnel beneath the dragon teeth, but they were well mined. After explosions and casualties, we couldn't break through, all the while our tanks and troops were stalled out in the open under fire.

My battalion was ordered to attack the Siegfried Line on foot. To reach attacking position, we marched through the night up a narrow forested canyon. I carried my machine gun, a load of ammunition, and one-day supply of rations. I had learned to sleep while I marched. Just before dawn, our lead platoon worked through a tangle of fallen pine trees and discarded war paraphernalia and came within sight of the German line of trenches and pillboxes uphill and ahead. As we advanced single file, we met Colonel Everett Simpson crouching behind a large rock with an open meadow to his front. The meadow was about fifty yards across. The colonel hollered to me.

"Okay, soldier, it's your turn. You run across that meadow as fast as you can, and then go into that fallen timber and work up the hill as hard as you can go. Don't stop, because they've got machine guns shooting down across the meadow at us." I studied the odds. Two out of every three men made it across without getting hit. The meadow was littered with American dead, gas masks and packs. "When you get to the other side," he continued, "you'll see some wounded guys in the trees there. Don't pay any attention to them, just go right on up to the front line." So I ran as fast as I could, made it across the meadow, and hit the ground near a thicket of pine trees and brush. Our medics were there in the trees busy attending to the wounded, and there were a lot of wounded. My companions and I hiked up the hill and saw a sight that I shall never forget. In the trenches were fifteen dead German infantrymen, half of them had been shot in the forehead right between their eyes. They had been in a trench dug in and shooting down at our front company. Our guys were such good marksmen that they shot them when they lifted their heads to peer out and take aim.

We had entered the "impenetrable" Siegfried Line. Our lead platoon attacked the trenches one by one and overran the concrete pillboxes. Some of the enemy got away on foot. Then it was my company's turn to take the lead and push beyond the Siegfried Line. We worked through the German defenses and took a trail along the mountainside away from fortifications. Sniper fire held us up, and we halted for a half-hour or so. We started cracking jokes and having fun with each other and tensions abated, and for a few minutes we were just a bunch of guys again.

Enemy soldiers moved across the canyon about a quarter mile away. We didn't shoot because we didn't want to be discovered. We were constantly advised to keep our bodies down low, and I gladly obeyed by lying down behind a log to rest. My friend Bill Steens sat on a fallen log and lit a cigarette. When Bang! Deadly cluster mortar shells exploded all around us. We called them screaming meemees because they came in on us with a screaming sound. One hit about ten feet from me and killed Bill Steens from the concussion. He was my best friend from Maryville, Missouri. We never knew who was going to get it next.

In a short time we were ordered forward again and only met token resistance. We heard that German artillery shells were rationed— more American casualties would have occurred if it hadn't been so, because some soldiers were careless.

As darkness set in, we set up a defense along the tree line and were warned to expect a German counterattack in the early morning hours. Totally exhausted, my buddy took the guard for the first half of the night while I slept. Toward morning, I had a good field of fire across a meadow for my machine gun. Before daylight, brush began to move. Images shifted around, and I tensed ready to shoot a burst of bullets when the images became clearer. It was deer out for an early breakfast. What a relief! With my battalion attacking the rear of the Siegfried Line, the enemy scattered in front of us toward the mountains and fled toward the Rhine.

That day we advanced down the mountain to Dorrenback and cautiously moved to the edge of the forest and entered Bergzabern. These were both mountain resort towns. Grape vineyards were growing on the hillsides and hot springs were advertised for tourists. We doubled back and scouted the town of Bollenborn. By then my one-day supply of rations was long gone and I was hungry and fatigued, though my body kept walking from force of habit.

All at once coming toward us out of the forest, was a line of German soldiers entering the grape vineyards ahead of us walking toward us in single file, and my companion and I set out to challenge them.

We suddenly stepped out in front of them with our guns aimed. Startled, their hands flew up, "Komerad, komerad." They cried the words we knew so well, "We surrender, we surrender." While my companion stood guard, I searched them one by one, and threw their weapons aside. One of the German soldiers speaking in English said, "I have a new Walther .32 caliber pistol hidden under my armpit." I took it and thanked him for telling me. Our battalion headquarters' officers had just entered the town in a jeep and I turned our prisoners over to them. Hitler had ordered German units never to surrender, but after the invasion of Southern France many thousands did.[1]

About this time I was just about starved. The cook's jeep pulled up by us and declared that breakfast would be ready soon—cooked powdered eggs and Spam, a most common front-line breakfast. After a few minutes, I had a friend take my post and I went around a building to the chow line. And ahead of me, OF ALL THE INSULTS! The surprise of the day! There were forty Germans in the chow line ahead of me! Then I learned that US propaganda leaflets had been dropped on the German defense positions inviting them to surrender and have a good breakfast with eggs, sausage and real American coffee. There they were with mess kits and cups in hand, drinking up our good, hot, South American coffee. Frankly, I was not surprised. We were all hungry and tired of fighting!

*

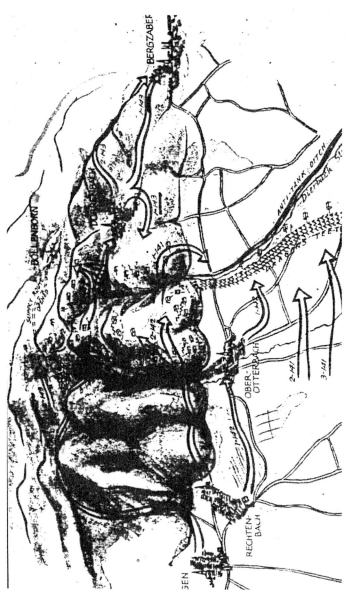

Siegfried Line - Germany's border defense between Belgium and France.
Sketch from *A Pictorial History of the 36th Division*

Editor's note: Darwin Baxter, recipient of the Bronze Star for leading attacks against the enemy, served in the 36th Army Infantry Division for thirty months and was in the field when the Germans surrendered on May 15, 1945. He then became a part of the occupational troops until discharged. Arriving home on January 2, 1946, on the following day entered college at Utah State University and graduated with a Bachelor of Science degree.

Born and raised on a ranch in Hyrum, Utah, Sergeant Baxter and his wife, Marjorie Bevan Baxter, live in Modesto, California, and have five children, nineteen grandchildren and three great-grandchildren. He is retired from the positions of school speech therapist, which he held for twenty-five years, and schoolteacher of high school and elementary grades.

I asked Sergeant Baxter about patriotism and his feelings about the flag and our country and received this response.

"After the war, I had a strong feeling of patriotism. When my country drafted me to face death every day for months, I felt I deserved the support of the people back home, including the news media, and I felt as a nation they had strongly supported our military actions. During the Vietnam War I was a pro-active patriot. I wrote letters and voiced my opinions on talk shows about my feelings of the sacred nature of our country and the value of a nation's whole-hearted support for its service men and women. During the Vietnam War, perhaps you remember Walter Kronkite reporting the antiwar demonstrations as if they had great merit, and then his reporting the ever-increasing numbers of dead every evening at the end of his national news program. In my opinion, we won all of the battles in Vietnam, but lost the battle on the home front, and that should be laid at the feet of our media people and some Hollywood movie stars.

"Which is more important, a soldier's right to have a country's moral support behind him while he's on the front lines? Or a country's right to freely oppose the military action?"

*****

[1] After the war, there was a great shortage of German men. The German parliament took a vote to make polygamy legal. It lost by only one vote.

CHAPTER 6

SERGEANT
LOUIS A. SLAMA

Sgt. Louis A. Slama
2nd Battalion, 508th Parachute Infantry,
82nd Airborne, U.S. Army

"IF YOU CUT MY ARM OFF, LET ME DIE, I'M A BASEBALL PLAYER."

THE INVASIONS OF HOLLAND, BELGIUM AND GERMANY

I was born and raised in Czechoslovakia, though I was adjusting my tie and military cap of the uniform of the United States 508th Parachute Infantry. If someone had told me when I was growing up in Bratislava across the Danube, a slingshot away from Vienna, Austria, that I would be parachuting out of an airplane, I wouldn't have believed it then.

When my father left Czechoslovakia to find work in the United States to save for the purchase of productive farmland in Bratislava on his return, I was just two. Years would pass without him until his photograph was all of Father I knew. Two years later, he wrote asking my mother to join him in New Jersey as he was unable to save enough without her help. My father's parents raised me and my sister Millie was raised by my mother's parents. We all lived in the little town of Gajare.

By 1933 political storms were thundering across Czechoslovakia as Hitler began arming three million Germans living in the Sudetenland, which was northern Czechoslovakia bordering Germany. Hitler's concentration camps were already annihilating political, religious, and ethnic opposition prior to Germany's lightning attacks into neighboring countries. Sandwiched between Germany, Austria, Poland, Hungary, and Ukraine, the Czechoslovakian government struggled to maintain autonomy at the same time the Sudetenland was unraveling the country's integrity.

Fearing war and the closure of borders, my parents had grave concern for us and appealed to the International Red Cross for our safe passage to the United States. The summer of 1934 when my sister Millie was fourteen and I was nine, we hugged grandparents and said farewell to cousins, aunts, and uncles, and I embraced my beloved dog for the last time. We traveled by train seven hundred kilometers north across Czechoslovakia to the German border, through Dresden, Leipzig, and Hanover to the port of Bremerhaven and boarded the German ship Beringgaria, for the three-week's voyage to New York.

My parents had become strangers to me, as my father had been gone seven years and my mother for five. My father's cherished dream of farmland in Bratislava had vanished and in its place were a United States' citizenship, a cold-water flat in Gullenberg, New Jersey, and a job as a laborer. My mother worked as a cleaning lady. After a long day she would come home and do the washing by hand on a washboard with water heated from the kitchen stove. My Saturday night bath was taken in the same washtub in the kitchen.

I began fourth grade that fall unable to speak English. Yet as a natural athlete with a ready smile, I rapidly integrated into the new school curriculum. Though my parents knew English, they spoke only Slovak to us so that we would remember our native tongue. With only Slovak newspapers in our home, my parents were unaware when my athletic achievements on occasion appeared in the local newspapers.

By the time I finished high school, I had become a recognized athlete in track, basketball, and football, and pitched baseball for the American Legion. Georgetown University, Manhattan University, and Dartmouth College sent me letters of interest proffering scholarships, but it was baseball that impassioned me. Elated over a successful try-out with the New York Giants, I decided to put the Giants' offer on hold, unable to ignore that Hitler had seized Czechoslovakia and the rest of eastern and western Europe. In September 1943 I decided to become a fighter pilot.

While taking my physical at Fort Dix, I was astonished when told, "You can't be a pilot, you're colorblind." Tail gunner wasn't an option since I had a phobia about tight places. Transferring to Camp Croft, South Carolina, I met Lambert Siniari, also from New Jersey, and we stuck together. While we were sitting in the PX one day, we noticed a sign JOIN THE PARATROOPERS. It was very appealing to us to make $50 a month extra jump pay, and we signed up for parachute training.

OPERATION MARKET-GARDEN

The 508th Airborne Parachute Infantry, a regiment of the 82nd Airborne, was nicknamed the Red Devils, which suited me fine, as I was a scrappy kid. My platoon leader, Lieutenant Loyd Pollette, nicknamed me The Kid. Lambert and I were both eighteen and the youngest guys in the platoon. Lieutenant Pollette was a real warrior, a guy we admired, and would follow him through hell, which we actually did since our first combat jump was the invasion of Holland, code-named Market-Garden.

Responding to political pressure from Washington, Allied Supreme Commander General Eisenhower had given the nod to Britain's Field Marshall Montgomery's plan to try and shorten the war two years by deploying 35,000 men, tanks and artillery behind enemy lines to cut off the entire German Army in the western Netherlands. The code name for the operation was Market-Garden—Market for the air drop and Garden for the ground forces of Britain's 30th Corps Armored Guard that would drive through the Netherlands and link up with the paratroopers in the target zone. Precision timing of the air invasion to capture bridges was crucial for the success of the ground troops.

The thrust of the paratroopers' mission was to keep open three large river bridges and five waterway passages for movement of ground troops. Three main targets would be divided among three airborne divisions with the British 1st Airborne taking the northern-most city of Arnhem, the American 101st Airborne covering the south-ern area around Eindhoven, and the American 82nd Airborne seizing control of the Grave Bridge and Nijmegen (pronounced Nimegan) bridges. The British 30th Corps tanks would then follow driving across the Zuider Zee to cut off an entire German army and destroy V-2 rocket launching sites located in western Holland.

While months were usually allowed for invasion preparations, Montgomery insisted these preparations be carried out in only one week's time before D-Day. The condensed schedule demanded irre-versible decisions from Montgomery, and he clung to presumptions that critically influenced the success of Market-Garden.

Presumption #1— To ensure surprise and success for Market-Garden, Montgomery didn't want preliminary reconnaissance un-dertaken at the drop zones since reliable Dutch Underground had reported Nijmegen and Arnhem, two cities eleven miles apart, were practically undefended. Germany had lost nearly four million men from their military by then and Montgomery exuded confidence that the paratroopers would meet little enemy resistance.

Presumption #2— In spite of giving Montgomery's generals only one week to orchestrate the invasion, he felt confident, even cocky, that this was adequate time since there had been several smaller operations recently cancelled at the last minute that had brought his troops to a state of readiness.

But after Montgomery's twenty-seven high-level staff officers heard the plan for Market-Garden they not only expressed grave concern, some predicted a massacre. In just one week's time they would have to mobilize 35,000 men, commandeer hundreds of transport planes from other air forces, manufacture hundreds more gliders to carry the heavy artillery, tanks, jeeps, trucks, ammunition and supplies, and position all of it sixty-four miles behind enemy lines. The planes would be flying over some of the heaviest antiaircraft concentrations in Europe and the paratroopers would be bailing out over enemy territory during daylight hours, heretofore not attempted.

Montgomery Ignored the Warnings— Finally, forty-eight hours prior to the mission, messages were received from Dutch Underground alerting Montgomery of German SS Panzer units amassing at Arnhem. Eisenhower's Chief of Staff General Bedell Smith challenged Montgomery to revise Market-Garden, but Montgomery ridiculed the idea. Reconnaissance photographs were dispatched to British airborne commander General Browning showing German tank positions at Arnhem. Browning thought the alarm was twaddle, and failing to respond to the warnings, briskly dismissed it with the reply that the tanks may not even be operable.

Finally on the eve of the mission, Supreme Headquarters Allied Expeditionary Forces (SHAEF) Intelligence issued the ominous warning that the 9th SS Panzer Division and possibly the 10th Panzer Division were seen approaching toward the Arnhem area. Even though the SS Panzer divisions were Hitler's crack elite tank corps, Montgomery disregarded the message and Market-Garden proceeded on schedule.

D-DAY—PARACHUTING BEHIND ENEMY LINES

I boarded a C-46 troop carrier weighted down, as we all were, carrying a five-pound mine strapped to my chest, a pound and a half Gammon grenade secured inside a sock strapped to my side, ammo magazines around my waist web belt, a .45 pistol, Tommy gun, C-rations stuffed in pockets, and a parachute. High explosive Gammon grenades could knock out a tank or a building. I discarded my reserve chute in the plane because jumping out at 500 feet didn't give us time for a second chute to open if the first one failed. Lastly, I taped a switchblade knife to the palm of my hand.

We were quiet on the flight over, most of us reigning in our fear, silently wishing it was a night jump that would afford protection from being shot at on the way down. Holland's farmlands were flooded by the North Sea from Germany's destructive attacks on the dikes of Holland. We approached the drop zone 500 to 700 feet off the ground. Suddenly we were hit by 20mm artillery fire and the guy sitting across from me was struck by flak and died instantly.

Just before jumping, we pushed out ahead of us color-coded parachute bundles all marked for platoons and squads containing 30mm mortars and other heavy equipment. The pilot gave the jump signal. It was 1:30 the afternoon of 17 September 1944. We hooked up in the plane, twelve men to each side of the aircraft, and jumped twelve guys in ten seconds—almost jumping on top of each other. My chute opened after a hundred-foot fall, and looking down, German artillery waited for me on the ground.

From two dozen Allied airfields, thousands of aircraft were launched and shuttled back and forth to the Holland drop zones carrying paratroopers. Thousands of parachutes darkened the sky from British 1st Airborne, and the American 101st Airborne and 82nd Airborne. Most of the 82nd Airborne paratroopers landed within two kilometers from the German border on the only high ground in the Netherlands south of Nijmegen. "The drop zone was occupied by most of an enemy antiaircraft artillery battalion, but the sight of the hordes of descending skytroopers scared most of the Germans away from their weapons... " (Lord 42). The 82nd Airborne alone successfully parachuted 7,467 paratroopers and men in gliders, and 70 tons of equipment during the three-day invasion.

I landed in a turnip field, cut through the parachute shrouds with the knife taped to my hand, and struggled to remove my old-style chute. My buddy Lambert landed nearby. We had jumped together and were committed to looking after each other. Our first mission was to secure the drop zone for the thousands of paratroopers and the 2500 gliders of the 325th Glider Regiment carrying men and big equipment that would land on the second and third days of the invasion. Shortly after landing in the drop zone, the Germans re-assembled, and we came under direct fire, counterattacked and began pushing them back into Nijmegen. Thousands of planes and descending parachutes covered the sky. Netherlanders, ecstatic and lighthearted, erupted in celebration in the streets of Nijmegen exhilarated by the invasion and obvious liberation. Others observed from roof ridges watching the parachutes descend seemingly oblivious that Germans still occupied Nijmegen and Arnhem and a fight could explode at any time. They crowded streets singing, jostling and kissing. They offered us beer, milk, apples, and scattered flowers on us. Jubilantly, they hugged us at the same time clogging streets and restricting our movement.

"F" Company was ordered to lead into Nijmegen, a city of 100,000, and secure the southwestern approaches to Nijmegen's bridges. It was about ten o'clock that same night and pitch dark when Orcott, Sanchez, Pop Hall, so nicknamed because he was the oldest at thirty-two, Lambert, and I walked single file in Nijmegen's southern outskirts with fixed bayonets. By then the revelers had gone home, the streets were empty and shutters were drawn for the blackout. Suddenly enemy MG42 (.42 caliber) machine guns flashed around us in the dark from the direction of a roadblock. We ran for cover. Pop Hall and I instinctively jumped behind a hedgerow out of the line of fire, and from our secured position, helped to knock out the roadblock killing fifteen Germans. None of us was hurt. We continued on down the dark road approaching the outskirts of Nijmegen. "F" Company set up a defensive perimeter and Lambert and I dug a foxhole and tried to sleep. The water table was high and by morning water had seeped in, and we were slumped down in a foot of water.

D-DAY + 1

Next morning two patrols were sent out again on sorties to infiltrate Nijmegen and take the bridge over the Maas-Waal Canal. I was in one patrol, Lambert in the other; it was the first time we were separated. Hernandez, Sanchez, Orcott, Klevanger, Sproul, Giegold and I went into the city single file. Dutch Underground appeared from behind closed shutters eager to inform us where the Germans were, always knowing their exact positions. House by house, yard by yard, we cleared out pockets of snipers and enemy roadblocks, pushing farther into Nijmegen.

Then Burns, the radioman, yelled in a shrill voice, "Lambert's hit!" I ran over to where he was lying. He looked peaceful, like he was sleeping, yet he had been shot through the neck, killed by a sniper's bullet. Lambert, my closest friend, was dead. Devastated that my hometown buddy was gone, I felt painfully alone, and my anger and sorrow churned within me until my emotions erupted and I wept.

We attacked the bridge over the Maas-Waal Canal simultaneously from both ends of the bridge. We lost three of our guys doing it. All during the fight my mind was going over my conversation to Lambert's mother, if I survived, and what I would say. I had reached for his dog tags for her, but they wouldn't let me have them.[1]

Lieutenant Pollette kept us on the move deeper into the heart of the city. Our prime objective was to safeguard and fortify the Nijmegen bridge until the British 30th Corps Armored Guard could cross and provide artillery support to the invasion. "F" Company would reinforce the 3rd Battalion at the bridge.

D Day + 2

Nijmegen Bridge

At 0330 in the morning we approached Nijmegen from the south on sunken roads and ditches that ran parallel to the river, taking advantage of darkness during the early morning hours. The Nijmegen bridge was actually three bridges, a railroad bridge and two side-by-side double-span highway bridges spanning 1,960 feet across the River Waal. Suddenly, from the opposite bank SS Panzer tank artillery hit our exposed flank, and sniper fire cut into us from bridge girders pinning us down. In a matter of minutes eight of our men lay dead and twelve wounded, cutting our effective strength in half. An 88mm shell exploded and decapitated Hernandez. Pollette called in for supporting artillery fire, but couldn't get any, and we moved back to a small group of shelled-out buildings on the south end of the bridges to reorganize and evacuate our wounded and dead.

The railway bridge had already been blown by the Germans, but we clung to our position on the southern end of the highway bridges. Bullets were flying around us. Our B.A.R. man was shot and killed while standing next to Pollette and me. As we waited for regiment reinforcements, we stayed out of the line of fire, as we were no match for the well fortified line of Panzer tanks perched on the opposite bank.

Timing was critical. The first of the British tanks would reach the bridge within hours, and we had to occupy it for the crossing. If we didn't hold both banks, the expected tank force would be sitting ducks for the Panzers. A desperate and daring plan took form. A thousand men of the 504th Regiment would cross the 400-yard wide Waal River in small boats a mile down river and attack the north end of the bridge while we defended the south end.

It took the greater part of a day for boats to be trucked in, and when they arrived there were only sixteen, not enough to ferry a thousand men and equipment across. Worse yet, they were awkward collapsible boats with canvas sides and flat plywood bottoms; some had four oars, others only two. Men would row against a river current running eight to ten miles an hour and attack in broad daylight in full view of enemy tanks. Disastrous losses were anticipated.

Meanwhile, there had been unexpected good fortune for the enemy. A briefcase found in one of the abandoned gliders was rushed to German General Kurt Student whose headquarters was nearby. In the briefcase was the complete enemy attack order for the operation. Incomprehensibly, an Allied officer had carried the top secret plan with him and left it in a glider. Montgomery's targets, objectives, and flight routes were all detailed. General Student sent it to the high command, Field Marshall Walther Model. Disbelieving his good fortune, Model thought it was intentionally planted in the glider. Too detailed to presume the plans were authentic, Field Marshall Model chose to ignore them. He gave an undeviating order to his subordinates not to blow up any of the bridges. The Fuhrer, he had emphatically announced, needed those bridges.

During the delay while waiting for boats, we had received artillery reinforcements. Our Sherman tanks began firing smoke bombs to develop a smoke screen across the river just before 260 men from "H" and "I" companies, headquarters staff and engineers from the 504th Regiment, manned the first wave. I held my breath as I watched the boats launch. There were sixteen men in each boat rowing against the current with oars and rifle butts, and in the excitement and haste often rowed out of sync. Some boats capsized when they hit the strong current. Others were blown out of the water by 20mm and

88mm blasts from the enemy. The smoke screen often obscured the vision of the men in the boats more than the enemy. Boats swamped and sank with no survivors; others uncontrollably circled in eddies in the current. Some men dove in and swam the 400 yard-wide river after observing the death and chaos.

Miraculously, some of the boats and men made it to the opposite shore. The survivors scrambled out, leaving a crew of three to row back to the south shore for another load. In this way the boats plied back and forth transporting men and equipment. Losses mounted at every crossing. Reaching the north shore, the survivors had to climb up the embankment 200 to 800 yards before they found cover. At that point without any regard for their own lives, they savagely attacked enemy tanks and soldiers out in the open. Three bloody hours later we held both sides of the bridges and tanks began crossing them. The casualties were catastrophic.

As the British tanks clanked across the bridge, German General Harmel gave the order to his demolition engineer to blow up the bridge. The plunger was rammed down—the detonators remained in place; the wires had been cut and the bridge saved.[2]

BEEK AND BLOODY VOXHILL

After taking the River Waal Bridge, the 508th Regiment withdrew to the highest ground outside of Nijmegen to a town called Beek along with part of the 504th Regiment.

It was the Germans that held the high ground at Beek and whoever holds the high ground controls the battleground. Our mission was to take Beek away from them. We set up a roadblock during the night and began clearing the enemy out of the town. After heavy fighting, we were successful in pushing the Germans out. After that the Germans came back and pushed us out, and that began the successive bloody battles for Beek.

Again we cleared enemy machine gun nests street by street, house by house in hand to hand combat. Sanchez and I dug a foxhole in a strategic spot on top of an embankment obscured by hedgerows. The steep embankment, supported by a retaining wall, sloped sharply down fifteen feet to a one-lane road. On the far side of the road were row houses. We got situated and waited in our foxhole on top of the embankment until we heard a German tank heading toward us firing horizontally down the road. It was time to use the Gammon grenade that was still tied to my body. Unwinding the fuse from the neck of the pound and a half round-shaped grenade, I waited for the tank to get directly below us. A German was on top of the tank directing fire, and when the tank was opposite me, I leaned over and yelled to the guy in German, "Hands up!" He turned just as I dropped the Gammon grenade on top of the tank. I dove for cover. The tank exploded, the gun turret blew off, and the crew killed.

For the fourth time we took the town back and set up a strong defense with the 1st and 3rd battalions, bivouacking just outside of Beek at Voxhill. Voxhill was a knoll of treacherous ground with three sides open devoid of any cover, while the Germans were entrenched with heavy artillery concealed in the woods in the fourth quadrant. We were ordered to hold Beek no matter what happened, and to us that meant the Germans had to kill every last one of us before we would give up any ground. So we dug deeper foxholes and added tunnels and were spread out around the top of the knoll. We were fearful that our dwindling ammunition supply might not hold out. Supply drops of ammo and food had consistently missed us and were dropped into enemy territory, and while the Germans were firing 88mm, 20mm, and screaming meemees at us, we had five light .30 caliber machine guns. Forced to stay low, we could only send out patrols to infiltrate their lines and find out when the Germans were regrouping to attack.

On the top of the knoll, Dick Zrama and I had taken cover in a foxhole when an 88mm exploded in front of our foxhole. Then another one exploded in back of us. They could see us!

Sergeant Rex Spivey from the next foxhole yelled, "Get the hell out of here—they've got us zeroed in!" As he yelled, the shell exploded and hit between our two foxholes and killed Spivey instantly. Dick Zrama was wounded in the groin and the explosion sent me cartwheeling through the air, head first sprawling in the dirt. I went deaf, and the force of the explosion blinded me temporarily, otherwise I didn't have a scratch.

Medics pulled Zrama and Spivey out. I was rolled back into a foxhole and in a couple of hours my hearing returned and so had my sight and I continued fighting. Our regimental command post took direct hits, our message center was demolished, concentrated barrages of artillery pounded us, and communication was out between regimental headquarters and the ground troops.

After three weeks of fighting, the Germans had had enough and abandoned their artillery and fled from the woods. It was over. Weary, unshaven, and bloody, we emerged. We called it Bloody Voxhill because half our men had been killed. There was not a tree left standing from the deadly battles fought between the enemy in the woods and our foxholes. I'm told by the guys of "F" Company who have gone back to Voxhill in recent years that the citizens of Beek kept the foxholes and war paraphernalia as we left them that October as a shrine to the Americans who died liberating the little town of Beek.

The strength of the 9th and 10th Panzer divisions overpowered Montgomery's strength and strategy, and Operation Market-Garden was unsuccessful in pushing the Germans out of the western Netherlands. Montgomery had "politely refused" to use the eager and excellent assistance of the Dutch Underground. The entire British 30th Corps Armored Guard, scheduled to arrive within forty-eight hours after the paratroopers landed, was detained by the enemy, beset by disasters en route, and arrived two and a half weeks late. Allied radio communications were out most of the time between tactical units on the ground and Allied headquarters in London, all the while the local Dutch telephone system continued to function perfectly. Had the local telephone system been used, potential disasters could have been averted, and pilots dropping canisters of ammo and supplies could have been provided with exact locations where battalions could pick them up. As it was, ninety percent of the ammo drops fell into enemy hands. Germans later reflected that it was an inexpensive battle for them since ample food and ammo were daily dropped to them by Allied aircraft.

Nijmegen remained an embattled city for another seven months. The British 1st Airborne had parachuted into two SS Panzer troops in Arnhem resulting in battles that claimed 10,000 British lives. There

were only 2,000 survivors. The city of Arnhem was flattened by Ger-
man artillery, and midst the ravaged city the citizens evacuated. It
wasn't liberated for another five months.

Only pockets of courageous men performing superhumanly pre-
vented total annihilation. However, Field Marshall Sir Bernard
Montgomery presents a rebuttal in his <u>Memoirs: Montgomery of</u>
<u>Alamein</u>.

"In my—prejudiced view, if the operation had been properly
backed from its inception, and given the aircraft, ground forces, and
administrative resources necessary for the job—it would have succeeded in spite of my mistakes, or the adverse weather, or the presence of the 2nd SS Panzer Corps in the Arnhem area. I remain Market-Garden's unrepentant advocate."

Prince Bernard and the Netherlands could hardly afford to en-
dure another of Montgomery's "successes."

November came and the battlegrounds in the Netherlands turned
static. Since the attempt to outflank the German armies had failed,
supplies and reinforcements intended for Montgomery were shifted
farther south to Belgium at the Battle of the Bulge. The British 2nd
Army and the Canadians replaced us in Holland, and we regrouped
outside of Nijmegen at a GI rest area where we showered and got
some hot food. Our regiment was pretty well banged up. It had rained
on and off since landing in Holland and our boots and feet stayed
wet and likewise our fatigues. Our regiment rested for a few weeks
at Sissone, just outside Rheims, France. We had a few games of
basketball, and got reinforcements prior to our next mission.

By Christmas Eve the 82nd Airborne was established along a ridge
a thousand yards south of the Belgian village of Goronne called
Their-du-Mont, near the infamous Siegfried Line.

BATTLE OF THE ARDENNES MOUNTAINS—THE BULGE

My peers now considered me a seasoned veteran, and I was given
the job as acting 2nd Platoon squad leader of "F" Company. I was
nineteen by then, but felt like one of the old guys like Pop Hall who
was thirty-two. Supply lines had been stretched to the breaking point,

and we had neither fire power heavier than bazookas and B.A.R.s, nor winter clothing heavier than our paratrooper jumpsuits. New snow blanketed Their-du-Mont, making it a miserable task to dig our foxholes through frozen ground. The enemy was preparing to attack and take Their-du-Mont with Panzer tanks and 88mm artillery, and we were ordered to withdraw during the night to prevent them from slaughtering us. My regiment, the 508th, covered the rear during the withdrawal of men of the 82nd Airborne. We stayed behind and blew up the bridges on the Salm River, the only place the Germans could cross. Our withdrawal was reluctant. Spilling blood a second time only to retake the same ground later didn't appeal to us.

It was cold as we trudged through the night. The mercury hovered around zero Fahrenheit. We took turns breaking trail through snow two to three feet deep through the mountains. The snow sparkled in the moonlight, and enemy V-2 rockets streaked across the black sky bound for Antwerp from launch sites in Germany. By four in the morning, the regiments of the 82nd had marched seven miles and were defensively positioned along a line near the villages of Basse Bodeux, Erria, and Villettes, half way between the Belgian villages of Goronne and Chevron.

We dug foxholes as well as we could in the snow-covered frozen ground, laid mine fields and piled extra ammo by guns. There would be no withdrawal from here. Then we waited. At dawn they attacked. We fought for three hours. Then resting in our foxholes, someone said it was Christmas Day. Having neither Christmas food nor mail, we spoke of home quietly and reverently to our buddies in their foxholes.

The heaviest fighting came after Christmas. By the first week of January we were ready to take the offensive, return to Their-du-Mont, and push the enemy back to Germany. By then we had received reinforcements and artillery batteries with 75mm, 105mm, and 155mm Howitzers.

On patrol in the outposts of the perimeter one night in late December near Erria, our squad was alerted to expect an attack. I peered out of my foxhole at about one or two in the morning just as the moon came up. I saw what looked to me like thousands of ants out on the snow all dressed in white marching toward us. Haystacks were immediately set ablaze so the enemy wouldn't have cover. I took the tripod off my .30 caliber machine gun to give it maneuverability and began feeding ammo while my buddy manned the machine gun. We sprayed the fields in a wide arc cutting down the Germans as they approached us in a massive attack. Our right flank was exposed and a tank clamored toward us. We ducked down as it went over our foxhole. We peered up and watched it go over us.

About a minute later my buddy cried, "Lou, I'm hit!"

"What happened?" I said as I grabbed him and heard gurgling in his lungs and felt warm blood in my hands. "Medic!" I yelled. The men of the 504th Regiment were also being hit hard, and all I heard were guys yelling, "Medic!" He died in my arms before a medic got there. I laid him down and started mowing with that .30 caliber machine gun, shooting so fast that the barrel got hot and glowed red in the night. Then the German tanks turned around and headed back toward my foxhole again. Just then out of the corner of my eye fifteen feet away from me a German jumped up and pointed a one-man bazooka at me. I moved the .30 caliber around and cut him through the middle before he could fire the bazooka, then ducked down just as another tank crossed by my foxhole.

Next morning I walked out in the field and there were about 150 dead Germans lying in the snow. I turned some of them over and they were just kids, maybe fifteen or sixteen years old. It looked like the last gasp of the German army.

We stopped them that night, but they came back again and the attacks continued for four days, back and forth.

I was stunned to learn that Lieutenant Pollette had been hit by an 88mm and died from his wounds. My emotions were not yet steeled to losing trusted friends. He was in "E" Company when it happened. After receiving the Distinguished Service Cross for bravery during the Maas-Waal Canal attack on the bridges, Pollette was transferred from our company to "E" Company and Lieutenant Owens took his place.

There were many of our guys killed, but that wasn't the worst of it. The snow was so deep that even with jeeps we couldn't locate all the wounded and they lay in the snow over night and froze to death. The zero temperature during the daytime fell much lower at night, and crouching in the foxhole for four days and nights took its toll on all of us. Besides the cold, the Germans had poisoned all the wells and there was no drinking water, and while eating snow temporarily satisfied us, we became dehydrated and a lot of us had diarrhea.

Toward the end of January we were on the offensive again and liberating small towns, pushing the Germans east toward the German border through their own Siegfried Line embattlements. At the outskirts of Medendorf, the enemy pinned us down with machine gun fire coming from a roadblock sandwiched between a group of houses. From behind the barricade, Germans fired .42 caliber machine guns a foot or two above the snow, cutting down any bodies that moved.

"Take your patrol and knock out that roadblock and machine gun nest up ahead," Lieutenant Owens yelled at me from fifty feet away.

"Hell, lieutenant, we have lost a lot of guys, we're down to half strength, and most of us have frozen feet. They'll kill us," I hollered.

"Look," he hollered back, "you gotta go get 'em!"

"Well," I hotly argued, "I don't think it's a good idea!" and I turned to my squad and said, "Don't do anything." Lieutenant Owens started out hotfooting down the road toward the ditch embankment where I was crouched. Rifle shots rang out and he hit the snow face down. Looking across the field, I thought he was dead.

"Who's going to go out and get him?" I asked my patrol. Nobody volunteered. So I crawled over the ditch embankment on my stomach and across the snow until I reached his boot and grabbed it and shook it. He was alive. I was sure he had been shot. The crotch of his pants was all bloody.

"You been shot in the rear?" I asked.

"No," came the terse reply. "I've got bleeding hemorrhoids, and I wouldn't tell anybody if I were you," he threatened. He didn't want it known because he would have been replaced. We both snaked back on our bellies across the field to the ditch embankment.

"Wait until nightfall to attack the roadblock," the lieutenant quietly conceded.

I was having severe attacks of diarrhea by then and pills issued me were not helping, so as a next best step, I devised a system where all my clothing layers dropped down at the same time, which helped the situation a little.

Later that night under cover of darkness, the squad crouch-ran and darted through the woods and approached the same roadblock from behind. The Germans had barbwired the perimeter of town and by the time we had cut our way through the wire, the Germans started raking us with 20mm mortars and MG42 machine guns. The woods held no protection. The 20mm shells cut through tree trunks, fell trees, and shrapnel ricocheted around us. Art Stein, my bazooka man, and I crawled forward about forty yards toward a house where a machine gun nest had been chattering. We looked up into the house and there were Germans sitting up in the loft manning a machine gun. I whispered to Stein:

"Give me that damn bazooka." I shoved a shell into it and pointed it out. The shell missed. Swearing, I rammed another shell in, this time taking quiet aim. The shell hit the corner of the house and the loft exploded into flames. At the same instant the explosion triggered a diarrhea attack, and I couldn't get my pants down in time!

After capturing the roadblock, the squad took German prisoners. Among those captured were Czechoslovakians in German uniforms fighting for Hitler. It was known I was Czechoslovakian as letters to my parents were always written in Slovak much to the discombobulated censors who were always hounding me to interpret them, so they could turn around and censor them. (They always believed what I said.) An order came down from the CO that they wanted me to interrogate the Czechs. I strode in among them and started talking Slovak to those scared guys, and they broke out in cheers and greetings and were so happy that somebody could speak their language. They had been put in the SS troops and ordered to fight on the front lines. If they had refused, the SS would have executed them.

Afterward, I went over to the Evac hospital for treatment of diarrhea, and learned I had a tenacious infection from eating snow. I was able to get a hot shower, eat some hot food and get some care for the troublesome Trenchfoot that we all had. Trenchfoot resembled frostbite. When I rejoined my outfit a short time later all the men of the 82nd Airborne were relieved from frontline fighting, and we rested billeted around the town of Chevron, Belgium. By that time the Battle of the Bulge battleground had extended forty miles wide and sixty miles deep.

"THEY'LL KILL US"

During the first week of February 1945, we were slogging our way through snow-covered mountains again, and through embattlements of metal dragons teeth, mines, and concrete pillboxes known as the Siegfried Line that separated the borders of Belgium and Germany. We crossed the Siegfried into Germany and approached the Ruhr River just as winter blizzards worsened. Snow got deeper and a lot of us suffered from frostbite. We were all weary. To stay warm we took sleeping bags off our dead buddies, cut the bottoms out so we could still walk, and wrapped them around us and zipped them up. We were warned never to take our boots off as our feet would swell from frostbite and we wouldn't get them on again. One morning when I awoke the lower half of my body was frozen, and I couldn't move. My buddies went to work on me rubbing my legs and flexing my knees until I got circulation flowing again.

The snow was up to our thighs and the ground was frozen solid, and we couldn't dig foxholes. All we could do was hollow out a hole in the snow, spread tree branches over the top, and squat down inside. By then half of my squad was replacements—half of the guys had been casualties!

We were dug in on top of Hill 404 and could look down on the Germans below us across the Ruhr River. Our objective on 9 February was to seize and control the main bridge over the Ruhr River so our tanks could cross later and attack Köln (Cologne), Germany. By 0200 the next morning I took my seven-man patrol and moved down the icy trail under cover of darkness to cross and control both ends of the bridge. When we came to the edge of the tree line there was an open flat area about 300 yards long. In a muted voice I said to my squad, "Single file until we get on the other side of the bridge." We were across the bridge when I heard one of my men fire his M1. More than a little annoyed, I didn't know what he saw to shoot at in the dark. But in the next moment the enemy exploded in front of us.

Our M1 rifles, machine guns, and my Tommy gun were no match for the 20mm mortars that started hitting around us.

I radioed Lieutenant Owens back on the other side, "We're getting the hell out of here, they're going to kill us!"

"Everybody get across the bridge!" I shouted to my squad. " I'll bring up the rear if they come out to cut us off." I was scared they would kill us. Until we got back over the bridge our guys couldn't shoot artillery back at the Germans. My men dashed over the bridge while I covered the rear with my Tommy gun. I was the last to cross. Hurriedly, I unhooked my web belt and gear and let it drop, tossed the Tommy gun, and ran zigzagging across the bridge, remembering my high school track record of a quarter mile in 49.525 seconds. The enemy 88mms started zeroing in on me. In a few seconds I was off the bridge, my feet hit solid ground on the other side. Then an 88mm shell whistled past me and exploded twenty feet away from me. I flew through the air and landed with a thump.

Numb, I wondered if I was dead—I felt life's blood slipping out of me. I thought, maybe this was it. My hands ran over body parts to see if I was in one piece. I could feel air coming out of my lungs through my chest, and my hands got sticky with blood. I hollered, "Medic!" Two guys came to get me. They filled me with morphine only a little faster than it was flowing out of my open wounds, and they lifted me onto a stretcher and carried me to an Evac hospital where they cut off my clothes. I had a gash that went from the middle of my chest around and underneath my arm. My left arm, shoulder, and left leg were broken and my left lung was punctured. I was rolled onto a gurney.

"Well, what'd you do, forget to duck?" the doc inquired.

In agony, I said, "Not really, but look—if you cut my arm off, forget it, let me die. I'm a baseball player, and I can't play baseball with only one arm."

After the initial patching up, I was flown to the 79th General Hospital in Ireland for reconstructive surgery to rebuild my side, broken shoulder, set my broken left arm and left leg, and I entered the world of white sheets and women nurses for a while. Soon after, I was flown to France where I recuperated in the 92nd Hospital outside of Rheims for three months. After recovery I was given a choice, "We

can ship you back home, or—you can go back to your outfit," the
doc had said. Without hesitation I responded, " I want to go back to
my outfit."

Meanwhile ten days after I was wounded, the 82nd Airborne had
captured the Ruhr River valley, war was winding down, and combat
was over for the men of the 82nd. After convalescing, I rejoined the
Red Devils of the 508th again in Frankfurt, Germany—Martin, Owens,
and others were there—and the 508th became special guard for General Eisenhower at SHAEF Headquarters in Frankfurt, Germany.

The Belgium Battle of the Bulge claimed 81,000 American casualties, including 19,000 dead. Germany suffered 100,000 dead,
wounded or captured.

THE LAST JUMP

At war's end in 1945, the 508th Regiment participated in a special
jump during festivities in Austria for Russian Field Marshall Zhukoff,
commander of the East German Zone. Because the jump was near
Vienna, I obtained special permission from battalion headquarters
to cross into bordering Czechoslovakia after the jump. It was only
fifty miles from Vienna to Bratislava, and I was allowed a week's
furlough before returning to my unit. My father had written my uncle stating where to meet me at the border on the appointed day.

I was excited—my pockets were stuffed with candy and cigarettes. I got to the barricade and looked beyond the border guards
and saw my uncle waiting for me on the other side. He waved. I was
happy he recognized me in my uniform. I returned his wave, anxious for the border guards to cease their authoritative paper shuffling. I could look across the Danube to the fields where I had roamed
as a kid.

But like so many others during those years, I was not allowed to
cross the Iron Curtain border. Anger and disappointment beset me.
My uncle and I waved, and wept, and shouted back and forth across
the border to one another.

*

Editor's Note:
Before our visit ended, I asked Sergeant Slama how he felt about his United States' citizenship and about this country. He told me of a poignant visit to Czechoslovakia.

In 1982 I was senior vice president and general manager of Ford, Bacon & Davis, an engineering company in Salt Lake City, whose parent company was Deutsche Babcock of Dusseldorf, Germany. One of the men employed by Deutsche Babcock was overseeing the engineering of a power plant being built outside of Prague, Czechoslovakia. My wife and I made the trip with him.

As we approached the border barricade at Vienna separating the free world and the Iron Curtain countries of Eastern Europe, there were barbwire and machine gun nests in guard towers and dogs patrolling the no-mans-land. As one of the guards took our passports inside, another jacked up our car to examine the undercarriage. I casually walked into the guardhouse and overheard disparaging words about my papers, passport, and about me among the guards. Addressing him in Slovak, I cut his comments short.

"Sir, I understand what you are saying about me."

"Oh" he said, "Pan Slama, do you understand Slovak?"

"Yes, I understand everything that's going on here," I said.

"Oh, good, good, good," he said.

Then I gave him a pack of cigarettes and we were allowed to pass.

We crossed the Danube and drove through farmlands to the town where I was born in Gajare on the outskirts of Bratislava. Driving into town we passed a little grotto of the Blessed Virgin. I remembered as a kid working with my grandfather on the farm, we would get up at three o'clock in the morning, get the horse hooked up to the plow and go out to the fields. As we had passed the grotto my grandfather and I had made the sign of the cross on the way to the fields, and again when we returned at night. It gave me a warm feeling to see it again. In Gajare I visited the Catholic Church where most of the town attended and inquired of a storekeeper if she knew where my father's sister lived.

"Do you know Mrs. Lawrenstovic?" I spoke in Slovak.

"Yes, yes, I know her. Are you American?" she said.

I told her I was.

"What is your name?"

"Slama," I said.

"Oh, I know the Slamas, you speak Slovak very well."

She directed me, and I stood in front of the house remembering it as a young boy. There had been two or three acres of land behind each house cultivated in potatoes and other garden produce that would be sold for cash. It all looked the same now. I knocked on the door. My aunt was a tiny little woman, now a widow. My uncle had been a schoolteacher, but after World War II had ended he opposed the Communists and the Russians sent him to a concentration camp in Siberia from which he never returned. She opened the door, and I spoke to her in Slovak.

"Auntie, do you know who I am?"

She looked at me and could see we were Americans, "No, I don't know who you are. Who are you?"

Since I knew I had a strong resemblance to her brother, I said, "Auntie take a good look at me."

She looked closely into my face and cried, "Aloiz!" –my name in Slovak before I changed it to Louis.

"Aloiz," she cried.

After introducing my wife and getting reacquainted, my aunt put on a babushka, knotting it under her chin, and we went to visit the graves of my four grandparents buried in the same cemetery. Each gravestone bore a chiseled portrait of the deceased—and then we visited my astonished cousins.

There were only a few townspeople that had abandoned their out-houses and remodeled their homes to accommodate indoor bathrooms. They waited in lines half block long for grocery goods, and seemed to live from day to day, hoping their essentials could somehow be met tomorrow. Preparing to leave, I handed my aunt some money, which she refused until we went inside the house, fearing her Communist neighbors might turn her in. Gratefully she said "This will buy extra things for me for the rest of the year."

Before our interview had ended, I asked Sergeant Slama how he felt when he saw the American flag?

"The American flag flies in front of my house every day. I have often thought about coming to this country and what it has given to my family and me. I could never have had this abundance in Czechoslovakia. I am angry when the press show pictures of people burning it, because I remember the many young men I served with who were looking forward to the rest of their lives, but who died for this country, and others who have suffered disfigurement. Every one of us respected and honored the flag and saluted it with dignity. I used to tell people, "If Hitler had won the war, you wouldn't have what you have right now.""

Sergeant Slama was recipient of the Bronze Star and Purple Heart, and his company received citations for the Holland invasion and the Battle of the Bulge in Belgium.

Louis Slama played for the New York Giants in the minor league during 1946, 1947, and 1948, never failing to bat a 300 average, yet because of his injuries that had reduced his stamina, he could not make it into the major league. In 1958 he graduated from Brooklyn Institute of Technology majoring in Civil Engineering, is a licensed engineer, and has an associate degree in architecture. Employed by Ford, Bacon & Davis for twelve years, he retired as president of the company.

Sergeant Slama and his wife Virginia Combi Slama have two daughters, Stephanie Poulsen, who has patented equipment presently used in open heart surgery, and JoAnn Lighty, Ph.D., who received a doctorate in chemical engineering, presently Assistant Dean of Chemical Engineering at the University of Utah, and on the national EPA committee in Washington D.C. The Slamas have four granddaughters.

*****

---

[1] Lambert Siniari was buried outside Nijmegen; later removed to Hammonton, New Jersey.

[2] To this day wreaths are laid at the foot of the Waal Bridge by grateful citizens of the Netherlands in memory of the Americans who died that day.

508th Reg. 82nd Airborne - Holland. Landed 7,467 paratroopers
and 70 tons of equipment during 3-day invasion.
Courtesy of Louis A. Slama

CHAPTER 7

CAPTAIN LEO O. FRAZIER

Capt. Leo O. Frazier
97th and 44th Bomb Groups,
Eighth Army Air Corps

THE EPIC RESCUE OF *MY GAL SAL;* AND THE GREAT ESCAPE

*With documentation and firsthand collaboration of Captain A. Y. Parunak
USN (Ret.), a principal participant in the Greenland rescue.*

ON THE WAY TO THE WAR

As our aircraft, *My Gal Sal*, approached Greenland for refueling, we established radio contact with BW-1 (Bluie West 1), code name for a secret air base at Narsarssuaq on the southwest tip of Greenland thirty miles inland from Julianehaab. BW-1 radioed back that the airfield was fogged in and to proceed north to BW-8 (Bluie West 8) code name for SondreStrömfjord on the west coast of Greenland above the Arctic circle, 400 to 450 miles farther. Our pilot was First Lieutenant Ralf Stinson. I was the navigator and this was my first important mission.

Nine B-17s of the 342nd Squadron, 97th Bomb Group, had taken off from Labrador for England traveling the Arctic route the morning of 26 June 1942[1] along with twenty-one other aircraft from the 97th Bomb Group. Though the Arctic air route was still in its infancy, it was attempted to shorten distances between the US and England in the operation called Bolero.

I plotted the new course to SondreStrömfjord, code named BW-8, as we flew north along the coastal fjords of western Greenland. For a time we skirted the rolling inbound fog, then gaining altitude and heading inland, we came out into blue sky and a view of the top of the world.

Our circumstances grew worse within minutes. At the same time we gained altitude, ice began forming on the aircraft wings, and because of our course change to elude the fog, we had exceeded our calculated fuel consumption. Radioman Laskowski began sending SOS signals, yet, we were unable to broadcast our accurate position because the needles on the compasses were senselessly gyrating in pendulum swings. We were lost. With fuel tanks nearing empty, I scrutinized the uneven snow and tacitly speculated on our chance of surviving in the Arctic.

By Accident I Visited the Arctic Ice Cap

At 9:30 P.M. (local time) Stinson flipped on the intercom.

"I'm going to try for a wheels-up landing on the smoothest stretch of snow I can find," he said, and warned us to get out with our belongings the instant we stopped, fearing the weight of the 10-ton B-17 might be greater than melting June ice could bear.

With my head between my knees, I braced against the bulkhead with other crewmembers, fearful we would be entombed within a cavernous crevasse. I waited for the inevitable crash at the same time praying for divine intervention.

Stinson nosed the plane onto an open stretch of Arctic snow and eased her down. The aircraft jolted and lurched, skidded and shuddered to a stop. We bolted for the hatch and jumped onto slushy snow as the plane settled and stabilized. The fuselage was damaged, the props twisted; she couldn't fly us out, but we were uninjured.

Crewmembers besides pilot First Lieutenant Stinson and myself, a second lieutenant, were second lieutenants Wilson McGough co-pilot and Donald Bone bombardier; sergeants Harvey Gordon ball turret gunner, Wayne Heckendorn waist gunner, Tom Laskowski radioman, Stephen Breining tail gunner, and John Patrick ground crew chief; and Corporal Carl Bauman flight engineer, along with U.S. Army passengers Kenneth Bright operations clerk, Charles Chapman armorer, and Captain Wendell Freeman Army security officer.

We surveyed damages and Lieutenant Stinson began assigning tasks when an argument erupted between Captain Wendell Freeman, one of the Army passengers, and pilot Stinson over who was in charge. Flexing his higher rank, Freeman took command and an argument exploded. The loyal crew backed their pilot. Crew chief Patrick intervened and eventually defused supercharged emotions, but Freeman continued to grump.

Addressing primary survival concerns, the pilot resumed assigning tasks. The undamaged radio, our only hope of rescue, required a power source to continue transmitting. Fortunately, tools were on board, and we used a hacksaw to remove twisted prop blades from #1 engine where the electrical generator was located. Patrick drained the residual fuel from empty aircraft tanks into one tank to fuel the generator. The engine was started up and left to idle to keep radio batteries charged. Forty gallons of fuel remained, and we hoped it would last until rescued. Laskowski began his steady vigil at the radio.

Food was critically short and Lieutenant Bone was appointed mess officer to ration the food found on board. Collected were C-rations, sandwiches, and a case of Baby Ruths that were divided equally thirteen ways to last five days, then wisely divided again to meagerly span fifteen.

Patrick removed the dish-like supercharger covers, drained engine oil into them and ignited oil for open-flame heaters, providing heat besides being able to melt snow for drinking water.

I worked over my charts and our last known position trying to calculate where we were, wondering what may have happened to the other planes in our squadron, and whether they were also somewhere on the ice.

Arctic birds flew over and caribou hovered at a distance unafraid and curious at the shining metal of our aircraft on the otherwise white expanse. There were no other signs of life. We were in a place that no man had seen.

Days were warm and surface snow became soft and slushy. Though the sun never sets during June in the Arctic, temperatures dipped below freezing during night hours. We huddled in the plane for warmth listening to the tapping of Laskowski continually cranking out SOS. During those long days and twilight nights, I prayed that we would receive help, and I know others did.

And then we waited.

THE STORY OF THE STRANDED CREW BECOMES
THE STORY OF THEIR RESCUERS

According to the pocket-sized flight log book of rescue pilot Lieutenant A. Y. Parunak USN, My Gal Sal made a forced landing approximately 65° 21' N, 49° 53' W, 100 to 120 miles southeast of BW-8 at an elevation of 3500 feet. Recently, he discussed problems of Arctic navigation with the author.

"As one approaches the poles (higher latitudes north or south) the normally steady magnetic compass, on its vertical axis, begins to not only yaw (swing) from side to side, but actually will go into large swings, called 'oscillation.' The magnetic properties of the compass are such that a magnetic 'dip' needle on a <u>horizontal</u> axis would by now be pointing down at the <u>magnetic</u> north or south pole. Actually, at a position <u>over</u> the pole the needle would point straight down. This confusion of a horizontally mounted compass ring (vertical axis) trying to react to a vertical force, will not only cause it to have severe oscillations, but finally goes into constant rotation like a slowly turning pin-wheel.

"The flight gyro-compass, due to the rotation of the earth, will slowly change heading. . . To reset it one needs a reference such as an Astro-compass, a non-rotating mechanical device which is used with any visible celestial body, be it stars, sun, planets, or even the moon. This requires the use of sighting of the celestial body by an octant. <u>Very few</u> of the early AF [B-17] navigators could properly use this instrument or reduce the readings to an azimuth."

Apparently, even the advanced navigational training Lieutenant Frazier had received as one of the top thirty of his class had not been adequate to navigate the Arctic regions.

THE RESCUE

To know the circumstances at BW-8 is to better understand why this was a remarkable rescue.

Bernt Balchen, a Norwegian with experience on Arctic expeditions and pilot for Admiral Byrd at the South Pole in 1929, was snatched up by the U.S. Army in July of 1941 to supervise construction of the BW-8 air field in Greenland. War with Germany was inevitable by then and Greenland was destined to play a part. Accompanying him to Greenland were thirty-two men who made up the core crew of this outpost, including sergeants Joseph Healey and Hendrik (Dutch) Dolleman, who had been with Balchen and Bryd in the Antarctic. Prior to their arrival, a consortium of US contractors had begun construction of the facility that would provide airfields, radio and meteorological equipment.[2]

The Army's Greenland plans neglected to provide search and rescue capabilities. However, Navy Commander-in-Chief Admiral Ernest J. King thought it prudent to provide his search and rescue people in Greenland at BW-1 and BW-8 within the flying route of Army Air Force Operation Bolero. Succinctly, the Navy had anticipated a need that the Army hadn't cared to acknowledge. See endnote 3.

"VOT ARE YOU HERE FOR?"

On 28 May, a month prior to receiving distress signals from My Gal Sal, three U.S. Navy Catalina PBY-5A's circled BW-8's airfield. While waving off bulldozers blading the airfield, the pilots landed the seaplanes on the gravel air strip. Balchen hadn't received word from the Army of an impending visit and was surprised to hear that twenty-one men had disembarked from three seaplanes on his air-field. Jumping into a jeep, dust billowed as he progressed over the seven to eight miles to the airfield. Meanwhile, Patrol Plane Commander Lieutenant A. Y. Parunak, natty in his navy aviator's winter green dress uniform and mirror shined dress shoes, waited by his plane watching the dust cloud approach. Aware that Balchen was a lieutenant colonel, he scanned the shirt collars for the silver leaves as several men approached, but found none. The man nearest to him reached out his hand.

"Velcome, I'm Bernt Balchen, up here ve don't vear insignia, vhere are you headed for?"

"Here," I replied.

"Vot are you here for?" Colonel Balchen, who had to anticipate every nail, board and potato to be delivered on a once-a-summer supply ship, then inquired, "Did you bring food?"

Parunak, with the designation Patrol Plane Commander received after extensive experience in long range seaplanes, mastering naval navigation, seamanship, aircraft engineering, emergency procedures, and international law, explained he was there by order of Navy Commander-in-Chief Admiral Ernest J. King and produced appropriate copies of Secret dispatches. Besides Admiral King's dispatches, Parunak's coveted appellation of Patrol Plane Commander came with recognition to proceed alone and to operate independently anywhere in the world.

From the start, the savvy Norwegian polar explorer, and the seaplane pilot who had amassed 2900 air hours, became an uncommon Army-Navy team. The aftereffect of their compatible natures and cooperative efforts resulted in a succession of unique rescues. Later, Balchen with irony would give them the moniker "The Greenland Salvage Company," likely rankling his boss Chief of Staff of the Army Henry "Hap" Arnold.

On 2 July, Balchen and Parunak had concluded the evacuation of thirteen men from B-17 Alabama Exterminator. Piloted by Lieutenant John Holmes of the 97ᵗʰ Bomb Group, The Alabama Extermina-

tor had run out of fuel and ditched on 26 June, off course, and 185 miles north of BW-8 near the Eskimo village of Egedesminde near Disko Island.

"Here ve go again," Balchen commented in his lyrical Norwegian accent after receiving a radio bearing on My Gal Sal. It would be the third lost plane rescue operation since Parunak arrived a month earlier, and wouldn't be the last.

Six PBYs, three each from BW-1 at Narsarssuaq on the southern tip of Greenland, and BW-8 at Sondre Strömfjord, began the hunt for My Gal Sal by flying a line search toward each other from their respective bases. A significant part of the rescue was the PBY (Patrol Bomber manufactured by Consolidated Aircraft Co. San Diego), a large twin-engine seaplane that could be tweaked by a competent pilot to stay airborne for almost twenty hours and cover approximately 2000 miles without refueling. Pilot Lieutenant George C. Atteberry USNR of BW-1 was first to spot My Gal Sal and drop emergency supplies. Balchen and Parunak resumed rescue operations since BW-8 was closer to the downed plane.

THE SEVENTH DAY AT THE CRIPPLED AIRCRAFT — 3 JULY

Meanwhile, unaware that our SOS had been received, I was out on the wing watching caribou trying to shoot one with a .45 pistol, when I heard the drone of an airplane engine. It came toward us then flew over and for an instant my heart stopped, as I thought it was going to leave us. Then the PBY banked and made another pass and dropped us a package containing Arctic sleeping bags, C-rations, and coffee with a note inside which read, "Sit tight." The pilot dipped the aircraft's wings and flew out of sight.

That afternoon pilot Parunak and passenger Balchen flew over My Gal Sal while plotting a rescue course. The ill-fated plane had landed in a heavily crevassed area of the ice cap. Flying over the crippled aircraft, they dropped additional packages containing food, sleeping bags, and a bottle of whiskey. "We radioed an admonition," Parunak recalls: "All hands stay with your plane. To keep them from straying, we purposely did not drop skis or snowshoes."

From his report written on 21 July 1942, Parunak described the difficulties of the rescue:

"Due to . . . mountainous terrain and crevasses, [the] rescue could be accomplished only by landing a plane on the ice cap. . . [However], the crevassed and slushy surface of the cap made it impossible to land on wheels.

"On July 3, while re-surveying for a new plan of rescue, it was observed that the melting ice was forming a lake of respectable size in a dimple on the cap at approximate position, Latitude 65° 27' N, Longitude 49° 29' W, distance about 12 miles from the B-17. From the color of the water and the formation of the surrounding ice, the depth was estimated to be sufficient to land a PBY as a seaplane."

As they flew back to BW-8, the rescue was similarly planned like others they had recently made. Parunak would have the plane stripped of unnecessary equipment to reduce weight and refuel with 500 gallons of gas, just enough to go to the lake and return. Balchen would select sergeant Dolleman to set up a tent at a base camp and Healey to accompany him on skis. They would ski to the aircraft while Parunak, piloting the PBY, would direct them overhead and ahead to give guidance over crevassed areas. Parunak chose copilot Ensign John C. Snyder, Aviation Machinist Mate Oliver L. Leininger, and radioman Frank R. McEnroe as his crewmembers.

Later on the same day (3 July 1942) with preparations completed, Parunak, Balchen and crewmen boarded the seaplane. Parunak circled the 12-ton seaplane over the small ice-melt lake. It was possible that the bottom of the lake was only a thin ice crust bridging crevasses that would not hold the weight of the aircraft, and the crew watched the water line with keen interest as the keel hit the water. Captain Parunak continues the story:

"The lake had been formed by a large dimple on the surface being filled with the melting surface ice melted by the sun's solar rays. It was oriented north and south about 12 air miles north of *My Gal Sal*. We made several low altitude timing runs and calculated its length: Distance = Rate x Time. The "distance" of length was 1.8 miles. Adequate to land and take off. Depth was judged by "seaman's eye": clear at the edges, darkening blue toward the center. Altitude of lake 4200 feet above sea level.

"There were two conditions that any experienced pilot would have to respect. (a) At that altitude the air is thinner, therefore greater speed is required to achieve the necessary lift. This requires increased power. (b) In order to minimize the hydraulic impact of landing a 25,000 pound aircraft on a lake where the bottom may give way, you "grease it on"—a power landing. Apparently, we did it right, but then this technique was not something new."

First Successful Landing and Take-off from the Ice Cap

Waiting only long enough to see the rubber raft inflated and Balchen, Healey and Dolleman paddling to the slick-edged lake, Parunak was airborne again. Dolleman set up camp. Balchen and Healey slipped into ski bindings, each with a sleeping bag and a day's rations, and skied west toward the coast to circumvent crevasses. After skiing many hours in difficult terrain with a storm descending, they returned to base camp and rested. On their second attempt, Balchen chose the direct and more hazardous route. When traversing swollen glacial rivers of melting ice, they linked up arms to maintain their footing on the slick porcelain-glazed river bottoms. They cautiously tested the snow ahead of them with poles to unearth hidden snow bridges.

Day Nine at MY GAL SAL — the Fourth of July

Meanwhile, we were convivially celebrating the Fourth of July and our imminent rescue with a mini-sized banquet. From C-rations we had saved a can of stew and a can of plum pudding which we now ceremoniously opened.

But by the following morning our jovial attitudes were replaced with uneasiness. It had been two days since the PBY had dropped the last supplies and note, and we were speculating what "sit tight" might mean. I sat out on the wing that morning scanning the horizon when there appeared two silhouettes trekking through the snow toward us. At about the same time, the PBY flew over and dropped additional provisions, thirteen pair of snowshoes, and 200 feet of rope.

Balchen and Healey arrived on skis exhausted. They immediately stripped off all their clothes, rolled naked in the snow, washed down with ice water, and got into sleeping bags. Balchen gave us clear instructions from his horizontal position, "Take only sleeping bag and one day's food ration, and have snowshoes on prepared to leave vhen ve vake up." Balchen's voice was never officious, but he was known to stab with a stare those that didn't follow his orders, ultimately allowing them to suffer resulting consequences. We were soon to know this iron man better.

While our rescuers slept, we made preparations. Now in good spirits, we configured our sleeping bags into backpacks all the while looking forward to a comfortable bed and different companions. Having been advised to travel light and to leave nonessentials behind, we nevertheless wanted to take souvenirs home with us. While we stuffed our pockets and packs with mementos, others loaded suitcases, and Harvey Gordon even salvaged the eight-day clock from the cockpit and wrapped it in his sleeping bag. Lastly, we dealt with the Top Secret Norden bombsight by destroying it with a volley from .45s and left it in the aircraft.

We had snowshoes on when our rescuers awoke. Balchen said we would have only short standing rests along the way to the lake—no sitting rests. He cautioned us about snow bridges that spanned crevasses, and for everyone's safety, we were all to tie into the 200-foot rope. Balchen set the pace in the lead while Healey brought up the rear. At 1:30 P.M. (local time) 5 July, we left the plane and struck out single file across the ice cap. We were light-hearted and happy starting out, but after wading through glacial rivers becoming soaked to our necks, we were tired and irritable and began throwing off the extra weight of precious mementos that we thought important at the start.

From the air, Parunak kept vigilance over the line of snowshoers and recorded the scene:

"On July 5-6 en route from *My Gal Sal* to lake, [I provided] guidance from air by direction in writing placed in green coffee cans; for more immediate guidance by zooming over the party rocking wings and heading to the desired course for safe walking.

"An amusing development took place en route. At each rest stop men began discarding item after item. I could look down the trail and identify the rest stops by the piles of abandoned treasures. While Balchen led the pack, Healey brought up the rear riding herd."

All of a sudden there was a scream as a man fell through a snow bridge into a crevasse.

Balchen related the scene later to Parunak who recorded it, observing Balchen's parlance:

"Suddenly... there vas a curdling scream for help. One of the crew had decided on his own that he vould not be tied onto the rope, but vould fake it. He had broken through an ice bridge, clinging vit his fingers to the edge of a crevasse hundreds of feet deep. So, hearing the screaming I skied back to the victim. I look at him hanging there and I say, 'Is something vong?'"

"Save me! Save me!" The man is screaming.

"I said to him, 'That's the vay you vanted it. Live vit it,' and I started to ski off to join the line. By now, the man is hysterical. I ski back and inquired, 'Are you ready to be tied in and do as you are told?'

"He promised pleadingly. I pulled him out.

"There vas a solemn quiet among the others. I didn't have to say anything. Ve move on as if nothing had happened."

DAY TEN

The midnight sun circled around the horizon as we trudged on through the night and early morning hours. Following Dolleman's smoke signals, we were guided to camp and arrived at 3:30 (local time) the morning of 6 July. It had taken fourteen hours of steady snowshoeing to travel twenty-six circuitous miles to the lake. We collapsed from exhaustion at the campsite unable to eat the hot pemmican stew Dolleman had prepared for us. Within an hour the PBY arrived and seven crewmembers, including myself, climbed aboard. In those early morning hours ice had formed at one end of the lake dangerously shortening the take off area. *From Parunak's log book:*

> "Take-off area was diminished to less than one mile by ice, which had formed and drifted into take-off area on the lake. . . I jettisoned about 600 lbs. of fuel to provide a margin of safety. Subsequent flights were under normal ice-free conditions."

Grateful to be alive, I expressed gratitude to our rescuers. On my arrival at BW- 8, I took a very welcome shower and received clean clothes. It was then that I learned three out of the first four planes from our squadron had made emergency landings. Luckily no lives had been lost.

DISAPPEARANCE OF THE DIMPLE MELT-WATER LAKE

Returning to the ice-melt lake, Parunak landed a second time that same day to recover five remaining fliers and Healey and Dolleman. Balchen wanted to stay behind alone and rest. In telling the rest of the story, Parunak recalls:

> "[Balchen]… had been on his feet for several days without rest and relished the chance to stay there alone. It became the fourth landing and takeoff from the dimple melt-water lake when I returned later that day to pick him up…

Subsequent flights were under normal ice-free conditions.

"On July 11 on our way to Kungyat Bay near BW-1 on the tip of Greenland, we [passenger Balchen and one other] chose to divert a bit and fly over *My Gal Sal*. The lake was no longer there, and there was no apparent crevasse. Naturally, there had to be a fault which caused the drainage."

The Arctic route was discontinued for a season. Military aircraft flew a safer route south from Florida over Trinidad and Venezuela to Brazil, then east from Natal, Brazil, across the narrowest section of the South Atlantic to Dakar, Senegal, Africa, north to England, a distance three or four times farther than the Arctic route.

THE GREAT ESCAPE

Lone Survivor

Promoted to first lieutenant, I was none the worse physically for my ten days on the ice cap. On temporary assignment on the Arctic flight, I was then assigned to the 44th Bomber Group of the Eighth Air Force as navigator on a B-24 stationed at Shipdam, England. Prior to our first combat mission, our B-24 was equipped at Belfast, Ireland, with bomb rack and steel armor plates for pilot and copilot seats.

Up at 4 A.M., I picked up breakfast, guns, and a parachute and climbed up in the B-24 before sun-up on my second mission. Forty aircraft took off on this mission and while in the air learned we were airborne more than an hour early because of a CO's scheduling error. We circled over England carrying 500-pound bombs and expending precious fuel until heading south toward German submarine pens in the southwest of France. On our return, fuel tanks were giving up their last few gallons when we finally sighted the coast of England, and we cried out in relief. The pilot requested I find the nearest airstrip.

"I've located one, but the runway is too short to land," I replied.

"No time for an alternate plan," the pilot retorted, "prepare for an emergency landing. I'm going in for a wheels-up landing." I braced myself thinking these belly landings were all too frequent. We were safe, but our group commander was later relieved of his command for the scheduling error.

It happened on my tenth mission over Germany. Reporting to the briefing room early on the morning of 8 March 1943, I searched for a volunteer copilot, bombardier, radio operator, and two gunners. Half our crew was missing or wounded from the day's previous mission. Because we were assured fighter protection and it was a short mission, five off-duty airmen volunteered to fill out our crew, and add an extra mission to their tallies. We lost our established position in the squadron because of this delay, and ended up in the dreaded number four spot, last, and below the other aircraft in the vulnerable position aptly named coffin corner.

At the point over the English Channel where we expected our fighter planes to join us and give cover to the target, none was in sight. We continued on. Below us the northern tip of France appeared hazy from our 20,000-foot view when the bombardier hollered dreaded words over the intercom.

"Fighters at 12 o'clock high!" Enemy planes dove in and around our aircraft from all sides. On first pass, our lead bomber flamed and went into a dive. A German pilot flew head-on through our formation, and I got a glimpse of him as he headed directly toward our right wing and hit us with a cannon shell into the cockpit. The alarm went off. Bail out!

Reaching up and pulling the handle to open the nose-wheel hatch, I sat on the edge of the aircraft with my legs dangling out over 20,000 feet of space. With right hand on the ripcord handle, I jumped, then blacked out from lack of oxygen. With no recollection of pulling the ripcord or falling through space, I regained consciousness half way down when I got oxygen back into my lungs. Two Messerschmitts circled above me, and I expected them to shoot, or spill my chute. Helpless, I floated down finally dropping onto a plowed field on my left arm. Waiting nearby, a truckload of Germans surrounded and pushed me into the back of a truck. Interrogated at their headquarters by an English speaking German, I gave name, rank and serial number according to the Geneva Convention rules, then was transferred to a hospital in Rouen, France, where my arm was splinted and a cut sutured over my right eye. A Red Cross nurse said she would notify my family I was a POW. I knew that news would grieve my parents. While in the hospital, two airmen from my bomber group on the same mission said no other parachutes left my aircraft. I was the lone survivor.

Transferred to Frankfurt, guards locked me in solitary. Interrogated daily, I gave name, rank, and serial number, but discovered they knew a great deal even though I remained silent. They knew I had graduated from South Summit High School in Kamas, Utah, and graduated from Brigham Young University majoring in banking and finance; when I was inducted into the Air Force and where I trained, but lost track after I was rescued from the ice cap.

$25 LEMON PIE

After ten days' interrogation, they trucked me, along with other airmen, to a new POW camp specifically for British and American airmen. Photographed and fingerprinted on 1 April 1943, they marched me into the compound emphatically declaring Stalag Luft 3 was my new home. Lieutenant Harold Spires was the first person that greeted me. We had been through navigation and flight training together.

"What are you doing here?" he asked.

"I'm here to collect the $120 you borrowed from me in our last crap game in Florida!" I laughingly replied.

American senior officer Lieutenant Colonel A. P. Clark[4] introduced me around, explained the camp regulations, and that we were called Kriegies. Our camp, surrounded by a stand of tall pines, was located sixty-five miles southeast of Berlin within a compound of thirty new barracks.

I moved into a room with Americans Shorty Spires, Bob Carlburg, and Charles Austin. The 18x15-foot room had a wood-burning stove, two double bunk beds, four small standing lockers, food cupboard, table and four stools. Each barracks housed twelve similar rooms with washroom, three or four basins, cold-water shower and two toilets that we were only allowed to use at night. During the day we used the latrines outdoors. When showering, we heated a basin of water on the stove to soap up, then rinsed off in a cold shower. With no heat in the washroom, it was chin quivering during winter.

They called me Cupboard Fuerher as I had the responsibility of gathering and dividing foodstuffs for the men in our room. I used a bartering system assigning points to each food item. Chocolate bars, coffee and cigarettes had the greatest exchange value. Weekly, two of us took turns cooking, washing dishes, sweeping floors, and standing in line for rations. I often cooked and requested special items from home: tooth powder without flavoring which was mostly soda that I used for baking, and food tablets that tasted like vanilla for flavoring desserts. I created pies and cakes that even guards coveted. Colonel Clark once offered me $25 for a slice of my lemon pie.

Blood sausage, bitter brown bread, soup, potatoes, rutabagas, and barley mush were the staples we ate. We stood in line twice daily for these rations. In addition, a Red Cross parcel came each week containing a can of Spam, corn beef, salmon or sardines, a jar of instant coffee, half pound sugar, jar of jam, and four-ounce Hershey chocolate bar, dried fruit—raisins or apricots, and small can of margarine. Usually the British Red Cross packages contained tea, and the Canadians got a can of bacon, box of hard biscuits, and a can of butter. I traded with Canadians for hard biscuits and butter for piecrusts. Besides Red Cross parcels, we were allowed a personal package from home every other month not to exceed eleven pounds, and tobacco companies shipped us boxes of cigarettes.

Parcel officers were POWs assigned to open our packages in front of guards. Jabbing each can with a sharp tool at least twice, the guards made sure cans contained only food. The canned goods often spoiled because we didn't have refrigeration. Guards confiscated items from our packages, so we contrived a color-coding system to bypass the inspection guards. When packages arrived tied with red string, the parcels were furtively concealed under the table. Those parcels frequently contained radios, compasses, wirelesses, and other equipment for our escape and were delivered unopened to Big X, the British officer in charge of all escapes.

TOM, DICK AND HARRY

Though you may think we had all the comforts of home without working, yet we were a disciplined group of chiefly American and British commissioned airmen with superior ranking officers, painstakingly preparing the massive escape of 250 men.

Big X and the escape committees were skilled in craftsmanship and mechanical adroitness, and we resolved to dig three escape tunnels simultaneously.

Tom, the name of the first tunnel we dug, originated beneath a wood stove in the barracks, and rested on a concrete pad 2 ½ x 2 ½ feet with a brick load-bearing support that extended to the ground with a hollow center. By lifting the stove off its pad in one of the barracks rooms, removing brickwork and chipping concrete, we tunneled through the hollow brick pier down a depth of 30 feet. It was night work. Each morning the brickwork and stove were carefully replaced on its pad to conceal the opening, all the while we deceptively kept a fire burning in the stove.

Dick, the name of the second tunnel, was dug beneath the theater building floor. The empty building had a stage and sloping theater floor, but didn't have seats. We crafted three hundred theater seats by salvaging wood crates from Red Cross parcels as our tunneling progressed beneath the floor. Guards gave us carpentry tools on the promise not to use them in escapes, which we honored.

Harry, our third tunnel, began in a barracks shower stall. After removing the drain cover, we tunneled down next to the waste water pipe. After a night's digging, the tunnel opening was sealed, grate cover replaced, and a splash of water tossed in to conceal it.

Guards expected escapes, and if time lapsed without an attempt, they became suspicious and began probing the ground with three-foot pointed iron rods, inspecting under barracks and disturbing our rooms. Though our tunnels were deep and couldn't be found by probing, nevertheless, we pacified the guards by arranging periodic planned escapes. After a POW escaped, he was recaptured, and after spending a few weeks in solitary, returned to camp without injury.

Sandy and rock-free soil greatly facilitated our digging, but disposing of fifty ton of soil undetected created a gigantic problem.

When spring came, the German Camp Commander provided a magnificent solution for us. We were instructed to cultivate our own vegetable gardens. The guards furnished hoes, rakes, spades, and seed, and we began spading 10 x 20-foot garden plots around each barracks where we surreptitiously began dumping the tunnel soil.

Our escape organization had crews for tunnel digging, intelligence, security, diversions, forging, and tailoring. Big T, the tailor's, first task was handcrafting bags containing one shovel-full of dirt. Generally made from old socks, bags were attached to waist belts and by pulling drawstrings the dirt spilled out beneath our long overcoats. Tunnel dirt was conspicuously a different color and plot cultivators had to vigilantly keep it spaded. Surrounding the outer perimeter of the compound was a dirt path next to a wire fence ten feet-high with three or four barbwires strung on the top, sloped inward with a guard tower every hundred yards. We tamped the tunnel dirt on this perimeter path. It was a common sight to see twenty or thirty of us wearing long overcoats on dirt-dumping duty with twenty or thirty men following scuffing feet and packing down dirt. Despite the apparent comedy, our dirt dumping didn't arouse suspicion.

Removing 1 x 4 slats from our bunk beds ingeniously supplied lumber to brace tunnel walls and ceilings in three simultaneously dug tunnels. With brace and bit, we drilled holes in the sideboards of our bunks and strung them with salvaged cord from Red Cross packages. Besides, it made our beds more comfortable, too. By pulling off attic timbers, subfloors, and boards behind cupboards, we stealthily supplied adequate lumber for bracing. True to our promise, tools and equipment used in the escape were never the same tools used for gardening or crafting theater seats.

The Scrounge Officer had a special group of airmen assisting him who spoke fluent German and by connivance and bribery persuaded guards to supply them with cameras, film, heavy picks, and short-handled shovels. Chocolate, American cigarettes, and especially coffee were coveted by the guards and used as bribes. Shorty Spires was in the Scrounge group, and because he was my roommate, we often entertained German guards in our room with a cup of coffee and cigarettes and in return received wire-cutters, guns, ammunition, and other escape implements.

OUR HOPE WAS ON HARRY

The master forger and his apprentices were adroitly handcrafting passports, visas, travel documents, photos and official seals. Though unhandy as a forger, I was unflinching as a guard, and when a fellow Kriegie signaled that a guard approached, I swiftly gathered inks, cameras, and documents and placed them in a violin case and hid it.

In September we allowed guards to find Dick, the tunnel beneath the theater, to relieve search pressure on our other two tunnels. Unfortunately, Tom was also found beneath the heating stove. But Harry, under the shower floor drain, remained undetected. When completed it would be thirty feet deep and extend a hundred twenty feet with the exit into the forest.

Winter snow made it impossible to dispose of dirt, especially after Tom and Dick were discovered, and we closed the tunnel for the winter and concentrated on manufacturing bellows to force air through the underground passage, and a four-wheeled flatbed sled with pulleys to move diggers in and dirt out. Tunnel digging began again around the clock late in January. By then "Big T" the tailor and his team had completed civilian clothes, and the master forger had completed travel documents prior to going blind from the strain and tediousness of crafting three sets of perfect documents for each of 250 men. The escape documents were dated 24 March 1944, the next moonless night, and we drew lots for the order in which we would exit through the tunnel.

With preparations completed, a great disappointment developed just a week before the escape. All the American prisoners in the camp were quite suddenly marched to an adjacent camp. Shorty Spires, Bob Carlburg, Charles Austin, and I, along with all the other Americans, were moved and our drawn escape numbers became crumpled mementos. It was a great disappointment, but it turned out to be a blessing in disguise.

On the appointed night, airmen dressed in civvies with travel documents dated 24 March 1944 in their pockets crouched against Harry waiting for the signal to exit. The first man broke through the end of the tunnel to the grassy surface, peered out, and was horrified to see the length of the tunnel was twenty feet short of the trees. Guard tower and rotating searchlight stood between them. While pondering their next move and considering the dated travel documents they carried, an air raid alarm sounded, and the tower searchlights switched off for the black-out. During these few minutes seventy-six men hastily hoisted themselves up onto the grass and ran to the edge of the forest.

The following morning twenty-three airmen were captured and returned back to the camp by guards. Then the worst news was announced in the camp. The Gestapo had captured fifty of our men, and because they were in civilian clothes and carried identification papers, they were accused of being spies. A few days later on 6 April, guards returned to us bloodstained clothes and fifty burial urns of ashes. The Gestapo had trucked them to a field and executed them. It was a dark day of mourning for us.

Two British and one Australian were able to escape to freedom.

SAVED BY HITLER

Morale was low during the winter of 1944-45. With our tunneling activity discovered, we settled into depression and a monotonous routine. The Red Cross supplied us with overcoats, knit wool caps, and some of us had wooden shoes that kept our feet warm. Issued two army blankets and two sheets, we sewed the edges of blankets together, stuffed shredded paper inside, and quilted them together with string acquired from parcels and needles sent from home. Ten thousand airmen were in camp by then, and we were forced to sleep eight to a room that had four bunks.

Encouraged by frequent US planes flying overhead, we speculated whether we would be liberated by Americans or captured by Russians, since we were only sixty-five miles southeast of Berlin, near the former Polish border. We feared the Russians more than our enemy the Germans. Some of us felt we might never see our families again if captured by the Russians.

While discussing escape plans in January 1945, we received surprise instructions from the guards: pack food and belongings and be ready to move out on a moment's notice to an undisclosed destination. We made a packsack by tying each pant leg off at the

From fire scorched and discolored documents retrieved by Allied forces later that year were minutes of a conference held at Berchtesgaden on 27 January 1945 which referred to the transfer of airmen at Stalag Luft 3. The minutes named those present: Adolf Hitler, Reichsmarshal Hermann Goering, Field Marshal Wilhelm Keitel, General Jodl, General Heinz Guderian, Foreign Officer Walther Hewel, Himmler's liaison man, Obergruppenfuehrer Hermann Fegelein, General Winter and about a dozen other Hitler aids. An excerpt from the minutes follows:

Goering: "... There are 10,000 captured air force officers at Sagan. Guard and transportation facilities are not available but it has been suggested that the prisoners be left behind for the Russians to take. They would get 10,000 fliers."

Hitler: "Why haven't they been sent away earlier? That is sheer stupidity."

Goering: "That is in the bailiwick of the army. We haven't anything to do with it. I can only report it."

Hitler: "They've got to be taken away, even if we have to march them on foot through the mud. We will give the Volkssturm the job. Anyone who tries to get away will be shot."

qtd. from Pierre J. Huss, byline Berchtesgaden, Germany.

bottom and stuffing them with food and clothing, placing a folded blanket in the crotch for padding, and hanging it around our shoulders. Six inches of snow had fallen, and we waterproofed our shoes with margarine.

At ten o'clock that night we evacuated camp. Germans marched us south all night and through the next day. On the second night Shorty slipped on ice, fell and hurt his back, and I carried his pack besides my own.

Curious villagers came out of their homes to have a look at us. It was only a short time before Shorty had made friends and traded part of a chocolate bar for a hand sleigh. We loaded our packs onto it and pulled the sleigh. On the third day we rested in an abandoned plant where there was water to wash. On the fourth day we marched to a railroad where forty men were crowded into each cattle car, leaving us only standing room. For eight days we traveled with no toilet and no water, finally being incarcerated into the atrocious

Dashua Concentration Camp thirty miles northeast of Munich, Germany. Regardless of our wretched treatment, we were grateful to be beyond the grasp of Russians.

Our only ration at Dashua we called Black Death, a broth made from dirty alfalfa with floating vermin. Most of us had dysentery, and we all had fleas. Barber tools were passed around one day and Shorty asked me to give him a crew cut, which I did. The next morning he was gone, and I never saw him again.

Early April we received news from Allied Forces to "Sit tight." The message seemed extremely familiar, like another I had received on Greenland. Then on 28 April 1945, General Patton's tank division rolled into camp and freed us.

*

Editor's Note:

Captain Leo Frazier was a POW for twenty-eight months and received the Air Medal with five oak leaf clusters and Purple Heart. During part of the time he was a POW, he continued his university studies at Brigham Young University's extension division, receiving courses of study pertaining to his major. He had graduated from Brigham Young University in 1940 majoring in banking and finance and joined the Army Air Corps directly following graduation, receiving his basic training at Oxnard, California, then at Ellington Field, Texas, for pilot training. He was unable to qualify as a pilot due to a failing in depth perception, but undaunted, he transferred to navigational school and received advanced navigational training at Kelly Field near San Antonio, Texas. As training progressed, it became more apparent that math calculations and charts were the navigator's tools and he didn't feel confident in math to make grade. Early on he went to his CO and requested a transfer to bombardier training. However, before the transfer came through, he had graduated as a navigator among the top thirty in his class.

Captain Frazier returned to Utah at the end of the war and married Roberta Hortin also of Oakley, Utah, where they presently reside. They have three children and ten grandchildren. Captain Frazier served for fourteen years as Summit County Assessor and Oakley's postmaster.

The Retired French Air Force Pilots and other French citizens still remembered the sacrifices Americans made for them during the war and honored Frazier and other American fliers during a ceremony in December 1996 when they unveiled a monument dedicated to them in Rouen, France. Unfortunately, Captain Frazier was unable to attend the ceremony in France, but the following year a representative from the Eighth Air Force, 44th Bomber Group, visited the Fourth of July Oakley Rodeo and to Frazier's astonishment publicly pinned a medal on his chest for his valor and service to the French during World War II.

*****

---

[1] According to Log Book of U.S. Coast Guard ship *Comanche* that was serving as both a visual aid-to-navigation and radio beacon at the entrance of fjord to BW-1, 5 B-17s were logged passing the ship morning of 26 June 1942, and 21 others between 4:30 P.M. and 9:16 P.M. using "local" time plus 3, mariner time calculated from Greenwich Civil Time.

[2] U.S. Coast Guard ships on Greenland's coast provided weather data and radio beacon services until facility was completed.

[3] Recognizing the mismatch of the young, inexperienced Army Air Force crews, [Admiral Ernest J.] King suggested to Gen[eral] "Hap" Arnold that King place navy navigators in the B17s solely to navigate the planes over the treacherous route to England. At that time naval pilots were required to be proficient in navigation particularly in the large seaplanes. King stressed to Arnold that the naval navigators would be limited to navigating. Gen[eral] Arnold strongly demurred. Yet Arnold did not possess any recognizable rescue capability to put in place. As King said it to me: "I told the General that he could stop me from putting navigators in his planes, but that they would undoubtedly need help, and he couldn't stop me from putting search and rescue forces in place, for he was going to need them. Records of A. Y. Parunak

[4] Lt. General A. P. Clark was Superintendent of the United States Air Force Academy from August 1970 to July 1974.

Greenland

Lt. Aram Y. Parunak, U.S. Navy, on ice cap lake, Greenland, 7/3/42 during rescue operation of B-17 crew. *Courtesy of A. Y. Parunak*

Lt. Col. Bernt Balchen, Army Air Corps, on Greenland rescue operation 7/3/42. *Courtesy of A. Y. Parunak*

Leo Frazier fingerprinted and photographed as POW
in Stalag Luft 3. *Courtesy of Leo O. Frazier*

Photo sewed on the bottom of one of Leo O. Frazier's letters to his parents.
Left to right Lt. Walker, Lt. Godky, Lt MacPhillamy, Lt. Wucken Fuss,
Lt. Frazier and Lt. Mooney. *Courtesy of Leo O. Frazier*

BRAVERY IS NOT THE ABSENCE OF FEAR,
IT'S THE ABILITY TO KEEP GOING IN THE
PRESENCE OF FEAR.

Unknown

KOREA

CHAPTER 8

SGT. CHARLES V.
"SKIP" ANDERSON

Sgt. Charles V. Anderson, 1st Bn, 7th
Regiment, 1st Marine Division

CHINESE TRAP AT CHOSIN RESERVOIR

HALF MILLION CHINESE PEASANT SOLDIERS WITH WOOD
BULLETS AND WOOD GRENADES AGAINST 15,000 MARINES
IN ONE OF THE BLOODIEST BATTLES IN THE ANNALS OF WAR

It was June of 1949, my junior year at high school had just ended, and a bunch of my friends and I were at the A&W Drive-in in Provo playing pinball machines, drinking coffee, smoking cigarettes, and contemplating what we were going to do in life. School had been out only a few days and none of us had a job.

Max hollered, "Let's go join the Navy!"

Well, we were in a convivial mood, our serious thoughts to that point had been pursuing fun, football, and girls, and we rather thought there was more of the same anywhere we went. We walked up to the post office on First North and First West to join the Navy. The recruiting chief was out to lunch, but a Marine sergeant was there who told us about traveling the world and getting an education and Marines were the greatest. I was seventeen years old then and it looked like an exciting life. Even though I was underage, my birth certificate underwent a stroke of the pen, and I was a Marine. My friend Bob Kensinger and I signed up for one year of active duty and six years in the Reserves. Lee Robertson and Max Hume waited past the noon hour until the recruiter returned and joined the Navy.

After boot camp I was fortunate to be stationed at the Marine barracks in Clearfield, Utah, at the Naval Supply Depot assigned to a hobby shop. In my estimation I had drawn guard duty more often than anyone else had, yet my active duty year in the Marines had been okay. Though I hadn't seen the other side of the world as the recruiter implied, I had the GI Bill that would pay for college tuition, and I was anxious for my discharge from active duty scheduled for 29 June 1950. Then four days before, on 25 June, my discharge paper was stamped "Indefinite Discharge" and unknown to me then I would be one of the Marines ensnared in a Chinese trap in North Korea.

During World War II, Japan had occupational forces in Korea that exploited the Koreans to the extent that when Roosevelt, Churchill, and Chiang Kai-shek met at a meeting in Cairo on 22 November 1943, they pledged to make Korea a free independent country after the war. In a treacherous move during the last week before the war's end, the Soviets maneuvered troops to the north side of the 38th parallel and seized the industrial and manufacturing center, and Korea's only petroleum and cement processing plants. On 25 June 1950 the Soviet-backed North Korean Communists attacked South Korea across the 38th parallel.

Within hours after this aggression, nineteen United Nations' countries gave their support to South Korea. Though the heaviest burden fell to the South Koreans, it nevertheless became America's war. Communist North Korea's army had Soviet-trained hard-core veterans supported by Soviet-made T-34 tanks, artillery and a small combat air force. The South Koreans had a national police force and a hurriedly trained conscripted army without adequate fire power or combat aircraft. Beaten back by North Korean superior fire power, within a week South Korea's Army of the Republic of Korea (ROK) was in full retreat to the southeastern tip of South Korea. With them were four under-strength U.S. Army peacekeeping divisions unprepared for combat and lacking heavy weapons against Soviet tanks.

Six weeks after General MacArthur was appointed commander of UN forces, the 1ˢᵗ Marine Division made an amphibious invasion on 15 September1950 at the west coast city of Inchon at the enemy's rear, recaptured Seoul, and the ROK army and UN forces in the south were able to push the Communists back north across the 38ᵗʰ parallel. Convinced that Korea was lost to any further Soviet gain, Stalin refused further arms or army to support the North Koreans. Meanwhile Chinese Communist Chairman Mao Tse-tung and members of the Chinese Central Committee felt threatened by America's intervention in Korea, augmented by the US support to Chiang Kai-shek's anti-communist government in Taiwan and by the presence of the U.S. Seventh Fleet in the Sea of Japan. Mao convinced the Chinese Central Committee it must defend China from further US aggression and secretly proceeded to make preparations for guerilla forces to enter North Korea.

After North Korea's Premier Kim Il-sung declared the 38ᵗʰ parallel the new north-south border thus creating opposing North and South governments, the UN queried the General Assembly whose members voted for unification of Korea and authorized MacArthur to "invade and conquer" North Korea. On receiving this mandate, MacArthur scheduled a bombing raid for 6 November to bomb the hydroelectric plant and bridges on the Yalu River to discourage Chinese intervention. The raid was approved by The Joint Chiefs of Staff contingent on aircraft flying five miles inside the Korean border and not destroying the power plant or transmission lines; consequently, aircraft failed to demolish the bridges.

Meanwhile, Mao had appointed Peng Te-huai as commander of the Chinese "Volunteer" People's Army, and on the night of 19 October General Peng began moving troops into Korea maintaining total radio silence. During October and November, half a million Chinese traveled south from Manchuria by night toward the Chosin Reservoir. Though MacArthur received intelligence reports from reconnaissance pilots of Chinese amassing in Manchuria, he displayed confidence that the Chinese would not cross the Yalu in sufficient strength to stop his troops from pushing the Communists north out of Korea across the Yalu River into Manchuria.

Since the first air attack was unsuccessful in destroying the Yalu bridges, MacArthur scheduled a second air attack for 15 November followed by an assault by surface troops. As if Mao himself had been sitting in the Oval Office and heard the scheduled attack for 15 November, he shrewdly ordered Peng to have his ten divisions hide in foxholes during daylight and essentially disappear off the landscape. MacArthur, aware of reports of their sudden disappearance, pondered whether the Chinese had actually been a threat after all. But without much hesitation chose to march troops into this presumed vacuum, intending to race to the Yalu River and get the war over by Christmas with the consequent admiration of his countrymen.

Mao had anticipated MacArthur's moves accurately. The UN ground forces continued to march north to encircle the Chosin Reservoir and Mao's trap was set.

I landed at Wonsan, Korea, 1 November 1950. Unknown to us, Mao's trap to ambush and annihilate us awaited our arrival a few miles north. I was in Charlie Company, 1st Battalion, 7th Marine Regiment, 1st Marine Division. We descended on rope netting over the sides of ships into Navy landing craft for an amphibious assault to the beach. The landing craft I was in hit the sea wall instead of the beach, so I climbed over the side of the boat confident I could wade ashore, jumped into the water and sank twelve or fifteen feet to the bottom. I thought I was going to drown with my sixty-five pound pack, twenty-pound Browning Automatic Rifle (B.A.R.) and ten pounds of ammo on my back. I drank seawater, struggled with my gear, got a gulp of air, and was finally able to swim to shore. I felt fortunate the enemy wasn't on the beach firing at us. That night we found a bombed-out warehouse for shelter, built a large fire, dried out our clothes and sleeping bags, and tried to dry out our boots. It was cold, a damp bone-chilling cold with the thermometer reading below freezing.

The next day we were immediately committed to combat and marched north. Our mission was to seize the coastal area and drive northerly toward Hamhung and Hungnam, two major commercial and industrial cities, attack north and capture the Chosin Reservoir power complex that supplied electricity to North Korea, Manchuria, and Siberia, then push on to the Yalu River. MacArthur had proffered we would be back home in time for Christmas dinner. We had heard rumors that Chinese were in the area, but not in any great number. However, later in the day Able and Baker companies encountered the enemy in brutal combat and they were outnumbered—61 Marines dead, 293 wounded; 622 enemy killed. Charlie Company, my company, had fewer casualties since the enemy in their haste had bypassed us to get to the valley below.

Daybreak of 3 November the regiment marched north with my company in the lead. We were attacked again that morning and suffered casualties. Able and Baker companies then took the lead and Charlie Company went to the rear, and the 1st Battalion continued to leapfrog north on the main supply route toward Koto-ri and Hagaru-ri with little contact with the enemy. Occasionally, we saw bodies of enemy soldiers apparently killed by our aircraft or frozen to death. There were foxholes dug by the enemy along the supply line route but they had become so commonplace no one reported them anymore since only a few enemy were confronted, and we believed the Communist North Koreans were retreating north in front of our forces.

The sub-zero north wind swept across the high plateau out of Siberia and Manchuria whipping the drifting snow in our faces. The daytime temperatures were below freezing and at night temperatures plummeted between 20 to 40 below zero with a chill factor of 70 below. Water froze in our canteens and C-rations froze solid in the cans; breath froze on our eyebrows and beards. I wore two pair long underwear, two pair wool pants, a wool shirt, fleece-lined jacket, parka, and wool hat with earflaps under my helmet, two pair wool sox and snowpacs. I weighed about a hundred forty pounds, and carried close to a hundred pounds of gear that I seldom removed or laid down. It took a bit of adjustment to become a bulky two hundred and forty pounds. Yet even with all that bulk it was not adequate to keep out the penetrating cold. We learned never to take off our knitted gloves worn under our canvas mittens as our naked hands would freeze instantly to our metal weapons and buckles. Many of the guys had diarrhea and those times were desperate occurrences with all the clothing layers coupled with fear of sniper fire. Few dared to bare precious parts for fear of frostbite, and urination was often hit or miss down an inside pant leg.

The mountainous country carved by great rivers and shaped like Florida's peninsula, juts out between the Yellow Sea on the west and Sea of Japan on the east. Koreans, living in small shacks, used ox carts for transport. On the only north-south road, which was our main supply route, two vehicles couldn't pass side by side. Grinding up mountainsides over slick, frozen ice ruts, our jeeps, trucks, bulldozers, and Howitzers inched toward the Chosin Reservoir at the 4,000-foot Taebek Plateau. As the crow flies, it was fifty miles farther to the Yalu River at the northern border of Korea. Our 3500-man regiment, led the way. My company was always out on point, our forty-man platoon on point of the point, and I felt I led in front of everyone. We climbed through unbroken snow, bivouacked on lonely ridges, and tried to stay warm at night when the temperature slid to 40 below Fahrenheit. After twenty-three days, we reached Hagaru-ri village where the division's new command headquarters was set up, and continued up the west side of the reservoir fourteen miles farther to the village of Yudam-ni. The cold made my eyes water and nose run, and mucus froze and caked in stubble of my beard. With only snow to slake our thirst and very little food not frozen, it was difficult just to survive.

As a private in a rifle squad of thirteen men in Charlie Company, I carried a B.A.R., a heavy submachine gun, upside-down at my waist with the sling around my neck. My knitted gloved trigger finger protruded out of my canvas mitten to the trigger. Seldom aiming, I could shoot instantly by spraying bullets over a target. It was slow to fire in sub-zero cold. We all had problems with guns freezing up, and often urinated on the frozen mechanisms to thaw them. When cleaning our machine guns and B.A.R.s with hair tonic that contained alcohol, we reduced malfunctions.

On 24 November Charlie Company was on patrol high in the mountains west of the main supply road into Yudam-ni. In the afternoon we became increasingly aware of fighting to the north of us and fired a few mortar rounds at enemy soldiers near the main road below and to the north of us, but I don't think we hurt anybody. MacArthur was certain Chinese wouldn't enter the war, especially a winter campaign, so we concluded the few visible enemy soldiers were North Koreans in retreat.

We spooked a deer out of the woods and some of the guys had fun taking potshots at it. It was long after dark when we came off patrol that night to a belated Thanksgiving dinner. By MacArthur's order, all fighting forces would have Thanksgiving dinner wherever they were. Marines had been eating in shifts, and by the time I got in the chow line that night the turkey was gone and only cold potatoes and cold coagulated gravy remained. What I didn't know then, was that the cold chow would be the most I would eat for the next ten days. Because the area was littered with turkey carcasses—enough turkey to feed several hundred men, this location was afterwards known as Turkey Hill.

The following day our entire company went on patrol on the west side of the main supply road a few miles south of Yudam-ni. The patrol barely got started when sniper fire pinned me to the ground. Not seeing him, I lay behind a rock wondering whether he was determined to kill me—maybe if I didn't shoot then he wouldn't shoot. While this improbability played in my brain, I rolled my sleeping bag out into the open. Immediately two shots rang out and hit close by the sleeping bag. The point hammered home, I never hesitated an instant to pull the trigger after that and felt stupid at my youthfulness. Since I couldn't survive without a sleeping bag, I was likewise glad it hadn't been perforated.

Then fighting decreased and we felt like the war might be over. When we came off patrol on the 26th from the foothills near Yudam-ni, my squad was ordered to stand guard at the Hagaru-ri command post while the remainder of Charlie Company went south three miles to Turkey Hill to guard the main supply route between Hagaru-ri and Yudam-ni.

On 27 November at midnight the Chinese planned to simultaneously attack the east, west, and south sides of the reservoir to "chop the snake in pieces." By this time, the 5ᵗʰ and 7ᵗʰ Marine regiments had arrived on the west side of the reservoir at Yudam-ni, and Don Faith's Task Force from the 31ˢᵗ and 32ⁿᵈ battalions/ 7ᵗʰ Army Infantry Division was half way up the east side of the reservoir. Because of poor communication, Commanding General Oliver P. Walker was unaware the Eighth Army that had plunged toward the Yalu farther to the west had already been attacked by Peng's army and was in full retreat. The Chinese were now poised to spring the trap that Mao had tactically prepared.

THE TWENTY-FOUR HOURS OF NOVEMBER 27-28

Then at two in the morning on the 27ᵗʰ my squad of thirteen men was ordered to rejoin the rest of Charlie Company. We loaded into a jeep pulling a trailer and headed three miles down the road to Turkey Hill. I was hunkered down in the trailer trying to stay warm as we neared Turkey Hill. All of a sudden, I heard several pops and looked up to see the jeep windshield disappear. We hadn't anticipated enemy action and had brazenly drove with headlights on. Appearing in our headlights were forty to fifty Chinese in white parkas setting up a command post. We leaped free of the vehicle. I rolled out of the trailer onto the edge of the road and lay behind a pile of rocks unable to see any of my squad in the dark, when I heard, "Fall back!" I jumped up, ran around a curve in the road, took cover, but decided to get off the road. I climbed up the cut bank where I could look down. Reaching the top, I stood up and looked directly into the barrel of a machine gun five feet away and a startled gunner. I heard rat-tat-tat and bullets flew between my legs. I darted and dove off the twelve-foot bank headfirst into the ditch and the fall knocked the wind out of me. Unconscious for a few minutes until I got my breath, panic rose within me as I got entangled in communication wires that lay in the ditch. The more I scrambled, the more I slid and hooked wires onto my gear that bound me down. Fear, magnified by my awkward helplessness, grew to frenzied terror and I felt I would go insane.

Savagely breaking away, I caught up with the rest of the squad and made it back to an aid station tent near Yudam-ni. Corpsmen treating the seriously wounded were too busy to treat the wound in my leg. I sat in the warming tent watching corpsmen juggle vials of morphine in their mouths to prevent it from freezing, and I got warm for the first time in several days. As the heat warmed my bones and calm returned to my soul, I began listening to the wounded men relate their stories, learning that half-hour after we were chased off the road, Chinese had attacked Charlie Company at Turkey Hill and they were now under siege.

By the morning of 28 November headquarters at Hamhung had received reports of the desperate fighting on both sides of the reservoir and at Hagaru-ri. However, General Almond ignored the fervor of the dispatches, concluding that it was the same old story—just a simple matter of loss of nerve by the Marines and GIs, and quipped, "Don't let a bunch of Chinese laundrymen stop you."

Cold had stanched the flow of blood on my leg, but the icy wind whipped through bullet holes in my pants, so during the morning I approached the supply dump for another pair. Flames licked at stacks of new wool pants, and I stammered in amazement, "Marines withdrawing?"

I scavenged a five-gallon can of sickbay alcohol and three new canteens in the dump and filled them with alcohol. Most of the time we ate snow, but it caused our lips to blister and bleed. Besides drinking alcohol, I ate Tootsie Rolls. During a roadblock and while we had a truck stopped, one of the guys went around to the back of the stopped truck and threw a large wooden box out that was full of Tootsie Rolls. Our squad ate Tootsie Rolls most of the time instead of frozen C-rations.

Late afternoon of the following day, we joined up with Able and Baker companies to relieve Charlie Company. Approaching Turkey Hill, the enemy had been firing down on the company from a high ridge for twenty-four hours. During the nights Charlie Company fought on without air support, but during the day Australians in F-51 Mustangs and Marines in Corsairs flew twenty feet off the ground strafing and spewing napalm over the enemy. All mortar men and non-combat support staff had been turned into riflemen by the time we arrived, and all had become casualties. Men in Charlie Company suffered losses to the extent that it ceased to function as a full strength rifle company after that.

29-30 NOVEMBER

On the evening of the 29th, we assembled with Commander of the 7th Marine Regiment Lieutenant Colonel Ray Davis who warned us what was ahead.

"If you want to live to see the light of day, you better dig in and fight like bastards because there are more than a hundred thousand Chinese on the other side of that hill west of us with orders to annihilate the 1st Marine Division," he said.

I figured we were out-numbered ten to one. Snow fell all day and an icy wind blew down our necks as we made defensive preparations. Because our shovels couldn't chip the frozen ground, we tore down a portion of a nearby building and stacked it up for protection.

We fought off the cold and nervously waited. Just before midnight we heard sounds of a thousand crunching feet on snow and the smell of garlic. Chinese charged screaming into our lines throwing wood grenades, blowing bugles and police whistles, and clanging cymbals. Some fired Nambu Japanese-made machine guns with wooden bullets—bullets that splintered into a thousand slivers when they hit flesh and bone. Others carried Thompson submachine guns that had been furnished to the Taiwan Nationalist Chinese by the United States. Some fired Soviet 7.62mm burp guns that fired 900 rounds per minute. Behind our abutment I mowed down wave after human wave of Chinese with my B.A.R. In hordes they came through our lines. Enemy dead fell on us, and piled in front of us so high they obscured our line of fire, and we had to push them away. The Chinese wore white cotton-quilted parkas, cotton gloves, silk stockings and what resembled tennis shoes on their feet and a sock-like necklace filled with dried corn, beans, garlic and a supply of wood grenades and wood bullets.

Some Marines were caught still in their sleeping bags, some with their boots off firing weapons barefoot in the snow. Colonel Davis' estimate of a hundred thousand Chinese was way short, I thought.

The barrel of my B.A.R. got extremely hot from continuous firing and burned my hands when in hand to hand fighting I wrested the barrel from attackers trying to seize my gun. The Chinese attacked through that hellish night until the first gray of dawn.

The Chinese blocked the main supply route from Koto-ri to Hagaru-ri cutting off supplies and replacements. At 1:55 P.M. 28 November reinforcements left Koto-ri to relieve Marines who were under fire and short on ammo at Hagaru-ri, a distance of only eleven miles. Reinforcements included 29 tanks and a composite regiment of 922 men from the Royal Marine 41 Commandos, 1st Marines, 31st Army Regiment, Division Headquarters and 1st Marine Service Battalion. Proceeding toward Hagaru-ri, they were attacked and surrounded on the road and fought until rifle ammo was low and bullets were handed out only two and three at a time. When vehicles were destroyed, when most of their officers were killed, their ammo spent, and many taken prisoner, they surrendered, though some miraculously escaped imprisonment. Survivors called it Hell Fire Valley. Chinese had chopped the column into five sections and overpowered the allied forces. Of the 922 men only 150 survivors arrived in Hagaru-ri from the Royal Marine 41 Commandos who had led the column and faired better than the rest. General Oliver P. Smith had ordered Commando CO Lieutenant Colonel Drysdale to get through to Hagaru-ri at all costs and the cost had been 750 dead, wounded, or at the mercy of Chinese.

That same night, during the midnight hours, survivors of the 31st and 32nd Infantry units of Don Faith's Task Force from the east side of the reservoir came staggering across the frozen ice making their way to the west side of the reservoir toward the safety of the Marine perimeter. Task Force Faith hadn't fared well. Survivors, numb from cold and wounds, came dragging across the ice on frozen feet, their bodies riddled with multiple shrapnel and bullet wounds. Some with broken legs crawled on frozen hands and knees without rifles dragging leg stumps that stained the snow crimson. It was 24 below zero that night.

Marine Colonel Olin Beall, his driver, Pfc. Ralph Milton, corpsmen Biebinger and Contreras, Corporal Howard, Lieutenant Hunt, and

Red Cross Field Director Lefevre remained out on the ice in jeeps and ambulances for the ensuing seventy-two hours to bodily pick up survivors. Snipers stalked the wounded. Colonel Beall, always identified by his two pearl-handled revolvers on his hips, crawled over the ice toward the wounded men, and dragged them back to waiting vehicles, rushed them into an aid station, and returned again to the ice to rescue more. During this life-saving effort Colonel Beall and his men rescued 323 Americans and ROKs from the annihilated Faith Task Force unit. By 5 December, only 353 of Faith's 3,000 men had been accounted for. The rest of his men were killed, captured, or left where they lay wounded on the sides of the road or in stalled trucks to die of wounds or freeze to death. Colonel Faith, who had valiantly led the retreat, lay dead somewhere on the east side of the reservoir with his men.

Joint Chiefs of Staff in Washington and at MacArthur's headquarters in Tokyo wrote off the 1ˢᵗ Marine Division, saying it was impossible for the Marines to break out of the Chinese trap.

BREAKOUT – 1 DECEMBER

A dozer scooped out a common grave for our eighty-five dead and buried them during the night. Able, Baker and Charlie companies assembled into one fighting unit and heard the breakout plan from Colonel Davis. We would shoot our way out and march, without vehicles, across two high mountain peaks, penetrate enemy lines and attack Toktong Pass to reinforce Fox Company that had been under siege for five days. Absolute silence was imperative for success, and we checked our gear for rattles by jumping up and down. The D-23 tank to lead the column mysteriously arrived without fuel or crew, and we scrambled to find fuel and siphoned a TD-18 dozer. There was not a surviving tank man to drive it and a team was flown in on one of the few helicopters in Korea to operate it.

The tank and walking wounded led the column followed by several thousand men and hundreds of vehicles of varying size and function. No one was considered wounded if able to fire a weapon. Wounded and dead filled trucks to overflowing, layered three and four deep. With no more space in trucks, we strapped them to hoods and fenders of trucks and jeeps. Colonels walked, their jeeps loaded with casualties. Howitzers followed in the rear, so that if stalled wouldn't halt the column.

Able-Baker-Charlie fighting unit of five hundred men then left the truck column on the road, headed east through deep trackless snow, and climbed the ridges to cross the mountains. We carried two 81mm heavy mortars and six .30 caliber machine guns with double crews. Every man carried one 81mm round, plus our own weapon, an extra bandoleer of ammo, and sleeping bag. Each man on the trail ahead of me packed snow in slippery lumpy humps. Stumbling, and losing balance, I went down silently cursing. Others slipped and fell uttering groans, spilling mortar shells in the snow, yet no audible words were uttered. Never having tents, we lay on the snow with feet in each other's armpits to protect them from freezing in minus 24 zero temperature. Admirably, Colonel Davis walked the ranks of his men making certain they didn't freeze in their own sweat from the day's arduous climb. He talked, cuffed his men, and made them repeat commands, always checking against the cold malaise that stiffens and stupefies. Two Marines went insane that night. We restrained them in makeshift straitjackets and gagged their hysterical cries— both died later.

At two in the morning, we heard Chinese talking and caught a whiff of garlic on the wind. They attacked from every direction blowing bugles and police whistles, fighting from behind every rock and tree. A few Chinese without rifles even fought us with rocks and tree limbs. Chinese stole green parkas and leather boots off American dead and wounded and wore them. It was difficult to identify the enemy. Three Marines were killed and nine wounded that night, and we placed them on litters and carried them down the mountain to the road below to be picked up by the retreating column. Climbing back up the mountain in a blizzard of swirling snow, each raspy breath was painful to our lungs in the polar air. Because compasses were useless among the mass of metal we bore, white phosphorous markers fired by our road-bound artillery guided us, otherwise nothing was visible in the darkness and swirling storm. By then we had been on the move for nearly twenty-six hours. Between Fox Company and us lay five miles of unknown country.

At Toktong Pass the initial Chinese attack on Fox Company had come at 2:30 A. M. 27 November and lasted with little relief through the night and the following five days. Two Chinese regiments had surrounded the 200-man company. Unable to withdraw, the Leathernecks fought on defending the main supply route they held that cut through the canyon's narrow pass called Toktong, and fought attackers hand-to-hand when the enemy charged with fixed bayonets. Support from a four-plane division of Royal Australian Air Force F-51 fighter-bombers and a pair of Marine Corsairs relieved their desperate fight during days, but nights they fought on without air support. Low on ammunition and food, water from a bubbling spring was obtained down the mountain at the risk of life.

We reached the mountaintop by daybreak. Men of Charlie Company led the attack south and secured the first ridge, and held that position until the other companies moved forward. Drawing enemy fire from several ridges, progress was slow. We were attacked continuously that morning and part of the afternoon from four different ridges. We chased a large number off one ridge and I thought they had retreated to the next hill. They left a Thompson machine gun and some other pieces of equipment when they retreated, and I sat down in a foxhole thinking they were gone, and I was safe for a few minutes' rest. Suddenly, the Chinese charged back up the hill again blowing horns and whistles, which was their communication system, and the sky was peppered with grenades. One landed in the hole I was in. Instantly jumping out, I lay to the side of the foxhole when another grenade landed at my side and exploded. My neck and arm burned and shrapnel pierced my left knee. The grenade in the hole didn't explode. Again chasing Chinese down off the mountain, I shot at them as they crossed a small gully and ran up the other side. Picking up a Thompson submachine gun at the top of the hill, I ran down the mountain shooting at them emptying the gun before throwing it away. A Chinese soldier raised up from behind a bush in front of me, and I shot him twice in the stomach with .45-caliber bullets.

He rolled over on his back his stomach ripped open. Garlic smell overpowered me, and I doubled over retching from the odor, overcome by horror.

When crossing the last mountain, survivors of Fox Company waved their arms and shouted as we came into view. Colonel Davis drew the rear company in closer as we marched on. Suddenly, Davis' radioman shouted to him.

"Colonel! Colonel! Fox Company on the radio!" Davis took the radio.

"This's Cap'n Barber, Fox Company" he heard on the other end, " Colonel Davis, if you need help, we can send a patrol out to you."

Davis, understanding the desperateness of the survivors at Fox Hill and moved by the valiant offer, declined. Then Captain Barber, with two fighters on station above him, called them down in explosive fury on our exposed rear.

After fierce fighting and machine gun fire, we cleared the enemy off the ridge. Fields surrounding Fox Company were covered with hundreds of dead and parts of dead, and men burned from napalm. Fox Company Marines had made barricades of frozen enemy bodies and from behind them the bloodstained wounded had set up their gun emplacements and fought the enemy that never quit attacking. Eighty survivors crawled out on frozen limbs from behind walls of enemy dead. We exchanged profane greetings in tones and ways that only Marines cared to show love and admiration toward each other. There were 118 casualties—26 dead, 89 wounded, and 3 missing.

For security, the men of Fox Company had tied empty C-ration cans together with parachute cord and strung them around their perimeter at night. Bazooka shells still inside their cardboard tube containers were then struck in the snow at a 45-degree angle pointing away from the perimeter circle. Detonation wires were run from each tube to a central battery inside the perimeter to the guy on watch. When the enemy tripped the cord, clanking cans alerted the watch, and by touching a wire onto the battery coming from the direction of a rattling can, a rocket would shoot off in that direction. Next morning I saw the young Chinese soldier that had tripped an alarm during the night. A rocket shell had hit him under his chin. A photograph was lying next to him—a photograph of a young man in uniform at a train station with a pretty girl, probably his sweetheart, presenting him with a long-stemmed rose as he was leaving on the train. The snow was stained red where he had convulsively flailed. He had ripped his clothes off his chest, and ripped the flesh off his ribs evidently trying to breathe. His face and lower jaw were gone, but his eyes were still hanging there. I had become fairly numb to the monstrousness of seeing and smelling the wounded and dead, but I felt real remorse over the death of this enemy soldier and my youthful heart wept.

We carried the wounded down off the hill on stretchers to the road below. I was angry at having to dodge sniper bullets while carrying wounded. With one hand still on the stretcher I put the B.A.R. to my shoulder and shot off about 20 rounds toward the direction of the snipers. The recoil from the rifle butt hit my shoulder and threw me on my back, the rounds flew skyward, the stretcher upended, and the wounded Marine lay agonizing out on the snow.

A plane flew over and dropped a parachute with supplies—with food, I hoped, and plodded toward it through six inches of new snow, bent over from the tiring weight of the B.A.R. sagging in my right arm, my parka hood partly obscuring my vision. I had eaten mostly Tootsie Rolls since Thanksgiving ten days ago, and I was exhausted and hungry. We were all hungry. By the time I reached the drop net and canister everything was gone with the exception of one tin and one box, and I reached down and picked them up: a tin of Spark Plug tobacco and a box of stationery. I opened up the can of chewing tobacco, and because of my hunger, chewed and swallowed it.

Late afternoon while stopping in a grove of aspen trees for the night, I checked my leg wounds, which were numb, though I had been able to keep up with my squad, I was glad to rest. Leaning my rifle up against the trunk of a tree, I began unbuckling the suspenders that held my ammunition belt. All at once there was machine gun fire and four bullets hit across my stomach. I hit the ground hard. Regaining consciousness, I was gasping for breath and heard someone yelling for a corpsman, and guessed this was it for me. When sitting up, I discovered that all four bullets had hit the two rifle magazines attached to my ammo belt and pieces of metal, bullets, and springs stuck out from the full magazines. Not one bullet had penetrated my skin—only my breath was knocked out of me. Yet I broke out in cold sweat knowing that if the slugs had hit two seconds later I likely would have been disemboweled. We all felt it was just a matter of time before we would be killed—and sometimes morosely wished a quick end to our anguish.

While remaining on high ridges engaging the enemy, the main Marine column was able to retreat on the road with a battalion on each flank. The long column of walking-wounded formed the lead rifle company with non-combat staff cooks, bakers, and truck drivers turned into riflemen holding off attackers from the rear. The column came into Hagaru-ri with windshields shot out and wounded men stacked like cordwood in trucks. Those lashed across truck hoods and fenders hadn't survived the jostling of rutted, icy roads and raw cold. On the last truck in the rear of the column a Marine had defiantly scratched, "Only 14 more shooting days until Xmas."

Meanwhile we continued south across the mountains until in sight of Hagaru-ri, then dropping down to the main supply road, came across the D-23 tank that had led the column out of Yudam-ni. It had been knocked off its track by a single shot from a .50 caliber rifle that lay discarded nearby. We destroyed the tank, setting it on fire, and heard bursts of ammunition explosions behind us as we plodded on.

A short distance before they got to Hagaru-ri, tiredness was replaced with pride and the Leathernecks fell into ranks, shouldered their weapons, and stepping smartly, men of the 7th Marine Regiment marched into Hagaru-ri.

We arrived at the north edge of Hagaru-ri sometime in the early hours of 4 December met by survivors of the 1st Regiment of British Royal Marines who had helped secure the town. The 1st Engineer Battalion had hurriedly constructed an airstrip to evacuate the first of 4,081 of the more seriously wounded, the pilots bravely taking off and landing through enemy fire.

After fighting continually for ten days and nights, I rested for a couple days and stocked up on needed equipment, getting rid of my B.A.R. that had grown so heavy and obtained a much lighter .30

caliber carbine with two 30-round magazines which I taped together.

On the evening of 6 December while in a warming tent, I decided to pull off my boots since I hadn't taken them off for about three weeks, not wanting to be caught in an attack fighting in snow with bare feet. I wanted to wash them and put on clean dry socks, but after warming my feet for awhile they began to swell and then blister and then turn black. They had frozen and soon not even a larger pair of boots could be pulled over them. I felt it had been a mistake to take them off, by then my hands were also swollen. Told I wouldn't be able to walk to Hamhung, I was air lifted with the intent to rejoin my regiment there. But by then my frozen feet began to thaw and blisters the size of tennis balls covered them. I regretted having to leave my unit, but the next morning I was evacuated to a hospital in Japan.

Charlie Company had so many casualties it ceased to exist and from my original rifle squad of thirteen men only two others and myself remained.

The ten Chinese divisions that had orders to annihilate the Marines at Yudam-ni attacked them from Hagaru-ri to Koto-ri and all the way to the sea. Following within the shadow of the Marines for protection were nearly a hundred thousand North Korean women, children, and old men carrying their wounded and belongings, some on foot, some pushing native sleds, some in bullock carts traveling across the mountainous seventy-eight miles to the sea. Marines shared their limited food and medicine with them, but they suffered great hardship and many died on the way. Corpsmen assisted two Korean women in giving birth on the road. When the Koreans arrived at the Port of Hamhung they boarded ships which the U.S. Navy provided and brought many to freedom.

Below Koto-ri, where the Chinese had dynamited a bridge which crossed over a 1500-foot gorge, engineers went to work and called in C-119s that dropped eight, 2-ton Treadway bridge sections secured by the biggest parachutes they could find. When the bridge was still seven feet short, the engineers devised a quick, though grisly, solution. Using dozers they scraped up the dead Chinese that had frozen hard as rocks, and stacked them in the void and the column crossed over them and proceeded south to Hungnam seaport where the Navy's Seventh Fleet was waiting to evacuate them. While marching south the Marines sang words to the Australian marching song, "Bless Em All" with their own prophetic words punched in:

Bless 'em all, Bless 'em all,
The Commies, the UN and all.
Bless General MacArthur and bless Harry, too
Bless the whole brass-hatted Tokyo crew.
For we're saying goodbye to it all,
We're Harry's "police force" on call.
So put your pack back on,
The next stop is Saigon
So cheer up me lads
Bless em all!

During the two-week battle on the west side of the reservoir the 15,000 men of the U.S Marines, British, and South Koreans suffered 12,000 casualties—3,000 killed, 6,000 wounded, an undetermined number missing in action and captured, and 3,000 with severely frozen hands and feet. Many with frozen limbs required amputation of hands or feet—some were quad amputees. The 3,000 men of Task Force Faith of the 31st and 32nd battalions/Seventh Army Division fared worse with more than 2,600 dead and only 385 survivors.

Chinese General Sung ordered his wounded soldiers to walk home alone over the mountains north to Manchuria and many died of wounds or froze to death en route. They had little medical aid available, their cotton quilted coats froze stiff, and cotton gloved hands froze to their weapons and fingers had to be broken to free them.

Colonel Davis later described the battle.

"At the Chosin Reservoir, where we were outnumbered ten to one, the Chinese generals prematurely boasted of the destruction of the 1st Marine Division. Yet, the opposite happened there. Although the Marines were forced to withdraw, we destroyed several Chinese divisions as we fought our way to the sea and escape. Our withdrawal was a successful one, but we paid a terrible price: casualties reduced the division to nearly half of its strength. The three rifle companies of 1st Battalion, 7th Marine Regiment, which I was privileged to command, endured losses of even greater proportion. 'B' Company... came off the Chosin Reservoir, and out of North Korea, with only twenty-seven men, the survivors of more than three hundred of its original Marines and their replacements." (qtd. in *Colder Than Hell*, Joseph Owen at pp. xii-xiii)

The Korean War ended three years later (1953) nearly the same place where it began. There were 157,530 American casualties— 33,629 killed in action and related causes, and 5,000 missing. Other UN forces incurred 16,532 casualties of them 3,094 died. South Korean military dead numbered 415,004. Civilian Korean deaths numbered 2 million. An estimate of Communist casualties was two million. (Chinese refused to release official casualty numbers.) Mao's favored commander of the Chinese Volunteer Army Peng Te-huai was ousted as defense minister in 1959 and ten years later was tortured to death.

The 1st Marine Division received the Presidential Unit Citation for this battle. There were 70 Navy Cross Citations and 17 Congressional Medal of Honor recipients, which was a number heretofore unheard of. Colonel Don Faith received the Medal of Honor posthumously for aggressively leading the retreat of the Infantry down the east side of the reservoir when approximately fifty percent of his task force were ROKs that had not been combat trained or disciplined. Not to be forgotten is the humanitarian assistance given by the Marines under fire to 91,000 refugees in aiding their escape to the sea that were then transported to safety by the U.S. Navy. Many Koreans and their descendents are able to live in freedom today because of this rescue effort. Colonel Beall was recipient of the Distinguished Service Cross—no other individual rescue effort equaled his in the Korean War. Colonel Ray Davis[1] received the Medal of Honor for valor in leading the attack south through the mountains. All the bodies of Marine dead were retrieved after the armistice in 1953. On the east side of the reservoir many hundreds of men were left where they lay.

Some historians reflect that the fighting at Chosin has no parallel in the annals of war.

*

"We were, in short, in a state of shameful unreadiness."
General Matthew Ridgeway

*

Editor's note:

Sergeant Anderson was airlifted out of Hagaru-ri and spent twelve months recovering from frozen hands, feet, and shrapnel wounds at hospitals in Tokyo and Honolulu, where the skin on his feet that turned black was shaved off as it developed.

Discharged from active duty on 6 April 1952 and from the Reserves in 1956, he enrolled at the University of Utah where he was advised he was unique to the school—being the first Korean veteran to attend, graduating in 1958 with a degree in civil engineering. He married Florence Howard from Sigurd, Utah, and they have four children, Charles Junior, Paula, Laura, Maria, and four grandchildren.

Sergeant Anderson worked for the Utah Highway Department for the next twenty-nine years—eleven of those years as Chief Engineer and Assistant Director of Transportation. He is presently retired and spends pleasure hours portrait painting. For many years since his service in Korea he was unable to endure the smell of garlic.

I asked Sergeant Anderson how he felt about fighting in Korea.

"I was at the Yokosuka Hospital when a doctor at the side of my bed said, 'I'm sorry, but we are going to have to amputate your feet.' There were probably hundreds of survivors of the reservoir that had their hands and feet amputated. Fortunately for me, he was talking to the Marine in the upper bunk.

"The war was a United Nations action. I don't recall seeing the American flag during the time I was in Korea. When I was evacuated out of Hamhung and arrived at the US air base near Fukuoka, Japan, I looked out the hospital window and saw the American flag flying. I became emotional at the sight of our flag. I was so relieved that I felt like kneeling down and kissing the ground in appreciation for all that it signified. This was the first time in many weeks that I felt safe.

"I wouldn't hesitate to fight for our country and do whatever was necessary in order to maintain stability in this country. I wouldn't want to experience the Chosin Reservoir battle again. For many years afterward, my youth masked my ravaged feelings of this experience. Yet even now, fifty years later, this epic battle has become the warp and woof of my fiber—the depths from which sensitivities resonate; the depths from which gratitude swells."

During a recent Orem City contest to design a felicitous monument to honor our war dead, Sergeant Anderson's design was chosen from thirteen entries. Presented with a $1,000 prize for the winning entry, he chose to contribute the sum toward construction of the estimated $50,000 monument. It will be erected at the Orem City Center, Orem, Utah.

*****

---

[1] Colonel Ray Davis later became a 4-star general and retired as Assistant Commandant of the Marine Corps.

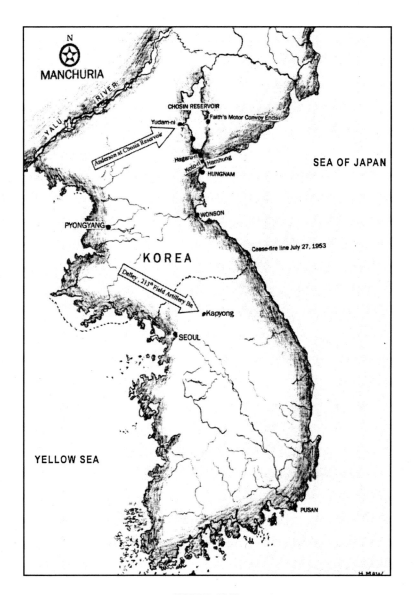

KOREA 1953

Chapter 9

Brig. General Frank J. Dalley
Commanding General XI Corps Artillery
Formerly Lt. Col. 213th Field Artillery Bn
Utah National Guard

Col. Max S. Dalley
Commander of 213th Field Artillery Bn
Name changed to 2nd Bn, 222nd Artillery
Utah National Guard

GENERAL FRANK J. DALLEY

9 Band-Aids and 9 Purple Hearts

"Major Max Dalley, we will rise each morning at 0300!" cranked out Lieutenant Colonel Frank Dalley.

Frank was my brother, two years older and a lieutenant colonel then. I had disagreed with him then and inquired, "Have you thought this over?" That's when he addressed me by my rank of major.

Frank continued, "You will stand-to and the rest of the men will stand-to."

A 3 A.M. stand-to meant to get out of the sack, put on your uniform and boots and assemble, often with nothing further to do until the sun came up. I obeyed the order. There was no doubt in anyone's mind Frank was the commanding officer, we all respected him. But sometimes in deference I would just slip on my boots and cover up with a long raincoat—that is until we got into the action.

I was Frank's operations officer and Major Pat Fenton of Cedar City, Utah, was his executive officer. The 213th Field Artillery Battalion of the Utah National Guard was made up of brothers, cousins, uncles, and friends all raised in Southern Utah just as Frank, Pat Fenton and I had been. We knew our "boys" well. We called them our boys because Frank, Pat, and I were in our middle or late thirties, as well as a few of the other officers, and were veterans of World War II. Major Pat Fenton was on Utah Beach during the invasion of Normandy and then in Belgium's Battle of the Bulge in the Ardennes. I was on Omaha Beach ten days after the invasion with the 83rd Infantry Division, and we advanced within a rifle shot of Berlin. Frank was a lieutenant colonel in the 640th Tank Destroyer Battalion in the Pacific. Our combat experiences had made us mature men among the youth under our command, most of them were just out of high school. Yet we all came from the same hardy southern Utah pioneer stock and our family histories intertwined like a patch of periwinkle. The men in Headquarters Battery were from Cedar City. "A" Battery was from Richfield, "B" Battery lived in St. George, "C" Battery from Fillmore, Service Battery from Beaver. Our engineers came from Lehi. Our military intelligence men, because of their experience in foreign countries and expertise with foreign languages, were chiefly returned missionaries of the Church of Jesus Christ of Latter-day Saints. The battalion acquired the name 213th Armored Field Artillery Battalion along its historic past, as well as other designations, yet it always carried the nickname Mormon Battalion.

The 213th Battalion had its beginnings elsewhere long before Utah was admitted to the Union. A Nauvoo, Illinois, militia called the Nauvoo Legion received its charter in December 1840 by the Illinois Legislature of which Abraham Lincoln was a member. In 1847 some of those same militiamen volunteered to serve in the conflict with Mexico. They formed a five hundred-man battalion, calling themselves the Mormon Battalion. They were on the plains of Kansas at the time en route with their families in oxen-pulled wagons, part of the Mormons' trek west to the territory of the western desert, when they responded to the U. S. Army's request. From Fort Leavenworth, Kansas, to San Diego, California, the men of the Mormon Battalion marched two thousand miles on foot—the longest forced march in history. The battalion fought in the Indian Wars. Again activated during the Civil War, it defended the telegraph lines between Salt Lake City and North Platte, Nebraska. In 1897 the battalion fought in the Spanish-American war. In 1918 it was activated and shipped to France during World War 1. In World War II, men of the battalion trained with wooden guns, as there were not enough rifles, then were transported directly to the Normandy invasion in France, entered the Battle of the Bulge in the Ardennes mountains of Belgium, and marched into Germany.

CITIZEN SOLDIERS

Max Dalley recalls: I never wanted to experience war again when I returned home from Europe in January 1945. I easily fell into the stride of teaching school and attending summer classes at the University of Southern California. I received a Master's in Education Administration in 1950 and moved back to Parowan, Utah, to teach school. I had married Roma Bentley in 1942, and we had two children, Robert and Mahlon by then. Meanwhile Frank was Commander of the 213th Field Artillery Battalion headquartered in Cedar City. Believing I would never have to go to war again, Frank persuaded me to join the Utah National Guard and become his operations and fire direction officer. As such I became a citizen-soldier putting aside my teaching responsibilities at times to dedicate a number of weekends each month for training and summer camps. This was true then and continues to be true of all National Guardsmen.

It was five years later that we were en route to Korea on the *U.S.S. General M C Meigs* that we laughed as we read President Harry

Truman's obvious untruth quoted in the *Stars & Stripes*. It read, "Truman says no National Guardsmen will go to Korea." The Guard was activated on 19 August 1950, one of the country's first.[1] We had by then received combat training, and were scheduled to arrive in Korea, via Japan, on 16 February 1951.

Frank shouldered the responsibility of the welfare of the six hundred men under his command like a father caring for his sons. This is Frank's story to tell, and I write only because he has passed on, yet perhaps it is even more fitting that men under his command tell this story.

After three weeks shaking down equipment and training, we were attached to the IX Army Corps and marched toward Kapyong with a mission to provide artillery support to the Army of the Republic of Korea's 6th Division, we referred to them as ROK/6th. The job of artillery batteries was to support with artillery the infantry's advance on the enemy. Our 105mm Howitzers could shell the enemy's position at a distance up to seven miles to soften up the enemy before the infantry advanced. Meanwhile the infantry would keep in close proximity ahead of us to protect our position. We had six 105mm Howitzers in each of A, B, and C batteries. That was a lot of firepower when they shot simultaneously, especially since one man could load a 37-pound shell every ten seconds. Each Howitzer had a gun registry of where and how often it had been fired. One of ours had been fired last at Anzio, Italy in 1943. We had a lot of leftover equipment.

But we had the best of some things. We had the best food in Korea. Pat Fenton went to all the batteries and ferreted out the best cooks, each battery having its own cook and mess. The food the Army distributed was good provided the cooks were gifted. Ours were, and we often had steaks, fresh eggs any time, and even warm, fresh Spudnuts, the donut of preference. Drinking water was trucked in and plentiful, and I don't recall ever having to carry a canteen. We were mighty grateful for the water trucks particularly during summer when the temperature reached 100 degrees and the air was heavy with humidity.

S-U-G-A-R!

Unlike other military units, likely because Frank and I were religious men, we adopted the code name of SUGAR, an acronym, though I can't exactly remember what each letter stood for, it meant haul-your-back-side-south in a hurry.

On the evening of 26 April we got into a hornet's nest. We were north of Kapyong to enforce firepower for the ROK/6th. That night our patrols returned with reports that thousands of Chinese were in the area. I went to see Frank. We were encamped at a place where we could get trapped because of the mountains surrounding us with only one narrow dirt road out. A forward air observer reported to us that the ROK/6th army had collapsed from an attack by several thousand Chinese and were retreating. In their haste, the ROK/6th men had not radioed us of their retreat nor warned us that our position was now perilously unprotected.

We were alone in the valley looking like duck decoys on a park pond. Radio communication was poor due to high mountains surrounding us, but we did get one garbled radio message from one of the outposts. We heard him holler S-U-G-A-R! Nobody knew exactly where the Chinese were, but we knew that SUGAR meant cover your backside and get out. Frank gave the order to withdraw at 8 P.M. We loaded up and got out. A few miles down the road we tried the radio again and learned there was a major withdrawal taking place. Before we withdrew, we shelled the area behind us to ensure the enemy wouldn't be on our tail. Captain Blaine Johnson was my assistant and gave fire direction that night. We sent off barrages of artillery fire that blanketed the hills with thousands of artillery rounds. We didn't know if we hit anything or not until the next day when we learned from General Hoag that they found North Korean soldiers dead scattered over the hillsides from our fire power that night. I attributed this to Captain Johnson who had figured the fire direction toward a likely trail the enemy would travel.

We then had to move our equipment quickly under blackout conditions onto a narrow mountain road crowded eight abreast with ROK troops that were also withdrawing. It was a precarious situation with enemy mortars coming in on us. During the night, we lost an M-7 self-propelled Howitzer, a half-track and trailer. That's when Frank issued the order that there would be a 3 A.M. stand-to so we would be alert to night attacks.

Besides the stand-to we had sentry watches and manned outposts. For that extra margin of safety, he sent out nightly patrols and forward observers and used strategy more characteristic to infantry units than artillery. Frank assured us we weren't going to be caught in our sleeping bags during an attack. Frank and I had a sixth sense when we were in a dangerous position, we also felt calm when things were safe. This was true when we were in World War II, as well as Korea.

Most of the Chinese used Russian-made rifles, machine guns, grenades and 37mm mortars. About twenty-five percent of the Chinese had no weapons, but had to wait to pick up a rifle from a fallen comrade.

We were artillery support for the 1st Marine Division, 24th Infantry Division, the 27th Commonwealth Brigade, and ROK army. We moved continually. We moved so often that we didn't dig foxholes, we just stretched a tarp off from the side of the halftrack and put our cots beneath.

We received orders to go to Kapyong again to close the perimeter; code name was Task Force Spoiler. When we got there, Frank sent out patrols that came back with the report there was a lot of enemy activity.

"NOBODY SLEEPS TONIGHT."

It was the night of 26/27 May when the patrols reported that there were a lot of Chinese in the hills ahead. Frank gave the order, "Nobody sleeps tonight." Battalion Headquarters, Headquarters Battery, and A Battery were encamped at the mouth of a narrow valley. Sandwiched in between them were the 21st Regiment's headquarters and their medical aid station. Batteries B and C were encamped some distance behind us assigned to provide artillery fire for the 21st Infantry that was engaged in an offensive attack. When the 21st Infantry moved forward in an attempt to encircle about 4000 Chinese, it had left us vulnerable to attack.

As the several thousand Chinese withdrew from the 21st Infantry's offensive thrust, they attempted to rejoin the main body of the Chinese army through the only escape route open to them. That escape route was directly through the narrow mouth of the valley occupied by 240 men of our Headquarters, Headquarters Battery, and Battery A.

As the Chinese funneled into this narrow escape route, they opened fire on us. Men from Headquarters and A batteries grabbed rifles and machine guns and set up defensive positions, and we fought the Chinese behind every sagebrush and rock. The trapped enemy fought fiercely to break their way through our camps to get to the valley below. At one point the attackers came within 20 feet from Battery A's switchboard. At the same time we were in hand-to-hand combat, we firmly held our ground so that B and C batteries could continue to give fire support to the 21st Infantry whose lines had been broken by the Chinese.

The massive attack went on all night and abated by 8 A.M. when the Chinese retreated back into the canyon behind them. Immediately, Captain Ray E. Cox, commanding officer of A Battery organized a combat patrol of 18 men and began chasing the retreating 4000 Chinese up the canyon, using a self-propelled open non-turreted Howitzer, like a tank, with a .50 caliber mounted machine gun. Flanking Captain Cox were men in two vehicles with mounted .50 caliber guns. Without regard for their own lives, they chased the Chinese up the draw destroying enemy machine gun nests in front of them and spraying machine gun fire on the hills surrounding the canyon. During the night, the 24th Marine Infantry Division sent three tanks up the valley to assist us. By then it was light enough for a forward observer to direct artillery fire from C Battery over the mountain into our valley directing 105mm shells that exploded beyond the retreating Chinese.

The enemy was forced then to turn away from the exploding artillery in front of them, and they headed back into the firing range of Captain Cox's 18-man combat patrol and our encampment, boxing them in. The retreating enemy that was trying to escape over mountain ridges scattered when we sent a barrage of shells exploding in their path. In the confusion and devastation with escape routes cut off, the Chinese began to surrender. Eventually over 2500 surrendered.

When the dust had cleared we returned to count the cost of the all-night attack—about 350 of the enemy had lost their lives and 831 initially surrendered. Chinese had attacked through the 24th Infantry Division's medical unit encamped nearby and killed seven or eight of its staff and wounded a dozen others, besides killing the wounded Chinese who had been receiving medical aid from us all the while they were shouting directions to their Chinese friends where to fire.

But when counting our casualties we discovered that not one of our men had been killed. Approximately 240 men, who fought off 3500 to 4000 Chinese, dusted off their fatigues and used Band-Aides to cover their scrapes. There were a few with more serious injuries, but Pat Fenton, executive officer, quipped, "We had just nine Band-Aids and nine purple hearts." Perhaps an exaggeration for those three or four who were more seriously wounded; however, it captured their feeling of gratitude that they had survived the night, all the while enabling B and C batteries to give continuous artillery fire to the 21st Infantry's position.

Frank penciled into his pocketsize hardbound war diary he carried around with him:

"May 27, 1951 – Sunday. Noon today moved on up to the first position we occupied in this area in Kapyong. Fired [at] about 200 Chinese just before dark. Lots of Chinese camped east of us tonight may give us trouble. About 2 A.M. this morning the [Chinese] hit our A Battery and surrounding units. The fight lasted until about 8 A.M. They [Chinese] started to surrender then and by night our battalion had killed 101 and captured over 800. There have been over 2500 captured in the area today. Two nice letters from Mary."

Mary was his wife, and they had three children at home Gardiner, Dennis, and Eugene.

We chose to bury the enemy dead before moving out.

Frank Brought Every Man Home

The battalion continued its artillery support in one combat scene after another. Its history in Korea has many other heroic stories from Operation Nomad, battle of White Horse Mountain, Old Baldy, and battle of the Kumsong Salient. Frank commanded the battalion on active duty in Korea from 19 August 1950 to 24 May 1952 when by then we were all rotated home. Frank brought every one of his 600 boys under his command back home to their families in Southern Utah. Later, Frank was promoted to Brigadier General and commanded the XI Army Corps, and I was promoted and commanded the 213th for ten years.

There were a number of combinations of brothers in our battalion, Frank and I weren't the only ones. Frank claimed that was the reason we took care of each other and definitely that was part of it, but I know that Frank was a good leader. He worried about all of us. When we shipped out he had weighed 187 pounds and had brown hair. But a year later he weighed only 147 pounds and his brown hair had all turned white due to the worry and stress over his men. He had a lot of help from Major General Hoag, commander of IX Corps, but I know Frank prayed a lot, too. Whenever the flaps were down on his tent, we knew we couldn't disturb him, unless it was an emergency. Executive Officer Pat Fenton said of Frank:

> "We had a great leader. Dalley would refuse an order he didn't believe in with no reprisals that I know of, because he was always right. One time when we were up north in Korea he was leading the battalion of 600 men and all the equipment to the next position. Captain Bill Firmage was Frank's driver and told this story about Frank:

>> We came to a fork in the road and Frank said, 'Stop the jeep, Bill.' And I stopped. Frank got out and went over into a rice paddy and knelt down and I could see he was offering up a prayer. It was not uncommon of him to pray for guidance.

>> After a time he got back in the jeep and said, 'Bill, we're going to the right.'

>> 'Well, the brigade commander said we're sup-

posed to go to the left—that's our next position area,'
I said.

'The commander upstairs told me to go right,'
Frank said.

"They took the right fork of the road. The next battalion observed orders and went left when they reached that fork, and were totally annihilated by the enemy."

During World War II, Frank saw active duty from 3 March 1941 until 19 January 1946 and was recipient of the Bronze Star in Korea. His military service spanned over thirty-five years.

When he returned from Korea, Frank was invited to speak on Edward R. Murrow's national radio program called "This I Believe." Frank was a humble man and didn't boast about the numbers of 240 of his men against 4000 enemy, or that he brought every man under his command back home. From a transcript of the radio broadcast, he reflected on service to his country.

Edward R. Murrow:

"This I believe—Colonel Dalley is one of thousands of Americans that has twice been interrupted by war. First inducted when a teacher in 1941, he saw service in the Pacific Theater. Four years after starting his new civilian career with the Utah State Employment Service, he was again inducted as commanding officer of a field artillery battalion and was sent to Korea. Here are the personal beliefs of Frank Dalley:

"Early in 1951 I found myself in Korea in command of a field artillery battalion with the immediate prospects of taking each man into battle against the Communists. Many of them were relatives of personal friends and practically all of them were from my hometown or nearby communities. With this to face, I knew I must have help. I was taught from childhood to seek help from God through prayer. I had always believed in God as the Supreme Being and believed in the power of prayer. But the events that happened early in my battalion's participation in the Korea War did much to strengthen this belief.

"Not long after arriving at the Front and during my battalion's first engagement with the enemy, we found ourselves separated from all friendly forces. The Republic of Korea forces we were supporting at that time fell back without warning us, making it possible for the Communist forces to practically surround us without being detected. When my liaison officer, who had been sent out to establish contact with the Korean forces, returned with the information that all the friendly forces had fallen back and we were alone, the extreme seriousness of our situation was immediately apparent to me. I was responsible for the safety of 600 men entrusted to me. For moments, I suppose I was almost dazed. Then instinctively, my thoughts turned to God and I knew that our safety was in the hands of our Maker. I humbly asked for help, as I know and felt that many of the others did who were near me. The change that took place in my feelings, and the events that took place almost immediately, are hard to explain. They made a lasting impression on me for I feel sure that I was guided by a Supreme Being.

"It became clear to me the course that we must follow, and all the men calmly responded to a rapid series of instructions. In almost superhuman time the battalion was assembled and headed for the temporary safety of friendly lines. Over 12-15 miles of rough steep canyon roads and for about nine grueling hours prayer remained in my heart. Although the situation was precarious, yet not once was the outcome doubtful to me. I feel positive that we were guided to safety.

"Through the war in the Pacific from 1942-1945 and again in Korea, I viewed the untold human suffering with horror as I realized that each individual regardless of race, color or creed, was a creature created by God to occupy an equal place on earth.

The thought that each underprivileged person was an individual loved of parents had a deep impression on me. In the battle zone one day I found two small Korean children huddled together beside what remained the only home their family had. They were disease ridden and almost famished from hunger. The father and mother had been killed and were lying in the ruin of their house. The picture of these two children returns to me often and at this scene I vowed to do whatever I could in my small way to relieve human suffering wherever I can. This is my belief.

"Edward R. Murrow: That was Frank Dalley of Cedar City, Utah."

Returning to Max Dalley's narrative:

On my return to Parowan I became principal of Parowan High School, and Roma and I had added three more children to our family, John, Laurene and Randy. I succeeded Frank as commanding officer of the 213th battalion[2] for the ensuing ten years as Frank was promoted to the U. S. Army IX Corps.

*

Editor's Note:

The battalion received the Presidential Unit Citation, the highest honor a unit can receive, along with the Korean Presidential Unit Citation, for the battle at Kapyong. Captain Ray Cox was the recipient of the Silver Star. Frank Dalley passed away in 1995 and is buried in his hometown of Summit, Utah.

The 213th Battalion continued on in Korea after the first group was rotated home and served 893 consecutive days in Korean combat, and its artillery exploded nearly quarter million rounds of ammunition. The battalion would be called up and serve again during the Vietnam War.

Utah's incumbent Governor Michael Leavitt was a member of the 213th Battalion, renamed 2nd Battalion, 222nd Artillery, and served from 1969 to 1975.

Lt. Col. Frank Dalley, Commander of 213ᵗʰ Field Artillery Bn
Photo by Max Bonzo

---

[1] This was due to our excellent firing scores.
[2] The battalion name was changed to 2ⁿᵈ Battalion, 222ⁿᵈ Field Artillery.

ONLY THOSE ARE FIT TO LIVE
WHO DO NOT FEAR TO DIE;
AND NONE ARE FIT TO DIE
WHO HAVE SHRUNK FROM THE JOY OF LIFE
AND THE DUTY OF LIFE.

Theodore Roosevelt,
qtd. in *Inscriptions of a Nation*, Clint W. Ensign

VIETNAM

CHAPTER 1O

SERGEANT
ROGER C. ALLEN

Sgt. Roger C. Allen
Mortar Platoon – Cu Chi, Vietnam
27th Army Infantry

LETTERS FROM VIETNAM

*R*oger Allen was married just twelve days before his induction into the Army. In his final year he was on active duty in the Mekong Delta, half way between Saigon and the Cambodian border along the Ho Chi Min Trail, South Vietnam. Keeping his promise, he wrote to his wife each day. Besides being poignant love letters to his adored wife, Roberta, his letters reveal the vivid day-to-day war. Here are excerpts from his letters along with recollections. The letters have consecutive dates with one exception.

The Viet Cong came down the Ho Chi Min Trail from northern Vietnam, crossed the border into Cambodia, continued down the trail within the protection of Cambodia, and then crossed back over into Vietnam around Saigon. The VC attacked, then retreated across the border, then attacked again. Our area of operation was between Saigon and Cambodia.

I was assigned the position of forward observer. I was the guy with a radio on my back next to the lieutenant. If we needed fire power, I called in the mortars. My lieutenant preferred to stay up front; consequently, I was usually where the action was. But it wasn't just the enemy who attacked us, the mosquitoes were big enough to carry us off, and the temperature and humidity were inclined to reach 100 simultaneously. At times my feet were wet for so long they looked permanently wrinkled.

20 Jan 68... We went out on sweep today and everything was going along O.K. when all of a sudden I heard this terrible boom! It was just on the other side of a hedgerow. One guy (Hosea) lost his leg and part of his intestines. He later died. Another guy, Jessie James, got some shrapnel in his leg, but was O.K. I found shrapnel all around the area. It was a 105mm round which Charlie [Viet Cong] had booby trapped. I was 10 ft. away from it. I can surely say the good Lord was with me today. I really don't see how I wasn't hit...

THE TET OFFENSIVE

30 Jan 68... It was water and mud to my waist all the way. About 7 o'clock at night we got in after being lost and trying to find our way back and being fired at.

31 Jan 68... Well what a day this has started out to be. We had to go help our ambush site because they sprung their ambush. We were fighting from 6 o'clock until about 8 o'clock. There were VC all over the place. The F.O. [Forward Observer] for 2nd Platoon called in some mortars and they hit our own men. 5 men were wounded. When the chopper came in to pick them up for the hospital, the VC opened up and killed two of our wounded. One was from our platoon. We captured two 75mm recoilless rifles and a bunch of small arms and web gear. The VC were all around us and running through the open field. Every time they got up and

started running, we would open fire...

I well remember we were out in the field and the enemy was all over. We were crouched behind a rice paddy dike, our only protection. A new forward observer was being trained in the second platoon when the intensive fighting of the Tet offensive hit us. The new guy called in for mortar fire on the enemy. Whenever we called in for mortar fire, they would always send marker rounds first so we could see if we had given the right coordinates and adjust it if we had to. I remember this new kid panicked and called in the coordinates and said, "Don't send markers, send live rounds. Send them right now!" Fighting was fierce and we thought we would all be shot dead in the next minute. I remember those rounds coming in and they didn't go where they were supposed to go, and they hit us. He screamed on the radio, "Stop firing! Stop firing!" Three of our men were killed. Three guys were dead and I was crouched next to them.

[Continuing with 31 Jan 68 letter]

The writing at the bottom of this page is from one of the Vietnamese girls, the scribbling is from the little boy who sat on my lap today. The Chinese-type writing is from another boy. The next line is from another boy. These are their names...

1 Feb 68... I had a little boy who wanted to sit on my lap all day. He was sure a cute kid. You get to feeling like you would like to bring about 50 home with you. We are by Saigon and people live a little nicer here than out in the farmlands. One thing the kids over here understand is Batman. He is a world famous person.

2 Feb 68... Just a few minutes ago I had a person placed in my custody. He was a boy without an I.D. card [suspected Viet Cong]. We started to move and we had gone about 100 meters when the boy took off. I hollered at him to stop, then started firing. He dodged left and right so I couldn't hit him. I ran after him and stayed up with him pretty good until he went through a hedgerow. I had a radio on my back and got slightly tangled up. I kept firing at him and he kept running

and ran past one of our men, but our guy didn't do anything. I took aim at him, but couldn't fire because our men were in front of me. I had to stop running because our men opened up [firing] and I had to get down. Needless to say the boy got away. I feel just terrible about it. . . It's just like the whole world has fallen in on me. . .

3 Feb 68 . . .We continued on our sweep. We got 5 more detainees [Viet Cong]. We were just about to our objective when we got in a firefight. B-3, that's our platoon, went around to the west side and started sweeping in to try and flush the enemy out, when all of a sudden a machine gun opened up on us and 3 men were hit. We fell behind a berm and returned fire. I pulled one kid down off the berm and we started giving him first aid. He was hit in the neck. Our machine gun was out front where it was dropped when the machine gunner got hit. Well, somebody had to go get it. I wished I could do something to make up for the VC getting away [yesterday], so I took off my equipment and while our men returned fire, I jumped up on the berm, ran out and got the machine gun and came back. That's the one time I was really scared.

That's not all—we were working around this guy that got hit in the neck when an RPG [enemy anti-tank weapon] round went off right by us. The guy with the neck wound was right at my feet and got killed. The medic got hit who was right to the side of me. In fact, I was the only one who didn't get hit out of about 5 guys . . . I bandaged up a couple of guys, then we started moving them out. . .   Well, I'll close for now . . . P.S. Since 29 Jan. until Feb. 1, we had killed 5800 VC in Vietnam, had 2500 detainees, most of which will be VC, and we have lost 500 friendly forces, 200 of them Americans. . . *[The following day after everyone was accounted for, there were three remaining in his platoon, a sergeant, rifleman and himself, the forward observer. They re-assigned a medic to make a 4-man platoon.]* We went back and looked at the area where we were hit yesterday and boy what a mess. Hootches were burned down and animals dead all over.

4 Feb 68. . . The last two nights I have been sleeping in a graveyard . . . I don't know how long we will be out here. I've heard it will be about two weeks... Somebody is in a firefight out to our west, and they are using all the helicopters, so we couldn't get any C-rations for dinner. Well, we went and got some bananas and killed a chicken . . . and cooked it in one of the hootches and ate it. . .

I was up in the area of the Hobo jungle close to the Cambodian border in an area that had been cleared of vegetation with Agent Orange. We were sneaking through the jungle looking for the enemy and were in a line ten, fifteen, twenty feet apart. We came to a clearing and about thirty feet ahead was a hedgerow and thicket and we headed toward it. In my position I had to make a decision whether I moved to the right or to the left around the thicket. I had the strong feeling to go right. I started to move right and in doing so the whole line swung right. As we got to the hedgerow the guy on my left went around it on the left side, and tripped a land mine. It went off and blew his leg, thigh and part of his arm off. He died right there.

5 Feb 68... We went through the area where Charlie company [the Viet Cong] got hit. We burned everything to the ground and destroyed everything we came across. We dug up one VC body and found another one. We found some machine guns and some new M-16s. The VC had our new M-16 before we did...

The Viet Cong didn't leave bodies behind unless they absolutely had to. They didn't want us to know who they were or how many had been wounded or killed. That day we ran across some graves and we had to dig up the bodies. I remember wearing a gas mask because the bodies were a couple of weeks old. We had to pull them out, identify about how old they were, what type of clothing they wore and whether they were regular army or guerilla army.

We were required to search through villages for signs to determine if the VC had been there. In one highly concentrated VC area the enemy had taken over a village. We received an order to go to the village and destroy it. We searched all the grass hootches and then burned the village to the ground. There was a beautiful gold-rimmed teapot that was in one of those homes. Whoever lived in the hut had a china closet of things like that, and it was all destroyed. It was a hard thing to do. I'm glad I only had to do that once.

6 Feb 68… I went into a little Vietnamese country store on the way today and bought me a U.S. Government pen for 20 cents and I got a toothbrush… We moved a little closer to the fighting. I heard Alpha company had 15 killed and about 35 wounded. It must be real bad where they're fighting. It's real demoralizing to keep going day and night for a long time. Well, we started into the area where they have been fighting all day but pulled back. We set up a perimeter with some tanks and APCs [Armored Personnel Carriers]. We have the VC boxed in, in this one area, and we [US] have bombed it all day, and put artillery in also.

7 Feb 68… Well, this morning was one of those mornings when you wake up and 10 minutes later the VCs are shooting at you. We got carbine fire and RPGs [enemy anti-tank weapon fire]. We moved out with the tanks about 10:00, and we started sweeping through the area where the VC were. About 2:00 we ran into them. We have just been sitting here— firing every once in a while and being fired at. It's really funny. Here we are with the VC firing at us, and just ahead of us are a bunch of GIs sleeping; I'm writing a letter; one kid is making some coffee—just like there wasn't even a war.

Well, we finally got back to base camp, we eagle flew in [via helicopter]. We are inside an ARVN [Army of Republic of South Viet Nam] compound. I got the news about the baby when I got here. I am so happy I could cry! I love you so much… I don't know what day it was born. They didn't say, they just said it was a boy and weighed 7 pounds and something... all I can say is, I love you... Love always, Roger.

8 Feb 68... I am having some flowers sent to you... I hope everything is all right at home and the two of you are doing all right... We are sitting here in the same area we were in yesterday... They are going to call artillery in on them so we are held up until they finish. The VC are really set in not giving up. There are supposed to be 1,000 VC and this is supposed to be their division headquarters. Well, we pulled back and are getting ready to be taken back to base camp...

We had a Vietnamese barber that would cut our hair. One night we were in a firefight close to camp, and after searching the area the next morning we found several Viet Cong dead from the fight. There was our barber, one of the VC dead. We never knew who the enemy was.

9 Feb 68... We are eating C-rations for every meal now because they can't get food into us. Things are still pretty bad over here. We spend our nights in the ARVN compound. Well, it's night now and we just got back from a firefight. We had two guys wounded. The first one got wounded in the chest (Holt was his name). The medic wasn't around, so I went up to him and got a bandage on him. The medic came and we carried him [Holt] back while the VC was shooting at us. Then another kid got hit in the rear (Higgs was his name). I went to help him. Second platoon had 2 killed in action, we had to leave them because we couldn't get to them without getting killed ourselves. We will go in tomorrow and get them... Love Daddy." *A post script:* '[They] have called air strikes in on the area where we got hit. They are dropping bombs and firing ammo into the area... We got hot chow tonight which we didn't expect. We had rice with chili on it. It really tasted good after eating C-rations.

10 Feb. 68... We have a sniper in the wood line who keeps sniping at us every once in a while... Yesterday we killed 148 VC that's pretty good, you know. We captured three 50-caliber machine guns and some big gun—I don't know what it is, and got some small arms, too.

11 Feb. 68... We have just sat around here in the ARVN compound this morning. They have been bombing the area where we were yesterday. We are going out again at 10:00. I haven't received any mail yet, but I think I will get some tomorrow. At least I hope so. The guys still want me back in weapons platoon, especially now I have a son, but I just don't feel right about going back, so I've stayed on line. . . Well we went back into the area today, but all we found was dead VC. We got our two men out that we had to leave behind. The VC must have gotten out last night some how. I got word this morning that Holt (the guy I patched up 2 days ago), died. I was real sad about it. . .

12 Feb 68. . . Charlie has a machine gun and we found out he has claymores pointed at us. The air strikes got rid of them though. A claymore will [spew shrapnel] 250 meters and so you can imagine what would have happened if 8 of those went off. We were lucky the VC never detonated them... Well, we got back in O.K. And again I thank the Lord for protecting my life because when we got off the chopper, we were walking down the road to our camp as some helicopters were bringing some more people in. Usually we stop, get down, and face out so the dust won't get in our eyes and all. Tonight, though, we started running up the road to get out of the way. Well, we got out of the way and I turned around and looked at the chopper that was landing where we would have stopped, and it just fell right out of the sky and turned over as it hit the ground. If we had stopped, it would have fallen right on us. There were 11 men on the chopper and all came out alive; one guy was hurt real bad, but the rest were pretty well O.K.

I got your Valentine today and my son's and also got the birth announcement. I was so happy about it. Now I know what day he was born! I sit here with the tears running over my cheeks, I thank the Lord for you and our son. I thank Him for every letter I get from you, because that is what keeps me going. It keeps my hopes up that there is something better than this is—a future, and that there is still love somewhere in this world of war. . . It's that one last link I have with my home, my country, and my loved ones I miss so much...

13 Feb 68... We got to shower and get clean clothes today. Just a little while ago they brought two of our guys back who were pretty drunk. We tucked them in and the one went to sleep, but Harvey was crying about Holt who got killed. They were close friends. I tried to ease his sorrow but didn't help much. . . I made some coffee for him.

14 Feb 68... Well today has been very exciting. This afternoon I went with a guy named Harvey so he wouldn't drink too much and get drunk like he did last night. We were down at a Vietnamese club. I had a few sodas and about 10:00 we started back. Harvey was going to go get some Boom Boom.

(In one area the venereal disease was so rampant the Army actually brought in women and announced those women had been checked out and were free of disease.)

[Continuing 14 Feb 68]:

After begging him not to, I started back to camp. His squad leader came after him, so together we went back and got him. When he found out his platoon sergeant had wanted him back, he blew up and he was going to go hit the sergeant. Well, I talked a blue streak trying to stop him. I even begged him to hit me instead. Sergeant Null [weapons platoon sergeant] came and talked to him and calmed him down quite a bit. Sergeant Null left me in charge of him to get him to bed. Well, he is calmed down a bit now. I think he feels worse about Holt being killed and blames himself for it . . . We have recommended that he see a psychiatrist and they are sending him in, in the morning. Sergeant Null told me tonight he was pulling me off line, that I had a wife and child to think of and he didn't want me out there. I told him that I wanted to stay. I love you and our son very much dear, but I love these guys I'm with, also. . .

15 Feb 68. . . I also got a picture of the baby. You know something? He does look like me! . . .Well, today I told my sergeant I wanted off line. Everybody wanted me to come off so bad. I even think you did although you wouldn't come right out and say it. . .

16 Feb 68, Dear Wife and Son: Well today was another bad day. We left the ARVN and went eagle flighting to the Saigon River. As soon as we landed and started to move, Charlie opened up on us and killed two of our men. I was 50 meters from the bunker, there were bunkers all along the coconut trees. Charlie had machine guns and... something hit me in the leg... I don't know what it was, but the only thing coming our way were bullets. It never left a mark. Boy I was sure praying! We pulled back and waited until they [U.S. helicopters with guns] came in with artillery and hit Charlie, then we started out to rescue a helicopter that had been shot down. The VC opened up on us again and they had us trapped in an open field. We laid there in the water with the sun beating down on us. We pulled back and waited for awhile until we [helicopters] bombed the place and put artillery in from our gun ships [helicopters with guns] and still the VC were there. We tried to go up and get our two men out who had been killed, but couldn't get to them. The grass had all been burned around the bodies and I suppose the bodies are burned some. The two men were Johnson, the one I said got ants in his eyes a few days ago, and Spellman, the new kid who came out from weapons platoon. We had to

leave them there for the night. This is the second time we have had to do that.

We were wet all day today. Everywhere I stepped there was water. I would sit and look at my little boy's picture today and take 2 father pills before looking, and two after. *[Candies his wife had sent him which she called father pills.]* How's that for a proud dad. I am so thrilled and happy, it just hasn't quite registered yet... Well, that's about all that has happened, except I found out our Vietnamese boy who was teaching me Vietnamese was killed during Tet [offensive] by the VC. It's too bad, he was a swell boy. Well, until tomorrow, my love. . .

17 Feb '68... We eagle flighted out... to where the VC had been yesterday. A few of us stayed behind to carry the two dead bodies out. We got Johnson and put him on a stretcher. It made me so sick. His head had a hole in it and the flies and bugs were crawling around in his brains and he had bullets in his legs and body. The smell was so bad I almost threw up two or three times. That wasn't the worst part though. We had to go and get the other guy—Spellman... I had to pick up his head, neck and right shoulder that was in one piece; his right arm and hand was in another piece— it stunk so bad and was a horrible sight to see. About thirty feet away, we found the rest of his body. It was the part from his last three ribs down. His body had been burned and it was real bad. After that we found his left hand over under a tree about 10 ft. away. After we got the bodies out, we had to go and get some equipment Charlie company had left behind, 5 M-16s, 1 M-60 machine gun, web gear, gas masks and other things. After we got all that done we went on with our mission. We swept down to the Saigon River then we came back to base camp. We are going to move tomorrow.

Well, that's about all that's happened today. I got your two pictures you sent. The baby looks real cute, but you really look like you had a baby. You better let your hair grow out a little more, you almost look bald. Well, keep that sweet son of mine happy till I return. Love always, Roger.

18 Feb 68… Well today we moved base camp. We got everything ready and then left on helicopters. We are now on the other side of Saigon by the Saigon River… We landed at our base camp and then went sweeping to the south.

One night we went out in the field and set up a new base camp, dug our bunker, put a roof on it, right on the perimeter. I had a hammock that I wanted to swing between two trees, and was going to sleep in that hammock during the night instead of the ground. We had been on patrol setting up ambushes outside of our perimeter the night before. The perimeter was the area around the camp where we would set up barbed wire and then set our bunkers just inside the barbed wire. This was true for each base camp we built so that if the enemy came in they would hit us first, before they hit our base camp. Because we had been out on patrol the night before, we knew we wouldn't have to go out again. We built our bunkers, ate our meal, and got ready to settle in, when our lieutenant came over and told us we had to go out on ambush again that night. We got very very upset! Thought it was very unfair we had to go again! It wasn't our turn! but we still had to go.

We left and went out from the perimeter a few hundred yards from the base camp and set up our ambush with claymore mines. A claymore mine looks like a waffle iron with legs that you set on the ground. It has an explosive that shoots forward with shrapnel. That night VC overran the perimeter and got inside the base camp and attacked. We could hear the explosions and could see flares off in the distance. We had to stay where we were in case the VC came through our area. After awhile the fighting subsided and the morning came. We broke camp and went back to base camp. The enemy had broken through into the base camp right where our bunker was. They had thrown a grenade into that bunker and three men had been killed. I don't know how many men we lost. There were Viet Cong bodies still lying on the ground next morning.

When we were flown in by helicopter into an area where we were fired on as we were landing, we called it a hot landing, and a couple of times we had hot landings. When we were coming in, the noise was so loud from the helicopter, we wouldn't know if we were being fired at until somebody dropped over. There was always apprehension as we flew into an area. You never really wanted to be the one sitting next to the door. We came into one area and it was a hot one, and one of our guys was shot and wounded as we landed. He wasn't killed. We pulled back out and called in air strikes.

19 Feb 68... About 2:00 in the morning we got mortared. I believe the VC were using recoilless rifles 60mm type. There were about 41 rounds that came in. Nobody was hurt though...

20 Feb 68... We got on line with Delta company and Recon [Reconnaissance]. We started moving out but hadn't gone very far when we got fire from the VC. So far Recon has got one VC (dead) and one AK 50. The VC had on GI web gear and GI hand grenades. Well, when we started to move after awhile, Charlie opened up on us and wounded two men. We fired for awhile, then pulled back to the road and called artillery in on the area. We saw about 20 VC when we moved back.

We pulled together and watched out for each other when bullets were flying around us. We had been in a firefight and as this one guy came jumping around trying to get behind something to protect himself, he sat in a cactus. Those spines went right in his rear end. There we were out on the battlefield, and he's got his pants pulled down and I'm pulling thorns out of his rear end while we were being shot at.

21 Feb 68... All the Vietnamese people are leaving the area we are going into. And those coming this way turn around and go back. There are probably VC ahead. . . Sure enough, we ran into some VCs and we had 3 guys wounded... Today was my last day on line.

22 Feb. 68... Well, today was my first day off line. I nearly went crazy. I read some of my book today, then I washed my socks, and tried to sleep, but couldn't.

I was eventually assigned as plotter in a fire direction center mortar platoon. When a forward observer radioed for mortars into an area, I would plot the coordinates and give the order to fire.

*

Editor's Note:

Sergeant Allen was gravely fearful when he was the only man assigned to combat in Vietnam from his training platoon. The rest were sent to non-combat countries. When his convictions overcame his fear, he was consoled that it would be all right. He seldom wrote or spoke of fear and only in passing mentioned he was a recipient of the Bronze Star. He became known among his platoon buddies, as the man bullets wouldn't hit after they observed death strike around him; consequently, his buddies looked to him to take the initiative when under fire. He served in the Army for twenty-three months, the last eleven in Vietnam.

Roger Allen and Roberta Hall Allen were married a few days prior to his induction into the Army. During the first two years of marriage they spent less than four and a half months together. They have been married for thirty-four years.

Sergeant Allen returned from the service and finished college at Utah State University in Logan majoring in accounting. He is presently a CPA for Cook Dorigatti & Associates in Logan, Utah. He and his wife were born and raised in Hyrum, Utah, and presently reside there and have four children and four grandchildren.

I asked Sergeant Allen how he felt about serving in the unwar, and how he felt about our country and the flag.

"I would have been happy not to go, but I didn't dodge the draft. I wasn't a protester. I might not have believed in the things that we were doing over there, but I felt that as an

American citizen I had a duty to uphold my country and a duty to uphold our commander-in-chief. And we were trying to do something for those people—it was too bad the Vietnamese couldn't catch the vision of it. When the war ended, when we came home, there was no fanfare, no tickertape parades, life just went on. But I'm still proud of the fact that I served.

"When I see the flag, especially on the Fourth of July with flag ceremonies, I can't help but have tears come to my eyes. I feel very patriotic. I put my life on the line for the flag and what it stands for—and for all the people who have fought the wars and conflicts ever since we became an independent nation. The red in the flag stands for the many people who have shed their blood, and I have deep respect for those people. I was lucky. I didn't have to give that much."

The majority of Vietnam veterans returned home unwilling—or unable to talk—mute. They fought to forget. And in the thirty years since, there are few men that have broken the deafening silence. When Veterans Day approaches some are consumed with remembering what they did, or could not do. Yet the unspeakable unwar for most veterans remains unspoken.

*****

CHAPTER 11

Lt. Colonel Jay Criddle Hess
Tactical Air Command
U.S. Air Force

LT. COLONEL
JAY C. HESS

I DREAMED OF STEEL CHARGERS WITH SKIES TO ROAM, BUT MOSTLY I DREAMED OF JUST GOING HOME

I was willing to die for my country. But I had made up my mind I wasn't going to be taken prisoner by the Vietnamese. Air Force survival school had convinced me of that.

"SHARK FOUR'S TORCHING!"

We briefed in the early morning hours of 24 August 1967, then held until noon for the weather to improve. On my thirty-third mission over North Vietnam, I was flying an F-105D Thunderchief. We called the Thunderchiefs Thuds, and my code name was Shark Four. Colonel Robert White[1] led the twenty-four-aircraft strike force from Takhli, Thailand, east toward the Gulf of Tonkin climbing to 18,000

October 1966
Dear Dad,
... You expressed an interest in my choice concerning the Air Force. I decided not to get out at the present time... The coming few months will surely bring a prolonged separation from Marge and the children, as I am one of the very few who has not been to South East Asia yet.

Despite these cinching reasons for doing otherwise, and not forgetting that I could easily be killed myself, or maybe more unfortunately be a prisoner of war, I've made the choice... There is no doubt that the moral condition of our mature population, and most assuredly those in the military, is at such a shocking low state that there could be no hope of the Lord helping us to protect our freedom if every one who loves peace and right decided to avoid the conflict.

Love, Jay.

feet to rendezvous with KC-135 tankers to refuel. Refueling twice more before they left us, we crossed the coast of Vietnam at 20,000 feet inbound toward the target, a railroad repair facility northeast of Hanoi near the China border. Power and maneuverability of the F-105 exhilarated my senses as I soared through the steel blue sky. With throttle full forward, I thrust it outboard to light the afterburner giving it 25,000 pounds of thrust and accelerated to Mach 0.9—near speed of sound—and climbed to 25,000 feet, enjoying the exquisite burst of power within my control. We located the target through a gap in the clouds, and I streaked through it descending to 12,000 feet releasing my six 750-pound bombs and pulled up off the target.

Suddenly, I was hit. Ground fire—37mm or 57mm, or was it the fin of a bomb in front of me I touched? It felt like hitting a guardrail in a car going 70 miles an hour, slowing my aircraft, and it began to tumble. But I regained control and had it flying smoothly again. Trailing a bit behind, and still near the target area, I instinctively pushed the throttle outboard to light the afterburner for maximum speed. Instead of thrust and swift ascent, the cockpit burst into flames. Fire obscured the instrument panel, and I couldn't see. The Thud pitched down violently and threw me up against the canopy. Through flames I could see that the control stick lay full back in my lap, but the aircraft wasn't responding. With my speed between 500 and 600 miles per hour, I estimated the altimeter now read 5000 feet, and I had less than five seconds before crashing into the ground. I heard in my earphones, "Shark Four's torching!" I pulled up the armrests, which started the ejection process, and reached for the trigger with my right hand, but it lay beyond my grasp as gravity had forced me up off the seat against the canopy. I was surprised at how quickly I had changed my mind about being a POW. Stretching and reaching again, the tip of my middle finger touched the trigger, the canopy flew off, and I went out with it. The air blast knocked me unconscious.

Regaining consciousness momentarily during the descent and looking down, a meandering stream followed the outline of a dirt road. Hearing rifle shots, and wondering if they were shooting at me, I raised my head to see if there were holes in my parachute, and discovered that fully half the panels were torn out of the canopy from the opening shock. Then I blacked out again.

I was face down in the dirt when I regained consciousness. At that moment I couldn't remember having flown that day or how I came to be on a trail leading to wooded mountains. Pushing up with my arms to get a good look around, somebody was crawling on hands and knees toward me to get a better look at the object that had fallen out of the sky. Reflexively my hand went for my .38 and aimed it. I eyed him over the sights and guessed he was about the age of Warren, my ten year-old son. I put my pistol away. He started yelling and screaming and as I looked around me, there were people everywhere. Yet for a second they hadn't seen me, and I reached for my radio to make a call, but all I got was the beep beep beep from the locator beacon attached to my parachute, and before I could turn it off women, children and uniformed soldiers were on me. I felt like a QB with the football on the bottom of a pile of linebackers.

My captors removed my weapon and began removing my clothing. I was certain they weren't acquainted with zippers when they began hacking off my G-suit with a machete like they were chopping down a tree. Before they hacked off my leg, I stood up and reached down to unzip it. My sudden movement startled the guy behind me, and he shot me in the back of the neck, and my knees buckled, and I slumped to the ground. The bullet grazed my neck and creased the side of my head. Besides the shock, the bullet wound added discomfort to my already painful neck that had been yanked and jerked during the swift ejection out of the cockpit. Yet, I felt fortunate to be alive.

As soon as my G-suit was off, they removed my flight boots and flight suit. Then hush came over the crowd as they took a good look at me standing barefoot in the dirt in my underwear. They later gave back my flight suit and my boots. A man in the crowd picked up my smoke flare and fumbled with it until he accidentally pulled the pin. When orange smoke spewed out and his eyes reflected complete surprise, then fear; and then a I'm-in-real-trouble-now look, I couldn't help but grin. The crowd scattered and took cover, and I stood alone.

A few seconds later a rifle-wielding oriental motioned me up the trail, and I began a hike that lasted all afternoon, crossing mountains and fording a stream where water reached my neck, then climbing up the stream's steep slippery bank onto a road. From there I was driven to a cave in the side of a mountain and taken inside and interrogated.

Electric power lines terminated at the cave's entrance and bare light bulbs hung from the ceiling. Smooth sand floors inside the cave made it easy walking. Classrooms off the main tunnel contained neatly aligned rows of wooden folding chairs. While waiting in the cave, I received first aid for my wounds and a large bowl of rice and fried chicken. I couldn't remember when I had eaten, and though it looked delicious, I couldn't eat. Frequently during the ensuing days and years when I was always hungry and thirsty I would think back on the delicious food I had turned away. Within thirty minutes a young oriental male walked in wearing a white short sleeve shirt, pressed slacks and shined shoes and said he was the interpreter. Accompanying him, a bearded man in peasant clothing began questioning me through the interpreter.

At twilight I stepped out of the cave led by my captors through a grove of trees to a neatly built three-room bamboo hut. The front door opened and we entered into a large room the width of the hut. As I stepped inside the room, photographers focused cameras and flash bulbs popped blinding me. There were two doors in the back wall and I was taken into the room on the right that led into an office where an oriental officer in full uniform sat behind a desk. A large picture of Chinese Communist leader MaoTse-tung hung on the wall behind him, surprising me since Ho Chi Minh was the Vietnamese leader, and I felt certain I bailed out over Vietnam. While the officer questioned in English, two large movie cameras focused on me. I stated only my name, rank, serial number and date of birth. Verbal pressure and threats repeatedly pressed for more information, but no physical force was exerted.

Darkness had descended, though light from a nearly full moon above the trees and mountain lighted a path as they led me to the middle of a cabbage patch. Not knowing what to expect next, a young girl drew near with a rifle pointing at me, and a flash bulb went off. My capture, it appeared, gave prominence to the villagers, and I surmised, provided valuable propaganda. A dozen more young girls entered the cabbage patch, lined up, and one at a time posed for cameras capturing me, the big American Air Pirate.

Two oversized jeeps arrived. The driver in the lead jeep drove ahead with a man yelling into a bullhorn to gather to see the spectacle. Driven to five or six pep rallies along the road while riding in the open backseat of the second jeep, they sandwiched me between interpreter and armed escort while a guard sat in the front seat with the driver. The pep rallies were not fun. The crowds excitably sang songs and hollered slogans, "We'll win, you'll lose," punctuated with propaganda hype, "Yankee American Air Pirate, Capitalist Aggressor, and Fascist" until they became frightening mobs. Lights blinded my eyes and I couldn't see the fast moving fist until it squarely hit my face and knocked me down. The guard standing next to me reprimanded the irate man for his violent action. I muttered, "If you don't want violence, don't incite the crowd."

Stopping at a wooden shack by the roadside with a telephone line strung to it, a uniformed soldier went in, and a long wait ensued before he returned. Guessing that Chinese originally captured me, I was now being placed in custody of Vietnamese. From that point on I received rough treatment. Placed in the back of an open pickup truck and blindfolded, my hands and feet were tied uncomfortably tight, and my boots removed. While bumping and bouncing along that dirt road in the dark guards in the truck repeatedly stomped on my bare feet. Peering under the blindfold near my nose, I could see that dawn of another day brightened the sky at the time the rough ride ended. As I waited in the truck tied up and blindfolded, someone put a CBU (cluster bomb) fragment in my hand and ran my fingers over it, and I felt his vengeful anger. After an hour I heard a helicopter descend and land a few feet away, and guessed I might be at Kep airfield. Still blindfolded I entered the door on the left rear side of the helicopter and sat on a bench-type seat. The aircrew came in after I was secured, walked past me and climbed up into the cockpit, and by the sound I identified the helicopter as Russian or Chinese.

Landing at Hanoi airport a short time later, young kids gathered and made my wait uncomfortable. Still blindfolded and bound, they pressed close against me twisting my ears, pinching my nose, and delighted in poking and hitting me. Departing the airport in a jeep, we later stopped outside an iron-barred gate of a high walled complex. I felt fortunate with only a grazing bullet wound and pondered how long I might be confined.

My feet were untied and within minutes led inside the green walls of the Knobby Room at New Guy Village at the Hoa Lo Prison that had been nicknamed Hanoi Hilton by Americans. They had also nicknamed buildings within the Hilton's perimeter—New Guy Village, Little Vegas, Unity, and Heartbreak. Detention camps in outlying areas were nicknamed Dogpatch, Plantation, Zoo, Alcatraz, and there were more. Additionally, they had caricatured each guard with an unmagnificent but appropriate tag: Dum Dum, Spot, Bug, Mickey Mouse, Lump, Buzzard, Snake, Colt 45, and others.

The guard discarded my clothes and handed me a pair of striped prison shorts. I stood barefoot, "Everything is gone," I whispered. "Separated from everything that counts—my wife, my children, and my home."

LEARNING THE ROPES AT THE HILTON

Fist-sized knobs of plaster protruded on the walls of the room. Later I knew why. The room was designed to acoustically muffle screams of its victims. Pig Eye, technician in the Knobby Room, received his orders from a sinister faced man we called The Cat, who was head of interrogation. Pig Eye and The Cat were a skillful team. Air Force Captain Konrad Trautman experienced the Rope Trick on thirteen separate occasions and describes it.

"Let me try to tell you what it really feels like when they tightly bind your wrists and elbows behind your back with nylon straps—then take the strap and pull the arms up, up your back, to the back of your head. If you can remember when you were a little boy, the fooling around you did, and someone grabs your hand and just twists your arm up to your back, and says: 'Say Uncle.' He does it with just one hand. And this, as you remember, is a very severe pain. Well, imagine this with both arms tied tight together—elbow to elbow, wrist to wrist—and then, using the leverage of his feet planted between your shoulder blades, with both hands, he pulls with all his might, 'til your arms are up and back over your head, forcing your head down between your feet, where your legs are between iron bars. The pain is literally beyond description. . . . If you scream, they pull the ropes even tighter. So you learn very quickly not to scream, and yet endure the pain. . .

"Besides the pain itself, you are tied up so tight that your windpipe becomes pinched and you breathe in gasps. You're trying to gulp in air, because your wind passage is being shrunken. Your throat, in a matter of 30 seconds, becomes completely dry, like it's been swabbed with cotton. . . .After about 10 or 15 minutes in this position, tied up so tightly, your nerves in your arms are pinched off, and then your whole upper torso becomes numb. It's a relief. You feel no more pain. . . .The breathing is still difficult, but the pain is gone. You've been anesthetized. However, when they release the ropes, the procedure works *completely* in the reverse."

There were other menacing tricks in their torture repertoire as evidenced by features of the Knobby Room—big meat hooks suspended from the ceiling, iron leg stocks and manacles. On the wall a large sign read "Lenient and Humane." The Cat stressed the lenient and humane treatment given prisoners and then asked us to repent and show remorse for bombing women, children and schools. Since our targets were always military installations, neither others nor I could feign remorse. He then attempted indoctrination into Vietnamese philosophy. "In America you are exploited. Enlisted people in America cannot afford bananas. In Vietnam everyone can have bananas. We have 4000 years of glorious Vietnamese history." The Vietnamese thought America was a terrible place since the only pictures of the United States they had viewed were of slums and polluted dock areas.

In the crucible of the Knobby Room I gave name, rank, serial number, and date of birth, but the cunning Pig Eye and The Cat were bent on torture and violently applied the Rope Trick. In the throes of the ropes I sweat from every pore. My thirst was incessant—my mouth and throat dry as parched earth—every pore pleading for water. Tortured until I lay on the floor deliriously hallucinating, I once dreamed I was swimming in a pool filled with orangeade. Feeling like a caged animal, I was given a few sips of water, occasionally a bowl of food, and defecating on the floor. After a few days, which seemed forever, a bowl of water with two or three leaves in it gave some relief to my thirst.

Tortured to the breaking point, Americans gave answers that were at best folklore and at worst distorted truth. The following year Lt. Cdr. Nels Tanner USN made the North Vietnamese a laughing stock when he told the inquisitors his fellow officers were Lt. Commanders Ben Casey and Clark Kent who had been court martialed for not wanting to bomb Vietnam. The Vietnamese never forgave Tanner because in their eagerness to ply that twit into propaganda they publicized it over international television. Results were horselaughs internationally that forever rankled the Vietnamese. But Tanner paid dearly, finally setting the record for 123 consecutive days in irons.

In another incident S. P. de Gonzalez was identified as a commander and when the propaganda-happy Cat announced it over the camp loudspeaker, the Americans responded with snickering that bespoke, "Gotcha again!" for when said fast it was none other than cartoon character Speedy Gonzalez. Marked for unrelenting torture were Lt. Col. Robby Risner USAF featured on the cover of Time magazine, Capt. John McCain USN, whose father was a Navy Admiral, and all senior ranking officers. Some Americans died during torture, others attempted suicide.

At the end of a week I was carried out of the Knobby Room and thrown into the unsplendid isolation of a 5 ½ x 7-foot dark, oppressively hot cell at Little Vegas. The iron door banged shut, bolted and locked behind me. I had a wood plank for my bed and a pail for personal waste. Permanently mounted at one end of the plank was a set of rusted old-style leg stocks shrilly testifying of anguishing prisoners. My clothing consisted of one pair of prison shorts. From a boarded-up window, nailed to the frame from the outside, a crack of light appeared where I could see a few green leaves on top of a tree and discover if it was day or night. During the first month, while peeking through this crack, two Americans and a guard moved across the walkway. One American wore prison shorts threadbare in the seat. It seemed like I had been there forever—maybe a month by then—yet my shorts still looked new. I wondered how long it would take to sit in shorts before the seat was worn through, and slumped down to the floor in despair, later learning Americans had been there three and four years before I arrived. With my arms and hands twisted and dysfunctional, I called out in prayer, and remembered a verse from Friedrich Nietzche, "He who has a why to live for, can bear almost any how." I had a lot to live for—a wife and five young children and I resolved to live.

TIME INVERTS AT THE ANNEX CAMP

After I had been in isolation for two months, I was moved into a cell at the camp called the Annex, and shared that cubicle with Konrad

Trautman USAF, Mike McGrath USN, and Gerry Gerndt USAF for the next two years. We felt we no longer had to fight survival alone, we were now a team. Trautman and I were both captains, though he was senior to me by a few months and became senior ranking officer of the cell. Within the 12 x 12-foot concrete cell, each of us had a pair of rubber-tire soled sandals, plate, cup, spoon, toothbrush, toothpaste, cotton blanket, and bar of soap. The bar of soap for washing and laundry had to last three months. The tube of toothpaste had to last a year; three pieces of toilet paper for ten days. We were allowed outside for a few minutes each day to wash and occasionally to bathe. We shared one personal convenience bucket that we kept in the corner of the cell. The stench seemed unrelenting, and though we emptied and rinsed it daily, it continued to ripen.

That first morning after the move we got up and heard church bells ringing from somewhere in the city of Hanoi. We knew it was Sunday morning and having a longing for home I said, "I think I would like to do some of the normal things that I did on Sundays."

Mike McGrath spoke up, "From what I've seen in the other camps I think most guys have some kind of church service on Sunday. In another compound they had pounded on the wall to make church call, then we all prayed together but in our individual cells."

We decided to pray together and were getting ready to stand up when Konrad stopped us saying, "Why don't we cover up a little bit out of respect?" I was pleased with that, and we got on our long-sleeved shirts and pajama-type bottoms, and since we all knew the Lord's Prayer, we prayed aloud:

"Our Father which art in heaven. Hallowed be thy name. Thy kingdom come, thy will be done on earth, as it is in heaven. Give us this day our daily bread. And forgive us our debts as we forgive our debtors. And lead us not into temptation, but deliver us from evil: for thine is the kingdom, and the power, and the glory, forever. Amen."[2]

Ready to sit down again, Konrad stopped us. "You guys, there is something else we ought to do. We ought to pledge allegiance to the flag."

We faced east which was toward home to where an American flag

was flying. With a hand placed over our heart we pledged together:
"I pledge allegiance to the flag of the United States of America and to the Republic for which it stands, one nation under God, indivisible with liberty and justice for all."

From that first Sunday it became our weekly routine, further embellishing our services with short sermons, each taking turns.

After that first day, part of each morning and afternoon was set aside for exercise as we tried to get body parts working again. Konrad, Mike, and I were still nursing wounds. Mike's arm was so mangled that the shoulder blade stuck out on top of his collarbone and the arm, which had rotated forward, hung on his chest. He had been in the Hilton for five months and was still in pain. Konrad, forced to march barefoot for miles through jungle to Hanoi after capture, had swollen feet of proportions that his toes were indiscernible on his feet. Gerry seemed to be in better health than the rest of us. Even though it had been two months since I received the bullet wound to my head, it remained infected and bled, and I had contusions and scabs on my legs and arms from resisting The Cat and Pig Eye. My arms had turned black when the ropes had been cinched down on my forearms that cut off circulation. Because of contraction of muscles and rotation of arms in the sockets, my hands were useless. I resolved to gently exercise them, but couldn't move my fingers. I would say, "Fingers move," but they lay limp and lifeless. November came and the turnkey brought in a razor, but I couldn't hold it. A month went by—December, a razor was brought in again—I could hold it but I couldn't unscrew the handle to put in a new blade. Then I got one finger flexed, but couldn't get it straightened back out. No way could I do a push-up, though later I did push-ups off my knees instead of my toes.

After exercise, about ten o'clock, we ate rice and swamp green soup. I concluded that the recipe for this swamp green soup was to mow lawn, dump grass clippings in boiling water, serve. But I ate it anyway, besides anything the other guys refused to eat, not knowing if there were leaner days ahead. Afternoons we exercised again and had school. Each of us had something to teach. Konrad spoke German, so we learned German. About four o'clock, we had rice and swamp green soup again. In the evening we tried to do something fun, tell a shoot-down story or tell about the first car we owned. Our mosquito netting had a duplicating pattern of square reinforced seams which made an adequate playing board for chess and checkers, and we chose different colored mortar and rocks for chessmen. Hungry most of the time, we agreed not to mention food, especially in the evening. That accounted for our daily routine, as we became part of the list of unknowns who blackened the walls with our sweaty backs.

Sleeping on a thin straw mat on the concrete floor, the nights from the time the sun went down until it got light in the mornings were elongated. We all had calluses on our thighs and on calves of our legs from turning to one side and then flailing to the other in our efforts to assuage discomfort. Then it was a long day from sun up until sundown. Time unbelievably stretched and inflated so that I felt that a day equaled a month back home. In summer we sweltered in sultry heat, and in winter shivered through cold nights. Words of familiar hymns or a prayer would comfort my spirit during those long nights "... The day is past and gone; the shadows of the evening fall; the night is coming on. Within my heart a welcome guest... O Savior stay this night with me... "[3] During this time there was screaming in the night from cells around us. That was not a fun thing to hear.

There were two cells in each building. I could press my cup to the wall with my ear against the cup, wrap my blanket over my head, and the sound was amplified enough so that I could hear the guy in the next cell. But I didn't know who occupied the remaining nine buildings at the Annex camp. When we were outside for a few minutes each day to wash we were the only ones out. The common wash area had a well, a table, and a rack where we stored our dishes after washing them, and knew there were many POWs by the number of dishes. We began drilling a hole with a nail into mortar of the brick wall near the sink where we all washed. Each time we went out to wash, we drilled it a little deeper, then plugged the hole with a glue mixture of sand, rice, and water. Eventually a small piece of toilet paper containing a message could be concealed in it, and word spread to other POWs through the walls that we had a message center established.

We began compiling a list of POWs, which was an important step since we didn't know who or how many were incarcerated. Sometimes we bypassed plugging the message in the hole when a POW could see the guard was taking his sieso (siesta), and on those occasions we threw it back and forth over the walls from our small walled-in area to the next. One day, after the POW list had lengthened, it inadvertently went over the ten-foot outside wall landing on a sidewalk. We had to begin again. Another day when it was thrown, it fell short and landed near a guard taking his sieso—miraculously a POW was able to get out of his cell and quietly recover it. Discovery meant torture and we had times of panic, but after many months the POW list was completed which had over a hundred and fifty names of Americans at the Annex. The list revealed Konrad was not only senior ranking officer of our cell, but over the rest of the Annex as well.

Besides the message center, POWs among the different camps were proficient in using a tap code and by this means could communicate with men in other buildings. The compound often resonated and reverberated like a colony of woodpeckers from the rhythmical tapping of a code on a wall, using a broom, or by a flash code utilizing a patch of sunlight under a cell door to flash shadows across it spelling out words and messages. An unusual message arrived one day to our room it read, "At Briarpatch a POW named Jerry acts crazy—rides a motorcycle." It occupied our minds and we made mental images of this guy riding his imaginary motorcycle in prison. "He used to wash the motorcycle in the courtyard. . . polish it and ride it everywhere he went—to bathe, to pick up his food—everywhere—making the noise of the engine with his lips. He was just having some fun. The Vietnamese thought he was crazy, and some of us did too, at first. Then word got around that the camp commander. . .called this man into an interrogation and told him that he could no longer be allowed to ride his motorcycle in the camp. 'There isn't room to maneuver it in here,' the serious faced Vietnamese commander said. 'Besides, we don't let the other prisoners ride their motorcycles and so you are not allowed to either.'" (Heslop 45) It felt good to laugh. This was a ridiculously absurd spoof by Jerry to trample the rules so stringently enforced on us. The rules were:

-You are the blackest of criminals. We are very lenient and humane, we'll keep you alive (though we wish you were dead), but we'll keep you alive.

-You criminals are under obligation to give full and clear written or oral answers to all questions raised by camp authorities. All attempts and tricks to evade answering questions will be considered manifestations of obstinacy and antagonism, which deserves strict punishment.

-Criminals must demonstrate a cautious and polite attitude to the officers and guards and stand at attention, bow a greeting, and await further orders.

-Criminals may sit only when permission is granted.

-Criminals must remain silent. No talking. Total silence is necessary at all times.

-If criminal is allowed to ask a question, he must say [the servile phrase] bao cao.

-Criminals may not bring into camp anything.

-Criminals must keep rooms clean.

-Criminals must go to bed and arise in accordance with the signal of the gong.

-If criminal tries to escape from the camp he will be seriously punished.

We were indignant about being called criminals since we were prisoners of war, but our captors wouldn't comply with Geneva Convention rules, consequently, guards referred to us as criminals—the blackest of criminals. Nevertheless, we took comfort in the fact that we were with other American POWs and guided by senior officers among us.

Senior ranking Colonel John Flynn USAF, isolated and ravaged by torture during most of his imprisonment was frequently unable to command. Other senior ranking officers who commanded were Cdr. James Stockdale USN,[4] Lt. Col. Robby Risner USAF, Cdr. Jerry Denton USN, Lt. Col. Hervey Stockman USAF, depending on who was able to command, or enduring torture or isolation unable to communicate. A senior ranking officer (SRO) commanded in each cell and an SRO was over each detention camp. The SROs made decisions and promoted military conduct within his sphere of authority, however, some men were arrogant and unwilling to bow to their captors or follow prison rules. If they were forced to lower their heads and bow ninety degrees to their captors, some were also disposed to impudently bow to the pig whose pen graced an outer wall of a cell and bow to the trees and to the well where we washed our shorts. The mocking mirth ignited their indomitably free spirits, as they continued to demonstrate in small ways their unwillingness to succumb to subjection.

THERE AIN'T NO WAY — BUT THERE WAS A WAY

As Christmas approached, I became too despondent to reflect on it. Christmas was home and my children and wife, and I couldn't contemplate it imprisoned, it was too painful. Regardless, Christmas Eve came anyway, and to everyone's astonishment, the camp radio in poorest fidelity played Christmas music. The peep hatch on the door opened and someone pushed in something. The minister of the Evangelical Church of the Democratic Republic of Vietnam had gifts. Four small plastic bags each containing a tangerine, a cookie and a few pieces of candy were pushed through the small opening. We stayed up late visiting about past Christmases, and I regretted that I hadn't promoted the spirit of Christmas.

When the camp gong dispelled the quiet of morning, we took advantage of its being Christmas morning and the four of us slept in. Startled by the sound of keys outside and a bang on the door, we scrambled to our feet. Konrad and I stumbled around looking for our missing Ho Chi Minh rubber-tire sandals. "Hurry" the other two whispered, "the turnkey is coming!" Each with one sandal on and one sandal off, bolted toward the door and then stopped in amazement. Across the room in the corner was a Christmas tree. Santa had been there! I felt the exquisite feeling of other Christmas mornings. For an instant through our sleepy eyes and hurried confusion, it was a Christmas tree. The guard yelled at us to line up, the spell was broken and the beautiful tree became a small broom placed handle down in a teapot with gauze from Mike's bandages wrapped and swaged like garlands. Tangerine peelings and candy wrappers stuck between broom straws imitated ornaments and scattered beneath were leaves stealthily gathered outside on previous days. The two missing sandals were in front of the tree with two colorfully wrapped candy pieces placed on them. I learned a valuable lesson that Christmas day—even when I think there is no way, there is a way. After that when I had a sock on Christmas Eve, I hung it on the mosquito net line. There was always something in it Christmas mornings. My companions knew I loved to fly fish and on one Christmas morning there were flies in my stocking—albeit dead houseflies, another year a needle made from a bone. The gifts we gave each other were thoughtful, though often imaginary and intangible, they were meaningful gifts given with ceremony and received with gratitude.

An event we seldom experienced was using a pencil. To write, I sharpened the end of a broom straw by rubbing it on concrete and making ink from brick dust and water, or on occasion, made ink from dye off the first washing of my prison clothes. One day Rabbit brought in pencils and paper and a letter from a lady in Michigan entitled, "To the Mothers in Vietnam." In it she expressed her compassion for sons killed in the war, "Our sons are dying, your sons are dying," and it was very sympathetic and compassionate.

"You tell us what you think about this and write it on this paper," Rabbit explained. I was resistive and chose not to write anything, and we all felt the same.

Next morning Rabbit came in screaming mad because we hadn't written anything. He commanded, "You write!"

Well, I thought we better write something, and I looked over on Mike's paper which read, "I don't have anything to say about that." So that's what we all wrote, and when Rabbit came back he appeared so happy that we had written something. Taking the papers out and shutting the door, we bent to a crack in the door and watched, and after taking a few steps he stopped and read them. I could see the red going up the back of his neck when furiously he read, "We don't have anything to say about that." He came back in.

"Put your hands up and keep them up, and you'll live this way the rest of the time you are here!" he demanded. And he slammed the door and went stomping out.

We put our arms down and all said, "Whow! That wasn't too bad."

In another minute Tonto opened the door and set up a machine gun on a tripod in the open doorway.

"You get over against wall and keep hands up. Don't lean against wall!" he commanded. So we stood all day with our hands up. When the gong clanged to go to bed, he said, "I put up machine gun, let you sleep." Man! I lay down on my concrete bed that had felt so hard before, and it felt like a pillow that night. I never slept so well in one night in my life.

The next morning the machine gun and Tonto returned and he barked, "Put hands up over head!" Day after day that went on with only a break at about ten o'clock for rice and swamp green soup, and four o'clock for rice and swamp green soup. We were not allowed time to relieve ourselves and after a while we started to smell so bad that Tonto moved farther and farther out into the hall. As the days wore on, he moved farther away and we learned to spread out along the wall. In doing this one guy was obscured from Tonto, and when he wasn't paying attention, we would rotate so each of us could put our arms down and get a little rest. It appeared that Rabbit was going to be true to his word because this went on every day for three or four weeks. Then, luckily, the Tet holiday came along and Tonto and machine gun didn't return. Vietnamese were big on self-torture stuff, there were many times that we had to kneel on concrete with hands over our heads for long periods of time, often a guard placed a pebble under our knees greatly increasing pain.

THE ESCAPE

After there had been a few unsuccessful escape attempts, orders came down from SRO Lt. Col. Risner that no escape attempt would be approved unless a prisoner had assistance from the outside because the odds of success were so poor. There was a bounty on each American of $1500, an incentive that made Vietnamese watchful of any man that stood a foot taller, besides we wore striped prison pajamas, and the Hanoi Hilton was in the center of downtown Hanoi, a city of three million people. Jungle lay beyond the city and we were all well aware of it. One morning draped over a fence in the courtyard, a poisonous snake that had been captured and killed in one of the cells the night before, captivated our attention as we watched it completely devoured by insects in three hours—totally, including skin and backbone—nothing remained of it. About this time the guard forgot to lock our cell at night. The thought of that unlocked door plagued us, and we discussed escape as the night wore on. All four of us concluded, so we make it out of the compound, then what?

But Capt. John Dramesi USAF in a cell next to ours, became obsessed with the Code of Conduct that required POWs to "make every effort to escape." He had a well thought out escape plan and patiently waited for a rainy night. One night in the middle of May of 1969, Dramesi climbed up through the air vent in the ceiling of his cell, and through a hole in the brick wall that adjoined our cell, threw a piece of mortar through the ventilating hole in our ceiling to talk to Konrad, SRO at the Annex.

"Is that you, Dramesi?" I responded.

He whispered, "Ask Trautman if Atterberry and I have permission to go tonight."

Between the order from SRO Risner not to escape unless there was help from the outside, and Dramesi's and Atterberry's[5] courage and determination to follow the Code of Conduct, Konrad could neither give his blessing nor give the order for them to stay put. Dramesi replied emphatically, "We're going tonight!"

Smearing their skin with a brown paste made of brick dust mixed with iodine to darken their skin color, Dramesi and Atteberry went up through the attic to the tile roof, climbed down the lightning rod, and dropped down between buildings. Each man had mosquito netting camouflaged with sticks, which he enveloped himself in. They inched their way among the shadows to the outside wall of the camp. Carrying a supply of food that their cellmates had helped them obtain during months of preparation, along with iodine pills for water purification, they climbed up on the outhouse roof, shinnied onto the top of the ten-foot wall surrounding the prison, shorted out electrified wires on the wall, then plunged off into a garbage bin of decaying fish heads in a downtown street. They stopped there to don a disguise. Turning their prison garb inside out, they fastened prison-made surgical masks over their faces—not uncommon for Vietnamese to protect themselves from disease on the streets. Months before they had stolen baskets and shoulder poles, and had woven hats from coarse broom straws, which they used and placed a coolie hat on their heads. Hiking on foot undiscovered before dawn, they covered four or five miles. But after daylight when search patrols were out, they were recaptured and placed in the infamous Room 18 of the building we nicknamed the Zoo.

During torture reprisals that followed, Atteberry's life ebbed and eventually slipped away after the first week. Dramesi endured severe torture and isolation throughout the summer months and early fall. Consequences of the escape attempt on the rest of us were enormous. Since Konrad was senior officer for the Annex and had the last word with Dramesi before escaping, he was pulled out of our cell and tortured. Vietnamese guards went from room to room pulling out senior officers one by one for torture until the entire prison had felt their wrath. Senior officer Major George Day USAF was beaten all day—he quit counting at three hundred blows, and then he was forced to kneel all night—that went on for four consecutive days and nights. Lt. Cdr. Eugene McDaniel USN suffered seven hundred lashes, given electric shocks, bound in irons and hung from the ceiling by his arms even though one arm had a compound fracture. The senior officers confined in handcuffs and leg stocks and on half rations for the next five months, were tortured until they cracked and divulged both communication and organization networks. The Vietnamese issued the men in leg stocks a bamboo tube to use to draw off their urine.

I likely escaped from the indiscriminate torture because of an infected thigh, swollen twice its size, and I couldn't walk, but guards came into the cell and plugged up light and ventilation holes—chinking up cracks, bricking up vents, and boarding up the window from the outside. The cells had previously been self-storage vaults, and in the heat of summer without any ventilation in our cell, the inside temperature likely rose to 130 degrees F. We all had unbearable heat rash that blistered, then festered, and felt like porcupine quills sticking everywhere. I slept with elbows bent and forearms upright, not bearing to have anything touch my skin. Adding discomfort, my infected eyes were swollen shut. Sun radiated all day on the outside walls and at night that heat radiated inside. The Vietnamese were sensitive about nudity and always bathed with their underclothes on; consequently, we were required to have shorts on at all times. During this hot time some of the guys took their shorts off and slept nude. Guards hauled one man out and beat him with a hose and when he returned his back resembled hamburger. Reprisals from the escape of Dramesi and Atteberry continued through the summer until fall, and before ending, we had experienced the most violent terror during our captivity.

THE ANODYNE FOR PAIN

With the coming of fall weather in 1969, The Cat announced major policy changes regarding prisoners, principally because Ho Chi Minh had died on 3 September 1969. He admitted some guards had far exceeded the accepted level of torture, and the brutality would stop. Prison rules slowly changed, but food improved immediately both in quality and quantity. Guards had confiscated our mail. Now, occasionally, we heard of one or two guys getting letters, then more frequently. However, as soon as we began receiving letters from home, they frequently contained devastatingly bad news about deaths in the family and tragic occurrences. On one day there were at least twelve men who received letters that read their wives had divorced them. Wives were tired of waiting, didn't know if we were alive and wanted to get on with living.

It was toward Christmas of that year when a guard came to our cell and motioned to me by putting his hand on his wrist which I interpreted to mean put on my long sleeved shirt and follow him to the office. They called me by the name of Xet. He sat down at a table.

"Would you like a letter?" he inquired. It was interesting as time progressed that some of the guards learned to speak English without an accent. I had been locked up about twenty-eight months by then without any word from home, and I didn't know if my wife Marjorie and children even knew whether I was alive.

"You bet," I said. He picked up a letter, not allowing me to touch it, but showing me the envelope. I didn't recognize the handwriting, and I was immediately dejected. Some of the guys had received letters from well-wishing strangers and they had been appreciated but were not what we wanted to receive. He let me read it if I gave it back.

It started out—

Dear Dad,
We all miss you. We are following your instructions.
I just got my Eagle last Sunday...

... Love, Cameron

This is from my oldest boy! No wonder I didn't recognize his writing, it has changed in two and a half years. "Following my instructions." Whow! I didn't think any of them heard one thing I said when I was home. This is good! I started to smile. I went back and told my cellmates, "Hey guys, my boy just got his Eagle Scout!" And all day I smiled and it filled my heart and by evening my face began to hurt and that was surprising to me. I didn't know that I had been using only frown muscles. That was all I could talk about to all the guys. I smiled all that day and the next day and the next. My face muscles were sore by the end of that time, and I thought that was humorous, too.

Dearest Marjorie, Cameron, Heather, Warren, Holly and Heidi,
Above all I seek for eternal life with all of you. These are important: temple marriage, mission, college. Press on. I had a slight flesh wound and last summer some sickness. All is well now.
Set goals, write history, take pictures twice a year.
Dec. 13, 1969
Jay Criddle Hess

To sow contention, the guards let some guys write a letter and denied others the same privilege, finally, I was allowed to write home. I could only write seven lines on their form, and it would be cut and censored unless I worded it carefully. I composed in my mind over and over what I would write. I wrote of things that I deemed important to my family and beyond the understanding of a Vietnamese censor.

I hoped Marjorie could read between the lines and know my anguish at not being with them.

On the stamp of one envelope pictured Neil Armstrong walking on the moon. This was surprising news that we had no knowledge of, and we discussed the ramifications for many days. The months slowly passed, each one identical with the last one until November.

THE SON TAY RAID—AND UNITY

On the night of 21 November 1970, aircraft and SAMS [Surface to Air Missiles] were exploding about twenty miles away, the ground shook, and it was an exciting night. I learned American commandos attacked Son Tay detention camp to rescue American POWs interned there. Sadly, four months earlier the POWs had been moved to other detention camps so there was no one to rescue. Afterwards the Vietnamese moved all prisoners from small outlying detention camps into Camp Unity at the Hanoi Hilton, including myself. Now there were fifty men to a room, sleeping twenty-five on each side of the room. It was great to meet everyone and put faces with names.

On the first day Captain Bob Purcell USAF, the SRO of the room, called everybody together and said Lt. Rod Knutson, Navy pilot from Montana, had something to announce. Rod got up,

"Okay guys I got something that's important to me. I've got a flag that I have flown every day in this POW camp." He showed a little piece of brown paper 2 ½ x 4 inches glued on a piece of wire. I had made small flags, I believe everyone had, and we respected his request. He hoisted it every morning on the wire that held the mosquito netting, and took it down every night. The guards often gave shakedown inspections, tore everything apart and confiscated stuff—somebody had made a deck of cards, or wrote a book on toilet paper, or secreted a nail—but they never discovered the flag, and we felt fortunate.

Of the many issues we wanted to protest two gave us the most irritation, being called a criminal and having our packages from home pilfered. But having to shower with our shorts on was the rule the men decided to test. Bug acquiesced without too much difficulty and constructed a fence around the area where we bathed. We felt that we had scored, and pondered what our resistance ought to be. Tension mounted when we asked for a Bible. Finally, Bug said, "Okay, we'll let you have a Bible. Choose one man and he can go out and copy from it for a half-hour and bring the copy back into the cell." I was chosen. I copied the Sermon on the Mount, then checked the 23rd Psalm to make sure we were saying that right. We had an argument about the names of Christ's disciples, and by the time I looked that up my thirty minutes were up.

A short time after that a guard pulled me out of cell 2 at Unity at the Hanoi Hilton and moved me to a detention camp that we called the Zoo, a few miles away on the outskirts of Hanoi. The move to the Zoo didn't appear to occur for any particular reason other than shuffling POWs about. However, a significant event occurred there. The cell had an open window with bars on it. Standing near the window one day looking out, a guard passed by and handed me a Bible through the window and whispered, "I will pick it up tomorrow morning." Oh, to have a book to read! And to have the Bible—it meant so much. I read it throughout that day and all through the night and finished it by the time the guard came the next day. While reading, I pictured events into plays with scenes and acts to remember it.

THE CHURCH RIOT, SKITS, AND SCHOOL

I was returned to Camp Unity after a couple of weeks just before the showdown began. Allowed to mill around buildings and talk quietly to one person at a time, we couldn't congregate in a group or hold meetings. SRO Stockdale agreed it was time to exert pressure to hold church meetings and committed, "Even if our new life of ease was at stake, so be it." It happened one day after Christmas when I heard someone singing from Building 4. The words were slurred, but I knew the tune and slowly it came back into my rusty mind, "When upon life's billows you are tempest tossed, when you are discouraged thinking all is lost, count your many blessing every doubt will fly, and you will be singing as the days go by."[6] It startled me and I proclaimed, I know that song! It was Jack Rollins getting his cell's choir ready for an unusual church service that week. Despite the ban on organized meetings and noise, with boldness his chorus sang out encouraging other rooms to sing out. It finally busted wide open on 7 February 1971, afterward called the Church Riot. One room sang The Star Spangled Banner, another room sang God Bless America with more volume, and another sang even louder America the Beautiful. The entire camp reverberated like a stadium cheering section. Then in the ruckus a guy in building 7 started chanting, "This's building number 7, number 7, number 7, and this went on through all the buildings and we were chanting as if we were in a stadium cheering section. Turnkeys Hawk and Ichabod tried to stop us, but couldn't. Soon Bug dispatched helmeted reinforcements with tear gas and bayonets and hauled many senior officers away putting them in leg irons for the next month. We had won some significant points and felt the score was now Lions 2, Christians 8.

Life significantly changed for the better after the Church Riot. Allowed to congregate for church meetings, entertainment, and educational classes, in the evenings we put on skits, plays, parodies, jokes, take-offs on television commercials, and musicals, and I don't believe I've laughed so hard before or since. Guys using falsetto voices spoke and sang girls' parts, costumes were imaginative, and the talent and ingenuity were enormous. We joked about our serious predicament and reveled in feelings of esprit de corps, and felt delicious excitement because it was beyond the guards' comprehension.

Besides entertainment, we organized educational classes every afternoon putting our minds to work advantaged by the high level of education present. One guy took a brick chip and wrote on the concrete floor, subjects. We then hollered out subjects we were competent to teach while he wrote them: Quantum Physics, Russian, German, Spanish, Evening at the Movies, History, Golf Instruction, How to Butcher Meat, Psychology, Religion, Sociology, Mathematics, Music, Geometry, Astronomy, and Wine Tasting. Then we took the brick chip and marked the subjects we were interested in learning about. The most popular subject was History and the second Religion. Obviously we didn't have textbooks and after heated arguments arose regarding facts, we agreed to settle on "Hanoi Facts," which amounted to the best information available from the group. The camaraderie that developed from entertainment, classes, and church meetings, improved our lives in the months to follow.

December of 1972 we heard the roar of jet engines overhead. Vietnamese fired missiles over our camp for the next ten days. Aircraft in flames tumbled from the sky and bombs exploded. Abruptly it stopped—it was quiet. Things changed. Guards no longer manned guard towers. Treatment improved measurably—guards brought baskets of bread and left them at the cell doors in the morning—we had craved bread the most and rarely had any. Cells were unlocked in the morning and we could come and go freely, only locked up at night. Once in a while a guard gave a prisoner a bottle of beer, or a Popsicle. We all received a banana. A few days later on Christmas, silence prevailed. Shortly after that we were allowed to stand in military formation in the courtyard for the first time. Rabbit announced there was a cease-fire, peace talks in Paris, and "You will be going home in thirty days." We heard it, but we didn't believe it, because in the past every time they had given us a banana we had got emotional and thought we were going home. The SRO organized us into the Fourth POW Wing and our motto became, "Return with Honor." Should release be imminent, we would follow accepted military procedure with no early releases, the sick and convalescent first, then sequentially each man according to the date of his capture.

I lay on my plank bed those last few weeks and thought of many things. I concluded you can't fight somebody else's war for them. The Vietnamese' measure of victory was when every American left their country, even if it meant fighting to the last man—or woman. No goals or measurements existed for victory for the United States forces, we had been sent over to help and our targets were politically plotted from the Oval Office.

Then I mused over hours and days that were in five and a half years. "Let me see," I calculated: "I had clocked 2,680 hours flying; I have been imprisoned about 2,029 days that's nearly 50,000 hours. That means I've spent 18 hours as a POW for each hour I spent in the cockpit—hmm that should get rid of any desire to fly again." Then while out in the courtyard a few days later two MiG-21s happened to fly low over the camp. In envy, I sighed, "Ah those lucky guys!"

America became so dear to me. Something happens to feelings about America when you leave it. It takes on the same special importance that you feel about your family, your hometown, your school, or your team. When you serve your country, you take pride in it and love it. I yearned for America.

Before I came back, I dreamed.
Some dreams put a smile on my face.
They were dreams of people and places and things.
My Favorite Things in America.

I dreamed of cool dawn air and of water,
of a home to build and a mountain stream,
of opportunities that I've let pass by,
of something to help me breathe, and to help the pain,
and of some way to help my friend.

I dreamed of evergreens flocked with snow,
contrails marking against the antiseptic blue of a free sky,
piercing through the gray and haze
to climb on top to that great sun-splashed vacant stage,
flashing craft alive to eager touch,
dives and zooms and lazy rolls and running free.

I dreamed of cherry trees in flowery blossom,
babbling meadow brooks,
fresh plowed field under a carpet and swirling cloud of seagulls,
the early morning call of the Redwing blackbird,
the smell of new mown hay,
the sight of brilliant autumn leaves
and sparkling untracked snow.

I dreamed of the sound of laughter and play and people.
It made me forget the doors I couldn't open,
the dirt, the heat,
the cold, the guards,
the wasted hours and days and weeks.

I dreamed of a hand to touch,
of people I love,
people—my people,
my friends, my family,
who are on my side—to help.

I dreamed of a book to read,
a song to sing,
a goal to reach, a task to do,
a lesson to learn,
Something to do.

I dreamed of steel chargers with skies to roam,
but mostly I dreamed of just going home.
Away from war and separation,
to my favorite things in America,

To Freedom—to say the things I want to say,
To Freedom—to go where I want to go and without fear,
To Freedom—to speak to God in my own way.
To Home.
To Freedom.
To America!

*

Editor's Note:

The North Vietnamese released Colonel Hess on 14 March 1973. He was awarded the Silver Star with Second Bronze Oak Leaf Cluster, the Legion of Merit, the Distinguished Flying Cross with Second Bronze Oak Leaf Cluster, the Air Medal with First Silver Oak Leaf Cluster, the Purple Heart with First Bronze Oak Leaf Cluster, the Bronze Star with First Bronze Oak Leaf Cluster and the Prisoner of War Medal.

Before his imprisonment, Colonel Hess attended Weber State University, Brigham Young University and University of Utah, and received a B.S. in Aeronautical Engineering from the Air Force Institute of Technology (AFIT) at Wright-Patterson AFB Ohio. He be-

came an aviation cadet in 1953, completing training at Columbus AFB Mississippi, Greenville AFB Mississippi, and Williams AFB Arizona. As a Second Lieutenant he was assigned to the Air Defense Command at MacDill AFB Florida, completed Combat Pilot Training at Moody AFB Georgia in 1956 stationed at Kinchloe AFB Michigan flying the F-89 and the F-102. After graduating from AFIT in 1962, he was assigned to the Tactical Air Command and stationed at George AFB California, Bitburg AB Germany, Cam Rahn Bay, South Vietnam, and Takhli Royal Thai AB Thailand flying the F-4 and F-105 when he was shot down.

"I spent most of my twenty active duty years waiting. At Bitburg Air Base Germany I waited on five minute alert near the end of the runway with my flight gear set up in the cockpit of an airplane that had a nuclear bomb in it.

"I waited behind locked doors for our longest war to end."

Colonel Hess retired from the United States Air Force on 1 November 1973, and continued his career as Air Force Junior ROTC Aerospace Science instructor at Clearfield High School, Clearfield, Utah for the ensuing twenty-two years. Presently married to Michelle Martin Hess of Layton, Utah, they are the parents of two daughters, Shantay, born on Veterans Day 1987, and Kenzley born in 1996, and reside at Farmington, Utah. He has five married children from a former marriage, Cameron Hess, Heather Nibley, Dr. Warren Hess, Holly Dunn, and Heidi Johnson, and has twenty-five grandchildren.

*****

---

[1] Colonel Robert White earned astronaut wings flying the X-15; later promoted to general.

[2] St. Matthew 6:9-13.

[3] *Abide With Me*, Hofford and Millard.

[4] Recipient of Medal of Honor for leading resistance among POWs—imprisoned in Vietnam for eight years.

[5] Capt. Edwin Atterberry USAF.

[6] *Count your Blessings*, Oatman and Excell

Major Jay C. Hess greeting daughter Heidi
after 5 ½ years as POW in Vietnam *Courtesy of Jay Hess*

Captain Jay C. Hess, "Shark Four"
Courtesy of Jay C. Hess

CHAPTER 12

COLONEL
PAUL H. JOHNSON

Col. Paul H. Johnson
POW Liaison Team
U.S. Army Military Police

THE LAST PLANE OUT

HANOI, NORTH VIETNAM—14 MARCH 1973

I was seated at the table under a canopy of camouflage netting on the tarmac's edge at Gia Lam airport. Seated at the table with me were twenty other officers representing North Vietnam, South Vietnam, Vietcong, and US. A curious crowd in a carnival atmosphere had gathered along the fence line to observe the release of American prisoners of war. A discordant conglomerate of four or five hundred international press with flash paraphernalia hovered.

Tension mounted and the crowd hushed when buses braked. It was noon, and the sun was jungle hot. One hundred and eight American POWs stepped out wearing new gray shirts, dark blue pants, and black shoes, carrying black gym bags. They marched up to a roped-off area on the tarmac in front of the table where we sat. Parked a hundred feet beyond our table was a C-141 aircraft.

Some airmen had been imprisoned for nine years. Time had stood still for these men bound in rat-infested holes—sweltering in summer, freezing in winter, while we were enmeshed in a race for manned-moon explorations.

I peered closely into faces of these men unaccustomed to sun who were suddenly on world's center stage. Their expressions were rigid, somber, perplexed, and uncertain. None smiled. Disappointment had been their daily fare. Each time they had been given the rare treat of a banana they thought the guards were fattening them up prior to release. Now, with emotions guarded they were unresponsive.

Commissar of North Vietnamese prison camps Major Bui, who had received the nickname of The Cat by the POWs, called out in flawless English, "Line up in a column of two and march forward." As they drew closer a few looked beyond our table at the C-141 and saw the American flag painted on the tail of the aircraft. The sight of the American flag rippled through the columns of men, and their stiffness vanished—some dared to grin; yet no man broke the silence.

"As your name is called step forward and go home," barked The Cat facing the POWs.

"Major H. C. Copeland." The Cat began calling out the list of 108 names.

A waiting Air Force general warmly shook both his hands and said, "Welcome home son," and motioned him toward the plane. As each man walked to the aircraft an American officer of the same rank greeted him. Each escort had been briefed on the airman's family and home status so that he could inform him during the flight to Clark Air Force Base in the Philippines.

The Cat continued, "Commander John McCain—step forward and go home."

McCain stepped forward limping and saluted the general.

"Commander McCain reporting for duty, sir."

Toward the end of the list was the name of a Utahn, imprisoned for five and a half years.

"Major Jay Hess—step forward and go home," The Cat called out.

Hess said later that he got a glimpse of the C-141 as the bus pulled up, and there arose within him exquisite feelings of joy when he saw the American flag on the aircraft. Hess stepped up smartly to the general, saluted.

"Major Hess reporting for duty, sir."[1] These were men who barely felt the pavement underfoot as they headed toward the aircraft. They were released according to the date they were captured adhering resolutely to their motto "Return with Honor," wishing no special concessions. This was the fifth and final group of men released from the infamous Hoa Lo Prison, renamed Hanoi Hilton by the five hundred American airmen from the Air Force, Navy and Marine Corps whose bloody backs had stained Hoa Lo's Knobby Room walls.

SAIGON THREE MONTHS EARLIER

When the Paris peace talks were wrapping up and the war was winding down, I was transferred from serving as a POW advisor at Phu Quoc Island in the Gulf of Siam to Saigon. There I became a team member on The Four Party Joint Military Commission to shut down the war—specifically to negotiate exchanges of American and Vietnamese POWs.

How do you end war? I searched the military manuals for subjects on shutting down war, and found only—How to Conduct a War. Our broad guidelines came from the Paris Peace Accords:

- Americans and Allied Forces must be out of Vietnam by 31 March 1973;

- Vietnamese Prisoners of War must be returned to the province where captured. No small task since we held 30,000 just on Phu Quoc Island and there were enemy POWs captured from one end of Vietnam to the other.

- Release of prisoners of war would be by The Four Party Military Commission representing governments of North Vietnam, South Vietnam, Provisional Revolutionary Government—generally known as Vietcong, and US.

There were about twenty teams—teams to locate downed aircraft, missing Americans, missing Vietcong, and missing Vietnamese, orphaned children, graves registration, and others. I was one of the officers assigned to the Prisoner of War Liaison Team. Our primary responsibility was to coordinate with our enemies the locations of POWs, ensure their safety, and transport them home.

We sat down with our enemies in Saigon. Most of the North Vietnamese were suave political military officers. They all spoke perfect English; most of them had been educated in the United States. From their arrogance they were apparently from the aristocratic ruling class. Ceremony precluded any business, and we learned it was prudent to observe their customs. The civilities as I perceived them, were to impress upon us they were our hosts and we the strangers in their land. Whether in the middle of a jungle clearing with only a handful of Vietnamese POWs to return, or amid more pleasant surroundings, the ceremony was the same. It began with three toasts with rice wine or ale. Usually a toast was made to President Nixon, another one to Ho Chi Minh. We refused to toast to Ho, —and so it went. The rice wine was very much like drinking kerosene with a dash of black powder. We learned early on to buy a large loaf of French bread and eat it before arriving. The bread efficiently absorbed the alcohol and kept us focused for business. There was an American refreshment table with Coca-Cola, 7-Up, Gingerale, Hershey chocolate bars, and American brand cigarettes.

Next came the presentation of credentials. Since there were actually five teams working on POW repatriation and team members rotated duties, we presented credentials at each meeting. The North Vietnamese quibbled over trivialities. Sometimes it was about our rank or titles, sometimes because we referred to prisoners as detainees, when they insisted they be called good Communists. Often we would have to ungraciously huff and bluff about bringing out our Protocol book before they would acquiesce. Finally, we were ready for business.

"How are we going to arrange releases for these prisoners? Where are Americans detained?" I inquired. Maps were unrolled and we discovered our immense task. There were fifteen imprisoned in the middle of the jungle here, and twenty-five in another spot over there, and small groups like that all over North Vietnam. There had been 771 Americans captured; 113 had died during imprisonment. Of the 658 that remained, approximately 500 were detained in and around Hanoi.[2]

We put into motion the POW exchanges combining them into one operation, arranging transportation for our men home and returning the North Vietnamese and Vietcong to the province in which they were captured. By helicopter our team, along with pilot and crew chief, landed in small clearings the size of a living room. The jungle forests had a triple canopy of foliage dense enough to land a helicopter on, had we wanted to land there. Our hosts insisted we conduct these exchanges without carrying sidearms and during those first few exchanges it was extremely unnerving to meet the Vietcong and North Vietnamese unarmed in the jungle. Occasionally, we encountered North Vietnamese that didn't want to go home. We placed them under protective guard so that their brothers wouldn't kill them, and then arranged their return to South Vietnam.

Regardless of remoteness of jungle exchanges, neither the carping over trivialities, nor toasting ceremonies, nor variety of refreshments ever changed. I was continually amazed to see ice on the refreshment table at every jungle exchange. I looked forward to the exchanges made at rubber plantations. Besides having well-cleared areas in the jungle for our helicopter to land, they were quiet, reminiscent of our languid Deep South, and had a fragrance deliciously like perfume.

OUR FIRST MEETING WITH AMERICAN POWS IN HANOI

Our Vietnamese hosts had invited us to events during the morning of 14 March 1973 prior to the release of the 108 American POWs at Gia Lam airport in the afternoon. The day began with a hosted grand tour of the very old, very tired, severely bombed city of Hanoi. Citizens were riding bicycles or cyclos; our motorized vehicles were the only ones on the streets. Some youths wore red kerchiefs or red armbands showing their revolutionary allegiance to the Communist Party.

At the conclusion of the tour we were driven to Hoa Binh Hotel for a mid-morning banquet. The special banquet was not just for my team; expected were generals and colonels from both North Vietnam and South Vietnam. These previously proclaimed enemies greeted and embraced one another happily and convivially. In many instances they were meeting for the first time. They had fought on opposite sides of the war for years.

I said to my interpreter, "I thought these men were enemies of each other?"

"Didn't all your American Civil War generals go to West Point?"

"Yes, they did," I recalled.

"These officers all went to the same military academy and graduated in the late 1950s," he said.

Then there was a pause and my interpreter faced me and said, "After all—there is only one stranger in our land."

I didn't feel unsafe, but I certainly felt unwelcome.

After the banquet, we were taken to see our American POWs detained in Hanoi. The Peace Accords stated POWs would be visited at the place of their last detention, which in this case was Hoa Lo Prison, but our cunning hosts had moved them several miles away from the rank prison to a pleasant building formerly housing military headquarters. The building was clean and open. Our hosts claimed this was where the POWs had been imprisoned, but the obvious tip-offs were that the fence surrounding the building was of residential height and there were no laundry or eating facilities.

We walked down the halls of unlocked cells to visit our American POWs. They were wearing striped pajama-like prison uniforms—new. We were not allowed to ask the questions we wanted to ask, like, How have you been treated? So we smiled and gave them a thumbs-up, though even that much communication was forbidden, but we did it. The men had been mistreated for so many years, they dared not hope, and consequently most of them didn't believe we were there to get them home. One airman turned around and faced the wall, unwilling to talk to us. Some sneered, some smiled but wouldn't speak, one slammed the door in our faces, and some gave digital greetings. They had gone through this rigmarole before a couple of years earlier when David Dellinger and Henry Fonda's daughter (whose name will never pass my lips again) were in the group that promised their release contingent on them signing confessions. Refusing to exchange honor for early release, they were locked up again. In the cell's dismal gloom they dealt with their discouragement privately.

We were finally jammed into a small room with the North Vietnamese officials, worldwide news, and four US POWs. "We would like to ask some questions," we began.

The senior spokesman was Navy Lieutenant Commander Claude Clower. He began, "Colonel Flynn is our spokesman and speaks for all of us, but he's not here."

He refused to answer any questions and that was the end of that—until around one o'clock that afternoon when we saw all 108 arrive at Gia Lam airport.

In the ensuing two weeks before I left Vietnam for the last time, our team examined empty US air bases and other vacated billeting facilities to ensure that all Americans had left Vietnam—and thus, the war shut down.

On 31 March 1973 I climbed aboard the last plane out.

31 MARCH 1993—TWENTY YEARS LATER

In honor of our forgotten POWs, I penned some thoughts that rushed to my mind one evening after the six o'clock news.

Homecoming + 20
31 March 1993

They didn't mention us today,
twenty years later—
those by-line hungry correspondents who
courted so much of their danger from Saigon's
cool and well-martinied lounges.
Now all proper anchor men and women, they
didn't remember us today, the POWs, twenty years later.

Most of us survived that green furnaced hell and the
interruptions of dedicated do-gooders of considerable
prominence who erected a profane dishonor over our
broken bodies in a hostile land
they could not understand.

I watched the network news tonight, waiting for some
remembrance if not for us, at least for fallen comrades.
Yet no mention forthcame as the well-starched deliveries
began from Peter, Dan and Tom, portraying this day as
another festering moment in our nation's dark journal.

But nothing of us, once claimed as heroes who
answered first to serve and then to endure—
How did we fall so far from grace, not worthy even of a
soundbite remembrance of our suffering? Our devotion?

We yet survive as our nation's scattered few.
Do we now embarrass your profession as but another
dark page better ignored in a nation's desire to
forget and flush away its mistakes?

And in collecting the proper items for tomorrow's news,
will you care enough to even bury us, your nation's living
dead?

Poem received Special Recognition by Utah State Poetry Society

This was Colonel Johnson's second tour of duty in Vietnam. During his first tour from 1967-68 his function was in the Military Police. On his return to the US in 1968 he was appointed Provost Marshal at Dugway Proving Grounds. In the spring of 1971 he graduated from the University of Georgia with a Masters of Public Administration and taught at the Military Police School until he received orders to return to Vietnam in October 1972. At that time he was assigned to assist as an advisor and oversee 30,000 North Vietnamese and Vietcong prisoners of war on Phu Quoc Island located ninety miles off the west coast of South Vietnam.

ENEMY POWS — OCTOBER 1972

Phu Quoc was a small island twenty miles long where approximately 29,000 able-bodied Vietcong (VC) males and 600 North Vietnamese Army (NVA) males were confined as prisoners of war. Our staff consisted of 25 U.S. Army advisors and several South Vietnamese Military Police units that served as guards. This was the central area for incarcerating enemy POWs.

The NVA were tough, mean, severe, well-disciplined soldiers, trained by the Chinese and Russians. They ate as little as possible to sustain life. When we offered them checkerboards and checkers, they declined preferring to make their own. They used their own blood to color the red squares of the checkerboards. We isolated them because they vexed the Vietcong. The NVA displayed superiority over their VC brothers by spurning them as undisciplined rabble. They had particularly ugly ways of dealing with informants.

We adhered rigidly to the 1949 Geneva Convention rules for protecting and providing for POWs; nevertheless, tragedies occurred. One night a Vietcong soldier left his camp after curfew, and appeared as though he was trying to escape. A guard shot him and seriously wounded him. Members of his compound demonstrated their feelings of unfairness by not releasing the victim for medical help; and they wouldn't allow us to remove him. Instead, they built a bier in the center of the compound and covered him with a blanket. Within twenty-four hours he was dead from his wounds exacerbated by sun and heat. That created an excuse for the NVA to demonstrate, and all 600 of them went on a hunger strike protesting the unfairness that a guard had shot a POW. They ate nothing for two weeks. Hunger strikes were very effective ways to demonstrate, because we provided fresh fish daily to feed the 30,000 POWs along with vegetables and rice. When they didn't eat the fish, it lay in the sun and became a putrid stinking mess.

The POWs lived in screened half-wall enclosures, had their own entertainment of usually one or two oriental plays a month, had books—Bibles and Korans and other reading material, and prepared their own food. They had a council of representatives that met with us to air grievances, and whatever they wanted they could have within reason. There were trusted POWs allowed to go into the jungle and cut wood for the camps. The jungle was a formidable barrier that some had to discover for themselves. One trusted POW who went woodcutting escaped. He hid in the jungle wearing only shorts, and after seven days insects had bit him over most of his body. He headed toward a village on the island seeking help. He knew his guard lived in the village, and he found the house and knocked on his door. The guard invited him in, and they sat down and ate lunch together. The escapee was grateful to be returned to camp.

Toward the end of the war when the POWs became aware they would soon be released, there were many attempted escapes and suicides. It made no sense to my western mind, so I inquired and was informed, "In our culture we are sent out to win the war or die in the attempt. We didn't die and we are a disgrace to our country. We will be looked upon as second class citizens for the rest of our lives because we were captured alive."

Sometimes the suicides were self-inflicted knife wounds, and other times we viewed them as "suicides at the hands of others," like the NVA soldier who, shortly before his release, walked out to the perimeter of the compound during the middle of the day where we had two rows of wire fences. He crawled up the first fence and down, then up the last fence and began to climb down the outside. The South Vietnamese guards hadn't given him much attention until he crawled down the outside fence. By then his friends were yelling, "Stop, Stop!" The escapee walked slowly away toward the jungle, when a guard finally shot and killed him.

In the spring of 1973, when the time arrived to release the enemy POWs and return them to the province where they were captured, we flew most of them to Quang Tri province, where the majority had been captured. We had provided them with proper dress, a khaki shirt, pants and sandals, or a pair of shorts, whichever they preferred, and a small 24-hour supply kit with food, cigarettes, candy bars, and a few hygienic supplies. They were given fingerprint cards, immunization cards, physical examinations, and all personal property and money that they arrived with. When they left Phu Quoc Island they were happy and fluttered South Vietnamese flags. When they disembarked on arrival in North Vietnam, they stomped on their flags, threw away their supply kits, and tore off the clothes we had provided. They didn't want to appear as though they had accepted good care from their captors.

I am frequently asked if there are still prisoners being held in Vietnam. We have a tendency to visualize Vietnam like a European battlefield, but it is much different. On occasions when we went into the jungle to look for escaped prisoners, we stumbled over knurled tree roots and branches in ankle deep swamp water, and slashed our way through vegetation as thick as a wall of spinach. I couldn't see the person who was next to me. You could easily trip, bang your head, drown and never be recovered. There were 3.4 million service personnel that came to Vietnam from 1961 to 1973, and 2,421[3] are still unaccounted. Personally, I don't believe the Vietnamese intentionally kept anybody. They wanted the Americans out of their country.

*

Editor's Note:

Colonel Johnson retired from active service on his return from the second Vietnam tour in the spring of 1973 and transferred to the Reserves. He received his Ph.D. from Sam Houston State University in Huntsville, Texas in 1975, pursued a teaching career, and is presently Associate Professor of Criminal Justice at Weber State University, Ogden, Utah.

Colonel Johnson and his wife, Dorothy Tucker Johnson, have resided in Utah for the past sixteen years. He has three children from a former marriage, Ellen McChesney, Gail Newton, Leah Johnson, and one granddaughter.

* * * * *

---

[1] He first learned he had been promoted to major.

[2] Figures from *Honor Bound, American Prisoners of War in Southeast Asia 1961-1973* p. 597

[3] Figures from *Encarta Encyclopedia* 1997.

Hanoi, North Vietnam – 14 March 1973. Release of American POWs; Lt. Cdr. John McCain USN shown in line, Major Jay C. Hess USAF in line. Major Paul H. Johnson seated at table. Photo by Major Paul H. Johnson

BIBLIOGRAPHY

<u>A Bridge Too Far</u>. Producer: Joseph E. Levine, Writer: Cornelius Ryan. MGM/United Artists.

Appleman, Roy E. <u>East of Chosin, Entrapment and Breakout in Korea, 1950</u>. Texas: Texas A&M University Press, 1987.

Allen, Roger C. Personal Interview 24 October 1999.

Anderson, C. V. Personal Interview 10 April 2000, 20 June 2000, 11 August 2000.

Aurthur, 1st Lt. Robert A., USMCR and 1st Lt. Kenneth Cohlmia USMCR. <u>The Third Marine Division:</u> Washington: Infantry Journal Inc., 1948.

Balchen, Bernt. <u>Come North With Me, an Autobiography.</u> New York: Dutton, 1958.

Balchen, Bernt, Major Corey Ford and Major Oliver La Farge. <u>War Below Zero.</u> Boston: Houghton Mifflin, 1944.

Barlow, Glade, Personal Interview 11 September 2000. Telephone Conversations and Correspondence March 2001.

Baxter, Louis M. Personal Interview 11 October 1999. <u>The War and I</u> [Notes from War Diary of Lou Baxter].

Baxter, J. Darwin. Telephone Interview 9 October 1999. Telephone Conversations and Correspondence 1999-2000.

Chang, Iris. <u>The Rape of Nanking: The Forgotten Holocaust of World War II.</u> New York: Penguin, 1998.

Cohen, Stan. <u>Destination: Tokyo: A Pictorial History of Doolittle's Tokyo Raid</u>. 8th ed. Missoula, Montana: Pictorial Histories Pub. Co., 1998.

Dalley, Col. Max. Personal Interview 11 September 2000. Telephone Conversations March 2001.

Dalley, General Frank. Personal Battlefield Diary.

<u>Destination: Tokyo: A Pictorial History of Doolittle's Tokyo Raid.</u> Producer/Writer Stan Cohen. Missoula, Montana: Pictorial Histories Pub. Co., 1985.

Dramesi, Lt. Col. John A. <u>Code of Honor</u>. New York: Norton, 1975.

238

Drendel, Lou. Walk Around: Boeing B-17 Flying Fortress. Texas: Squadron/Signal Pub., 1998.

Fenton, Pat. Personal Interview 11 September 2000.

Frazier, Roberta. Personal Interviews 27 March 2000 and March 2001, and Collected Journal and Newspaper Clippings.

Frazier, Leo O. Personal Interview 27 March 2000.

Glines, Carroll V. Four Came Home: The Gripping Story of the Survivors of Jimmy Doolittle's Two Lost Crews. Missoula, Montana: Pictorial Histories Pub., 1995.

— Polar Aviator, Smithsonian Institution Press, Washington 1999

Grier, Bauduy. Personal Interviews 11 November 2000, 6 January 2001.

Hammel, Eric. Chosin, Heroic Ordeal of the Korean War. New York: Vanguard Press, 1981.

Heslop, J. M. and Dell R. Van Orden. POW. From the Shadow of Death. Salt Lake City: Deseret Book, 1973.

Hess, Jay C. Personal Interviews 10 April 2000 and 4 May 2000.

Hickey, Lawrence J. Warpath Across the Pacific. Colorado: Int'l Research & Publishing Corp., 1984.

Isaacs, Arnold R., Gordon Hardy, and MacAlister Brown. Pawns of War. Boston: Boston Publishing Co., 1987.

Knight, Clayton, and Robert C. Durham. Hitch your Wagon – The Story of Bernt Balchen. Pennsylvania: Bell Publishing, 1950.

Kehr, William Hale. "Stalag Luft III Branch." Ensign Magazine July 1982: 34-38.

Kimmett, Larry, and Margaret Regis. The Attack on Pearl Harbor. Seattle: Navigator Publishing, 1992.

Lawson, Capt. Ted. Thirty Seconds Over Tokyo. New York: Random House, 1943.

Leckie, Robert, The March to Glory. New York: Bantam Books, 1960.

Lord, II, William G. History of the 508th Parachute Infantry. Nashville: Battery Press, 1977.

Mitchell, W. A. Outlines of the World's Military History. West Point, New York: Military Service Publish. 1929.

Nielsen, Chase J. Personal Interviews 19 October 1999 and 22 January 2000. Videotaped Lecture, Hill Air Force Base 2 December 95. Lecture, Hill Air Force Base, Ogden, Utah, 4 April 2000.

Owen, Joseph R. Colder Than Hell. A Marine Rifle Company at Chosin Reservoir. New York: Ivy Books, 1996.

Parkinson, Grant P. Personal Interviews 20 November 1999, 22 January 2000.

Parunak, Capt. A. Y. USN (Ret.). Telephone Conversations and Correspondence February, March, April, July, 2001.

Prados, John. The Hidden History of the Vietnam War. Chicago: Ivan R. Dee, 1995.

Return With Honor. Produced and Directed by Freida Lee Mock and Terry Sanders. American Film Foundation, 1998.

Roberts, Col. Dan. Personal Interview 27 April 2000.

Rochester, Stuart I., and Frederick Kiley. Honor Bound. American Prisoners of War in Southeast Asia 1961-1973. Annapolis, Maryland: Naval Institute Press, 1999.

Ryan, Cornelius. A Bridge Too Far. New York: Simon & Schuster, 1974.

Salter, Mark. Faith of My Fathers. New York: Random House, 1999.

Santoli, Al. Everything We Had. The Oral History of The Vietnam War by Thirty-three American Soldiers Who Fought it. Canada: Random House, 1981.

Slama, Louis. Personal Interviews 15 September 2000, 18 November 2000, 4 December 2000.

Spence, Jonathan D. Mao Zedong New York: Penguin Putnam, 1999.

— The Search for Modern China. New York: Norton, 1991.

Taub, Capt. Donald M. USCG (Ret.) Telephone Conversations and Correspondence March 2001.

"The Saga of My Gal Sal." Life Magazine 20 Nov. 1964: 106B-114.

The Great Escape. Producer John Sturges. MGM, 1963.

The Hanoi Hilton. Directed and Written by Lionel Chetwynd. Warner Home Video.

Thirty Seconds Over Tokyo. Producer: Mervyn LeRoy, Writer: Capt. Ted Lawson. MGM 1944, 1999.

Tindall, George B., and David E. Shi. <u>America</u>. 2nd ed. New York: Norton, 1989.

Toland, John. <u>In Mortal Combat, Korea, 1950-1953</u>. New York: Quill, William Morrow, 1991.

Wallace, James. "Bloody Chosin: The Blind Lead the Brave." <u>U.S.News & World Report</u> 25 June 1990: 37-43.

Whitlow, Capt. Robert H. USMCR. <u>U.S. Marines in Vietnam. The Advisory & Combat Assistance Era. 1954-1964</u>. Washington, D.C.: Headquarters, U.S. Marine Corps, 1977

ISBN 1553692928-6

9 781553 692928